The *New* AR-15 Complete Owner's Guide

by

Walt Kuleck
with
Greg King

THE *NEW* AR-15 COMPLETE OWNER'S GUIDE

All rights reserved. No part of this book may be reproduced or transmitted in any form or by any means, electronic or mechanical, including photocopying, recording, or by any information storage and retrieval system without the express written permission from the author, except in the case of brief quotations embodied in critical essays and reviews.

Copyright ©2014 by Walter J. Kuleck

Second Printing — February 2015

ISBN 978-1-888722-19-2

Published by:

Scott A. Duff Publications
PO Box 414
Export PA 15632

724-327-8246

Visit our web site at: www.scott-duff.com

Printed by:
Fotorecord Print Center
Greensburg, Pennsylvania 15601

THE *NEW* AR-15 COMPLETE OWNER'S GUIDE

This book is dedicated to

Dick Seelinger

. . . whose passing created an empty place
in the hearts of all who knew him.

THE *NEW* AR-15 COMPLETE OWNER'S GUIDE

Other books by Walt Kuleck available from Scott A. Duff Publications:

The M1911 Complete Assembly Guide
The M1911 Complete Owner's Guide
The AR-15 Complete Assembly Guide
The M1 Garand Complete Assembly Guide
The M14 Complete Assembly Guide

Additional books in the Owner's Guide series available from Scott A. Duff Publications:

The M1 Garand Owner's Guide
The M1 Carbine Owner's Guide
The M14 Owner's Guide and Match Conditioning Instructions

Other books available from Scott A. Duff Publications:

The M1 Garand: World War II
The M1 Garand: Post World War II
The M1 Garand: Serial Numbers and Data Sheets
American Military Bayonets of the 20th Century
Rock Island Rifles Model 1903
United States Rifle Model of 1917
US Infantry Weapons in Combat
Arms For The Nation - Springfield Armory Longarms

THE *NEW* AR-15 COMPLETE OWNER'S GUIDE

We Were Not Alone

We would like to acknowledge the generosity of:

AMBI Products and Mike and Theresa Brown
ArmaLite and Mark Westrom and Ronald Elbe
David J. Baker and Roger E. Lake, coauthors of **Paradox,
   The Story of Col. G.V. Fosbery, Holland & Holland, and the Paradox**
Clem Boyd and Lucid Manufacturing
Brownells, Inc. and Larry Weeks
Peter Pi and Mike Shovel, CorBon/Dakota Ammo
Bill Geissele, Geissele Automatics
Randy Luth and Luth-AR
Maklarbak Defense ApS and Michael Klarborg
Manta Rails and Frank Michal
Drake Oldham, Drake's Gun Works, *www.drakesgunworks.com*
Eric King, who contributed a fully equipped shop

During the preparation of this book we received help from:

Rita, Tom, Chuck, Gary, Doug, Mike and Bob, the crew of Dick's Gun Room in
    Cuyahoga Falls, Ohio—one of the last old-time gun shops!
Frank Iannamico, *machinegunbooks.com*
Richard and Sherrie Linke, Arlans Guns & Ammo Shop, Kent, Ohio
Alexander MacKenzie, SANHS
Paul B. Miller
MidwayUSA
Jack Gooldy, Davidson's, Inc.
Mike Fifer, Mark Gurney, and Beth McAllister, Sturm, Ruger, Inc.

...and W. Clint McKee, Service Rifle Mentor Extraordinaire

Please Help Support

Please help support the Jeff Cooper Legacy Foundation:

http://www.jeffcooperfoundation.org/

Its mission:
To preserve, protect, and defend the principle of self-reliance and the individual right of self-defense as espoused by Jeff Cooper. The Foundation will provide scholarships for firearms training in the Cooper tradition as well as preserve his writings and his personal collections for posterity.

THE *NEW* AR-15 COMPLETE OWNER'S GUIDE
Contents

We Were Not Alone v
Please Help Support vi
CHAPTER 1: Introduction 1
WHY A "***NEW***" AR-15 COMPLETE OWNER'S GUIDE? 1
PURPOSE 2
CHAPTER 2: History 5
INTRODUCTION 5
    Gene Stoner 5
    Birth of the AR-15: ArmaLite and the Stoner Years 7
    Colt Buys in and the Vietnam Era 13
    Grenada to Desert Storm 19
THE CARBINE ERA 27
THE FUTURE BECKONS 39
    ArmaLite's Later Years 39
AN INTERLUDE 45
    SULLIVAN'S SURPRISE 45
    STONER'S SECRET 51
    Gene Stoner's Patent Claims 56
    JOHNSON'S JEREMIAD 61
Technical Note 54: Direct Impingement versus Piston Drive 58
Back to Colt and the AR-15: the M16 for the Civilian Market 65
Others Enter the Market; Lots and Lots of Others! 71
The AR-15: an Engineering Perspective 71
A Sidebar on Legislation 78
Some Comments on the "Flat Top" 77
In Conclusion 77
CHAPTER 3: Selecting 79
The Infinitely Variable AR-15 79
Defining Your Purpose 81
    Defensive Rifle: Close Quarters 81
    Defensive Rifle: Long Range 87
    Hunting Rifle: Varmint 89
    Hunting Rifle: Small Game 91
    Hunting Rifle: Deer-Size Game 91
    Target Rifle: CMP/NRA Service Rifle Competition 93

THE *NEW* AR-15 COMPLETE OWNER'S GUIDE

- A Sidebar on Why the M16/AR-15 superseded the M14/M1A 93
- Returning to the CMP/NRA Service Rifle 95
- Target Rifle: NRA Match Rifle Competition 95
- Action Shooting/Three Gun/IPSC Competition 95
- Fun Shooting 95

Understanding, Evaluating and Selecting Your AR-15: 97
Conclusions 97

CHAPTER 4: Details 99
- The Barrel 99
- Muzzle Devices 109
- Handguards and Float Tubes 109
  - Float Tubes: First, "DCM/CMP Legal"; Then, The Dam Broke 113
- The Upper Receiver 117
- Sight Options 121
- The Lower Receiver 125
- Triggers 127
- Pistol Grips and Trigger Guards 131
- Butt Stocks 135

CHAPTER 5: The Rifle Complete 139
- So...You Want A Carbine? 139
- TECHNICAL NOTE 104: 140
- The Benchmark Carbine: Colt LE6920 149
- Colt LE6920 Gallery 150
- ArmaLite's Solution to the Carbine "Problem": 153
- THE EXTERNAL PISTON AR: 157
  - Introduction 157
  - OK, So All External Piston Systems are the Same, Right? 159
  - Ruger's SR-556: Our External Piston Exemplar 159
  - But...do we really need an external piston system in our AR? 161

CHAPTER 6: Chamberings and Cartridges 165
- The AR: Flexible Launch Platform 165
- Military 5.56-MM Cartridges 167
- .223 Remington: Most Versatile Cartridge of All Time? 169
- *Deja Vu* All Over Again: The .308 AR 173
  - Genesis of the "Big Block" ARs 173
  - Knight and Stoner Lead the Way 175

THE *NEW* AR-15 COMPLETE OWNER'S GUIDE

    ArmaLite Recreates the AR-10 177
    Bushmaster Has a FAL Moment; Rock River Steps In 181
    DPMS Goes Back to Basics 183
    Fulton Armory Wades In 185
    Ruger Combines Paradigms 185
  Closing Thoughts 187

CHAPTER 7: Accessories and Accoutrements 189
  Introduction 189
  Magazines 193
    ArmaLite's Recommended Magazine Evaluation Protocol 198
      INSPECTION: 198
      TESTING THE MAGAZINE: 198
      MONITORING AFTER THE TEST: 198
  Slings 199
  Lights and Lasers 201
  Other Neat Stuff 205

CHAPTER 8: Operating 207
  Principles of Operation 207
  Normal Operation 209
  Preventive Maintenance Checks and Services 210
  Operation: Loading and Chambering a Round 211
  Immediate Action 214
  Remedial Action 215
    Bullet Stuck in Bore 215
  Troubleshooting 216
  If All Else Fails 217
  Clear Your Rifle 222
  Disassembly 223
    The "Buddy System" 224
  Reassembly 227
  Magazine Disassembly and Reassembly 229
    GI-Pattern Magazine 230
    Polymer Magazine (Magpul PMag) 232

CHAPTER 9: Maintenance 235
  Cool Tools 235
    Cleaning 235

THE *NEW* AR-15 COMPLETE OWNER'S GUIDE

- Out in the Field 237
- In the Shop 239
- Lubrication 247

CHAPTER 10: Forbidden Fruit 249
- Why Can't You Have a Suppressed Full Auto Shorty? 249
- Silencers/Sound Suppressors 251
- Short Barreled Rifles/SBRs 251
- Select Fire and Full Auto 253

CHAPTER 11: Interesting Stuff Not Elsewhere Classified 259
- Old School Optics 259
- Old School Night Vision 260
- Charging Handle Variations 261
- Potpourri 262
- Magazine Loading Made Easy 263
- Chinese Copies 264
- Disappearing Act 265
- 20th Century Mag Change 266
- 21st Century Mag Change 266
- Paradigm Shift! 267
- NEVER HAVE AN EMPTY GUN! 267
- No More Just Hangin' Around 268
- OUCH!! 268
- From Russia with Love 268
- A Promising Second Act 269
- Double Your Pleasure, Double Your Fun! 269
- Get a Grip 270
- Cool to the Touch 271
- The "Last AR" 272

CHAPTER 12: The Future 275
- The Last of the Line? 275
- We've Never had it Better 275
- What We Can Look Forward To 275
- The Future is Up to You... 275

INTRODUCTION

CHAPTER 1

INTRODUCTION

WHY A *"NEW"* AR-15 COMPLETE OWNER'S GUIDE?

In the years following the first publication of **The AR-15 Complete Owner's Guide** the universe of the AR-15 has changed dramatically, by both evolution and revolution. The **Guide** was first written in the chronological dead center of the original Clinton Crime Bill's Assault Weapons Ban. While the Ban "sunset" in 2004, the threat, and the ban in several states, remains.

A major consequence of the Ban was the emphasis on working with "pre-ban," that is, "grandfathered" AR-15-type rifles. Once such a rifle was acquired, the owner could assemble all manner of upper receivers to the lower, without regard to the restrictions on new rifles imposed by the Ban. Because the Ban addressed certain cosmetic, or as we term them, "Dreaded Ugly Evil" features, it was still possible to acquire or assemble an AR-15-type rifle so long as the number of proscribed features was not exceeded. Sadly, legislative proposals to completely ban the AR-15-type rifle continue to rear their ugly heads.

During the dark days of the Ban, the modularity of the AR-15 became paramount. Many owners had more than one upper for each of their lowers, because unrestricted lowers were fixed in supply and much in demand. With the sunset of the Ban in 2004, the trend began for owners to acquire complete rifles for different purposes rather than switching uppers, and potentially butt stocks, on a singular lower. Thus, rather than an adaptable "Swiss Army Knife" rifle, the AR-15 has become a complete set of knives, each one to meet a specific need. Thanks to the Army's gradual shift to the M4 Carbine, that set tends to have mostly 16"-barreled AR variants. The AR-15 world has truly evolved.

A more recent trend in the AR-15 world is the plethora of different chamberings available for even the "small block" AR-15, not to mention the "big block" AR-10-types. Working within the restricted envelope afforded by the magazine dimensions and bolt face size of the AR-15, chamberings in calibers from .20 (.204 Ruger) up to .50 in addition to the original 5.56-MM/.223 can be found in AR-15 rifles. The merits of these rounds, whether as special-purpose cartridges or as replacements for the 5.56-MM/.223, will likely be debated for a long time to come.

Moving up in size to the AR-10-type rifles, we found them first offered in 7.62MM/.308 Winchester. The natural progression was then to chamber these larger rifles in cartridges based on the .308 case, such as .243 Winchester. A variety of cartridges suited for the larger magazine well and bolt face of the AR-10 has thus emerged, all the way from .243 to the short Magnum .30's. Thus, not only does the AR owner have to decide the configuration of his intended rifle, which generally today means, "Which float tube do I use?", but he or she also has to decide on a chassis size and caliber. Decisions, decisions.

Now, if that weren't enough, a revolution erupted in the wake of general derision toward the original Stoner internal piston operating principle. The Stoner system's design exhausts its operating gas in the upper receiver, leading to an untidy mess at best and function-inhibiting fouling at its worst, or so "they" claim. Thus, a bewildering array of external-piston-based gas systems has emerged, drawing operating principles from the Garand (both gas port and gas trap), the FAL, the M1 Carbine, the AK-47, and probably even the White cutoff and expansion system found in the M14. None of these systems exhaust their operating gas into the receiver; none of these systems has any commonality with any other. Each is idiosyncratic; should the owner need parts, the hope is that the original vendor is still in business, and still offers that particular system (or at least its components). We shall delve into the gas piston morass to some extent, but we wonder; what if the gas piston AR had come first? Then we might have seen the emergence of an innovative entrepreneur with a revolutionary idea: toss the complexity and cost of the external piston systems in favor of a slim gas tube that allows the bolt carrier to act as its own "piston." This would dramatically reduce the parts count while allowing the barrel to be truly free floated, constrained only by that delicate little flexible gas tube. One can imagine this new concept taking over the AR market by storm!

Thus, evolution and revolution; time for a "new" *Owner's Guide*.

PURPOSE

While we've brought the content of **The New AR-15 Complete Owner's Guide** into the 21st century, the purpose we set out for the original Guide is largely unchanged: to build a foundation for understanding, evaluating and selecting AR-15 rifles, components and accessories. We'll cover the AR-15 .223/5.56-MM rifle and carbine. It's for everyone interested in this, the most versatile rifle system ever developed, whether contemplating one's first AR-15 or one's tenth.

We'll be using certain conventions and following a regular structure throughout this book. "AR-15" should be taken to mean "AR-15® –type rifle," whether by Colt ("AR-15®" is a Colt registered trademark), Armalite, Bushmaster, DMPS, Ruger or others. "Rifle" should generally be taken to mean both rifle and carbine versions, though specific carbine issues will be addressed. ".223/5.56-MM" encompasses both the military 5.56-MM and commercial .223 Remington cartridges.

Because of the AR-15 rifle system's versatility, we'll be defining four general areas of AR-15 applications: Defensive Rifle, Hunting Rifle, Competition Rifle, and "Just Plain Fun"! Inevitably, within the Defensive and Hunting categories there will be an extensive range of configurations. We'll do our best to address the specific needs of the broadest range of users we can.

Within these pages you will find a straightforward, uncomplicated approach to AR-15 ownership and use. Based on your needs and desires, we'll help you think through your configuration and choice of AR-15s. Once you have your rifle, you'll find useful information to help you operate, maintain and troubleshoot it. So, let's begin our journey of discovery into the magnificent world of the AR-15!

INTRODUCTION

*Yep, the Four Guys are back in The Garage. Readers of **The M1911 Complete Assembly Guide** will recognize the setting!*

THE *NEW* AR-15 COMPLETE OWNER'S GUIDE
AR-10/15 Family Tree?

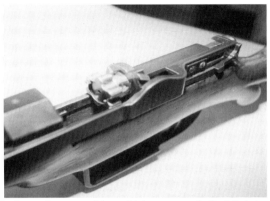

Fosbery shotgun with multi-lug rotary bolt. Ministry of Defence Pattern room, Nottingham, England collection.

Lewis Gun

Model 1941 Johnson Rifle, caliber .30-06. William H. Thomas, Jr. collection.

Fallschirmjaeger 42 (FG 42). Photo courtesy of machinegunbooks.com.

HISTORY
CHAPTER 2
HISTORY

INTRODUCTION
Gene Stoner

The AR-15 is often considered to be the creation of one man, Eugene Stoner. It was, and it wasn't. Stoner's genius was in his creative combination of existing operating principles with an appreciation of the new manufacturing materials and processes becoming available after World War II.

The roots of the AR-15, as with so many achievements, are to be found stemming from many minds and many countries. The AR-15 draws on the multi-lug rotary bolt of Fosbery and MacLean through Lewis and Johnson, Sauve's break-open architecture and the straight-line stock of the Johnson Machine Rifle Model of 1941 and the German FG 42. Stoner's true brilliance was in combining these and other elements with a barrel-extension bolt lock recess that made the use of lightweight, relatively insubstantial materials and structure truly practical for the first time. His masterstroke was the expanding bolt carrier assembly; more on this, later.

Stoner's unique design philosophy, most fully expressed in the AR-15, is his crowning achievement and lasting legacy. Each AR-15 and M16 in the hands of free men and women is his memorial.

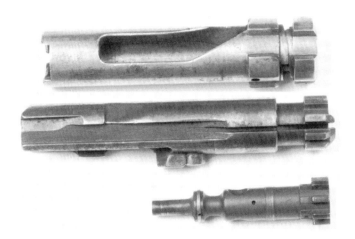

Comparison of bolts and locking lugs. Top: Lewis Gun bolt (reversed for comparative purposes), Middle: Johnson rifle bolt, Bottom: AR-15 bolt.

John Garand's T20E2, the select-fire box magazine Garand. Cancelled with the defeat of Japan in 1945. Springfield Armory National Historic Site (SANHS) photograph.

One version of the SPIW, this from Springfield Armory with a semiautomatic grenade launcher "area weapon." SANHS photograph.

M14NM by TRW. Walt Kuleck collection.

HISTORY

Birth of the AR-15: ArmaLite and the Stoner Years

The story begins sometime in the early 1950's. We may never know the exact sequence of events, but the major players include Jacques S. Michault, COL Rene Studler, Dr. Frederick Carten, George Sullivan and Richard S. Boutelle. The context includes Project SALVO, SCHV, the Lightweight Rifle project, SPIW, the Hitchman report, the Hall study, and more. The threads intertwine in such a way that the emergence of the M16 as our standard rifle seems incredible.

Donald L. Hall of Aberdeen Proving Ground's Ballistics Research Laboratory (BRL) began one thread. His 1952 BRL Memorandum Report 593, "An Effectiveness Study of the Infantry Rifle," was a theoretical study of the interrelationships among hit probability, wounding ability, and rifle and ammunition weight for rifles of calibers ranging from .21 to .30. He concluded that at a combined rifle/ammunition weight of fifteen pounds, "a man carrying the cal. .21 rifle would have an expectation of killing about 2.5 as many targets as with the M1 Rifle." Close on the heels of Hall's study was the Hitchman report, a follow-on to BGEN S.L.A. Marshall's report for the Operations Research Office, "Commentary on Infantry Operations and Weapons Usage in Korea." Combining Marshall's data with WWII experience, Hitchman concluded that riflemen rarely engaged targets beyond 300 yards, and that due to terrain and visibility, marksmanship deteriorated significantly beyond 100 yards.

The logical conclusion from these reports and studies was that a flat-shooting, multiple projectile weapon would be more effective than existing small arms concepts. A small-caliber, high-velocity (SCHV) cartridge would make range estimation unnecessary up to 300 yards. Multiple projectiles, whether as a salvo (hence Project SALVO), i.e., several at once, or serially in rapid sequence, would increase hit probability. Project SALVO led to multibarreled and multiprojectile efforts, including a duplex (two bullets in one case) round in 7.62MM standardized as the M198. The ultimate end of this thread was the SPIW, or Special Purpose Individual Weapon, a combination point (via serial flechettes) and area (via a grenade launcher) arm. The irony of the SPIW is that the M16, intended as a stopgap until the perfection of the SPIW, in fact supplanted it. While the SPIW's technical difficulties proved to be nearly insurmountable, the final blow was economic: the ammunition was estimated to have cost $1 per round—in 1950's dollars! The only vestige of the SPIW that remains is its area-fire weapon concept, articulated in the M203 grenade launcher adapted to the M16.

A second thread begins sometime before WWII in Germany. There, the rapid pace of weapons development accelerated even further during the war as materials and facilities shortages combined to drive the development of "quick and dirty" arms manufacture. The Germans pioneered the use of stampings, plastics and machine-screw-fabricated components in their desperate attempts to meet the needs of the Wehrmacht. After the war, COL Studler, the US Army's driver of small arms development, and Jacques Michault of Sidem International, S.A. (appointed by the US to supply infantry weapons to West Germany), met in Europe during discussions to rearm the West German Bundeswehr. "In the course of these discussions, COL Studler and Jacques Michault became interested in the field of lighter and shorter infantry weapons manufactured and assembled from stamped metal parts, and, possibly, alloys." (**Black Rifle**, p. 19) Studler's enthusiasm for these new approaches led to his singular support of Harvey's T25/T47 during the "lightweight rifle" competition to come.

THE *NEW* AR-15 COMPLETE OWNER'S GUIDE

ArmaLite AR-10 rifle, 7.62MM, 1956. SANHS photograph.

HISTORY

Michault later met another figure in the AR-15 story, George Sullivan, an aeronautical engineer and patent attorney working for Lockheed Aircraft. Michault described what he had learned about the German techniques to Sullivan, while Sullivan told Michault about American materials advancements, including high-strength aluminum alloys, and reinforced and expandable plastics. "Together, [Michault and Sullivan] conceived the idea of an aluminum rifle using a stock of fiberglass constructed like a helicopter rotor blade and with a straight in-line design which would require a higher sight. It was suggested that the sight could be used as a combination of carrying handle and scope mount. The idea of the AR-10 was born." (**Black Rifle**, p. 20)

In 1953, George Sullivan met a Fairchild Engine and Airplane Corporation executive at an aviation conference; Sullivan described his futuristic rifle concept and his partnership with Michault in a Hollywood machine shop. This meeting was followed by discussions with Richard S. Boutelle, Fairchild's president. Fairchild was looking for diversification, and in those early Cold War years, with many nations rearming with weapons more modern than WWII leftovers, small arms must have seemed to have been a promising industry. The result was the formation, on 1 October 1954, of the ArmaLite Division of Fairchild. Sullivan was president while he appointed his brother-in-law, Charles Dorchester, the plant manager. An ex-Marine ex-Army Ordnance technician named Eugene Stoner was brought in as chief engineer.

Independently, Stoner had been working on an aluminum-receivered .30-'06 autoloading rifle, while Sullivan and Dorchester had already prototyped a bolt action rifle intended to be the progenitor of a wide range of ultra lightweight super modern rifles and shotguns. ArmaLite was to be their design studio, creating and perfecting arms to be manufactured under license elsewhere.

Yet another thread started with the combat arms' demand for a select-fire battle rifle; the T20E2, a Garand with full-automatic capability and a 20-round box magazine was still-born, but the "Lightweight Rifle" project continued. As its 7.62MM round was based on a shortened Cal..30 cartridge with nearly equal power, the "lightweight rifle" was hardly an improvement on the Garand, and proved just as difficult to control in automatic fire as the T20. The "winner" of the prolonged lightweight rifle project was the T44, standardized as the M14, a small step indeed from the M1, as it was essentially a Garand with select fire, 20-round box magazine, roller bolt lug and White-type cutoff-and-expansion gas system. With 20 rounds in the magazine it was longer and heavier than a loaded Garand! When, after its adoption in 1957, production difficulties created a scandal worthy of Congressional investigation, the M14 was on life support.

Thus, the prolonged development of the SPIW and the stumbling of the M14 opened a window of opportunity for the AR-15. The need of GEN Curtis LeMay's Strategic Air Command security forces to replace their aging M1 Carbines coupled with the requirements of the Special Forces engaged in Vietnam's jungles created a demand for a high-performance, truly lightweight rifle. The AR-15 filled the bill with its "SCHV" 5.56-MM round, select fire capability, light weight and easy handling.

THE *NEW* AR-15 COMPLETE OWNER'S GUIDE

Artillerie Inrichtingen (Dutch) AR-10. Photographs courtesy of machinegunbooks.com.

HISTORY

But how did the AR-15 arrive on the scene to hit that window of opportunity? Sullivan, Stoner and the ArmaLite team had pinned their hopes on a 7.62MM NATO-chambered rifle. After all, NATO had adopted the US-mandated 7.62x51mm cartridge, and armies across the free world would need new rifles to suit. ArmaLite's 7.62MM AR-10 was the company's first offering in the battle rifle field, previewing the features and configuration that would later become the hallmarks of the AR-15. But due to bad timing, fierce competition in the US (from the T44/M14) and Europe (from the FN-FAL), and the limited resources of the ArmaLite/Fairchild team, the AR-10 saw only limited production, and that in the Netherlands. The AR-10 was not adopted by any major army and only a few thousand were ever manufactured.

In the US, the M14 had won the battle but was about to lose the war. Dr. Frederick Carten, COL Studler's civilian deputy and successor as head of the Office of the Chief of Ordnance (OCO), did all he could to sabotage the M14's competitors, including denying funding for the SCHV research that had been proposed by Aberdeen Proving Ground. In Dr. Carten's world, the US Army would rely on the "full power" 7.62MM cartridge. But Carten was to eventually fall afoul of the "old boy network."

When the commanding officer of the Continental Army Command (CONARC), GEN Jacob L. Devers, retired and joined ArmaLite as the company's Military Liaison Officer, ArmaLite evidently opened a "back channel" to the OCO. During a visit in 1957 to OCO to "post mortem" a disastrous AR-10 trial at Springfield Armory, GEN Devers requested and received a briefing on the Project SALVO SCHV tests. In January 1957, AR-10 S/N 1002 had suffered a burst barrel due to faulty material (416 stainless, both selection and fabrication), which sealed the AR-10's fate as a viable competitor to the T44/M14. Meanwhile, GEN Willard G. Wyman, then-commander of CONARC, had been impressed by a 1956 demonstration of the AR-10 prototypes at Fort Monroe, CONARC HQ. Somehow, the letter requesting further research funding for SCHV (said funding having been rejected by Dr. Carten) found its way to GEN Wyman around the time that Gene Stoner paid a call on the General. It must have been Kismet.

The Infantry Board had become convinced that a Cal..22 rifle with a 300-yard practical combat range was the way of the future; however, they felt that CONARC would prefer a 400-yard requirement, and eventually the Board and CONARC compromised on 500 yards. Really! This requirement became the basis for the AR-15.

The story of the development of a Cal..22 version of the AR-10 could fill a book by itself. Suffice it to say that the .222 Remington Special (later to evolve into the .223) AR-15 prototype demonstrated to GEN Wyman was the first trickle in what was to become a torrent. CONARC submitted a request to the Army Adjutant General for ten of the new ArmaLite rifles on 6 May 1957. The M14 had been standardized just five days before. Though no one knew it at the time, the M14's days were numbered; it was to be the shortest-lived standard US rifle, replaced by what has become the longest-lived: the M16/M4.

Dr. Carten and the OCO were also victims of the success of the AR-15. Their stubborn resistance to the AR-15, including assiduously stacking the deck in the various trials of the ArmaLite, caused a terminal loss of credibility and eventually the demise of the OCO, but

THE *NEW* AR-15 COMPLETE OWNER'S GUIDE

A rack of military Colt ArmaLite AR-15s and variations of M16s at the Ministry of Defence Pattern Room, Nottingham, England. Walt Kuleck photograph.

ArmaLite AR-15 rifle, caliber .223, note the early "duck bill" type flash suppressor, 1963. SANHS photograph.

HISTORY

not before Carten in February 1959 convinced GEN Maxwell Taylor, Chief of Staff of the Army, that "only the M14 is suitable for Army use." Was ArmaLite about to snatch defeat from the jaws of victory?

Colt Buys in and the Vietnam Era

During the prolonged trials (and tribulations) of the AR-15 as it fell into, and then out of, favor, Fairchild's Board of Directors was growing tired of the ongoing investment in rifle development with no returns in sight. A "world tour" with the AR-10 had failed to bring large orders. Even if sales were made, there was no manufacturing arrangement beyond the ill-fated Artillerie Inrichtingen (A-I, of Hembrug-Zaandam in the Netherlands) agreement to manufacture AR-10s in quantity. A-I soured on the ArmaLite program in 1961 when, due to personal animosity between A-I's director, Hans Jungeling, and the Dutch Minister of Defense, the FN-FAL was adopted by the Netherlands and the AR-10 rejected. A-I ceased production soon after with a total of approximately 6,000 AR-10s having been made. Fairchild's Board refused, in their view, to throw good money after bad by investing in a factory to build ARs. In point of fact, Fairchild itself was on the brink of bankruptcy and in need of cash.

During the early days of ArmaLite and its "outsourcing" business model, foreign sales efforts were contracted out in four sectors. ArmaLite reserved the US for itself. Sidem International (Michault's company) covered Western Europe and North Africa. Sam Cummings of Interarms took all of South America, all of Africa south of the Sahara, and the Scandinavian countries of Norway, Sweden and Finland. Finally, the Baltimore-based sales agency of Cooper-Macdonald, Inc. took Southeast Asia as its territory.

Since 1948, Cooper-Macdonald had represented Colt handguns (and later Remington arms and ammunition) in Southeast Asia. Richard Boutelle, still president of Fairchild, gave Bobby Macdonald of Cooper-Macdonald an additional mission: find a licensee to tool up and make the AR-15 in quantity. Macdonald mentioned the matter to his friend, Fred Roff, then sales manager and later president of Colt's Patent Fire Arms Manufacturing Company. Colt was definitely interested, since coincidentally Colt's was going through a crisis of its own, due to the post-Korean War collapse of its military and civilian arms markets. It too was on the edge of bankruptcy. The prospect of large military AR-15 contracts was too good to pass up.

So Fairchild, reorganized as Fairchild Stratos, and Colt, newly acquired (for the value of its inventory only!) by a New York investor, signed an agreement on 22 September, 1958 to license Gene Stoner's gas system patent and the AR-10 and AR-15 designs that used it. The first money—$5,000—changed hands on 19 February 1959. Colt was in the ArmaLite business!

The money was for Bobby Macdonald to take AR-15 S/N 00004 (along with an AR-10 that was studiously ignored by ArmaLite/Colt's sales prospects) on its own "world tour," primarily through Southeast Asia. Military officials in the Philippines, Malaya, India, Singapore, Burma, Australia and elsewhere were enthusiastic. Here at last was a service rifle suited for the small stature of the Asian, for example. It was easy to shoot and extremely

THE *NEW* AR-15 COMPLETE OWNER'S GUIDE

An early production Colt ArmaLite AR-15 rifle, caliber .223, featuring many early design components including "duck bill" type flash suppressor; delta-shaped charging handle, pinned buffer tube, drilled selector & push pins, and waffle pattern magazine. SANHS photograph.

reliable during Macdonald's demonstrations. But the orders ran in the teens and twenties for "evaluation" only, not in the thousands and hundreds of thousands; there was "a fly in the ointment." To qualify for US Mutual Aid funding, a weapon had to be standard US military hardware. Foreign governments were loath to spend their own money for the AR-15 when they could have M1 Rifles, M1/M2 Carbines, and BARs for, well, free!

NOTE:
> In the 1980's, Northrop Aircraft found itself in a similar quandary. Its new F-20 Tigershark was arguably head and shoulders over the previous-generation F-16, but foreign governments were reluctant to buy an aircraft not used by the USAF. The third and last and only surviving F-20 today lies forlornly displayed in a museum.

Now Colt and Fairchild were desperate. Colt had already "wasted" $100,000 tooling up for the AR-10, a rifle nobody wanted. Now they had a rifle everybody wanted, but wouldn't buy unless it were a US standard. Desperate times led to desperate measures.

Richard Boutelle (remember, Fairchild was an airplane company) had become a friend of GEN Curtis LeMay, whose SAC security forces were lumbered with M2 Carbines. On the Fourth of July, 1960 (Boutelle's birthday), Bobby Macdonald arranged for a party at Boutelle's farm outside Hagerstown, Maryland, with GEN LeMay as featured guest. There, the famous watermelon shoot took place. After GEN LeMay had blown up two watermelons (the SCHV bullet literally turned them inside out) with an AR-15, events were set into motion that forced Carten's and OCO's hand. They could not refuse the Air Force, particularly now that Colt was involved. ArmaLite could be dismissed out of hand, but Colt had credibility—and some congressmen who wanted to know why Carten was boycotting the ArmaLite rifle.

Eventually the AR-15 passed its early trials and a buy by the Air Force resulted. But, events in a small country in Southeast Asia were to begin driving the AR-15 program. The AR was quickly recognized as eminently suitable for the short-range nature of the fighting in Vietnam. Kennedy's pet Special Forces could get pretty much whatever they wanted, and they wanted the AR-15! The little rifle was much better suited to the average Army of the Republic of Vietnam (ARVN) troop than an M1 Rifle, while being much more powerful than the M1/M2 Carbine. Suddenly, from being unable to sell AR-15s, Colt was unable to handle the torrent of orders that came pouring forth from the Army! The M16 became a de facto standard in 1964, the same year that M14 production was halted after just over 1.3 million M14s had been built.

Stevens and Ezell document in **The Black Rifle** the woes of the early years of the M16 Rifle in exhaustive detail. However, we can abstract two highlights of that unfortunate record. The first has to do with the M16 and its ammunition as a system.

Gene Stoner had designed more than a rifle when he designed the AR-15; he had designed a rifle/ammunition system, whose effectiveness was based on how the rifle and its ammunition worked as an ensemble. Remington, initial supplier of M193 ball (the standardized 55-gr 5.56-MM cartridge), found it too difficult to manufacture Stoner's original bullet, with its 7-caliber ogive and 9-degree boattail. Remington could not achieve consistent accuracy with the deliberately marginal stability afforded by the M16's original 1-in-14 twist (see

THE *NEW* AR-15 COMPLETE OWNER'S GUIDE

(NY12-Aug. 17) READY TO GO--Tough looking U.S. First Infantry Division soldier awaits airlift into enemy territory. He is a member of a special reconnaissance platoon trained to go on long patrols without being resupplied. These special troops wear soft hats instead of helmets in order to be as quiet as possible when moving through enemy-controlled areas. They search in small groups for information about the enemy and fight only when there is no other alternative.(APWirephoto)ph4-

HISTORY

Chapter 4 for more on rifling twist). The intention was marginal stability in air followed by instability after penetrating target media, for tumbling and enhanced wound effect. Thus, Remington changed the bullet to one with a shorter ogive and boattail. This began several years of tail chasing; the revised bullet's inferior exterior ballistics required higher muzzle velocity to have the same effect as the original bullet at 300 yards. This higher velocity could not be achieved with the original powder used by Remington (IMR-4475) without exceeding the specified 52,000-psi chamber pressure limit.

As a consequence of the need to maintain muzzle velocity levels without increasing chamber pressure levels, a sordid tale followed of new powders that resulted in higher cyclic rates, which in turn led to function difficulties including extraction failures and bolt carrier bounce. One result of the increased cyclic rate was the bolt opening while the cartridge case was still obturated (tightly gripping the walls of the chamber). As the AR's rotary bolt does not afford primary extraction (the leveraging effect given by the helix angle of the bolt lugs of an M1 or M14, for example), the relatively weak extractor spring would allow the extractor claw to jump the cartridge case rim and leave the cartridge case in the chamber.

NOTE:
> At around this time Kalashnikov was also working on the problem of bolt bounce in the AKM (the milled-receiver AK-47). His solution comprised a five-part assembly often mischaracterized as a cyclic rate reducer.

Stoner's rifle was tuned to very specific ammunition characteristics, which meant that changes in ammunition could and did cause major deterioration in rifle function. Thus, this ongoing "development process" took place at a time when the demand for rifles for Vietnam, coupled with an ineffective M16 project management structure, meant that rather than engineers in the laboratory perfecting the M16, US soldiers in combat uncovered the M16's inevitable flaws—alas, all too often at the cost of their lives. Note that the M1 Rifle was developed over a span of nearly 20 years. Its refinement process included a major gas system redesign (and retrofit) four years after its initial adoption! In contrast, the M16 was fielded with essentially no further development after its original design was frozen in 1958.

Concurrently with the emergence of the cyclic rate/component stress/extraction failure issue, the M16 fell prey to its own press releases; from the original User's Manual:

> *Corrosion resistant materials facilitate the assembly and interchangeability of parts and reduce the service and maintenance of the Colt AR-15 to an absolute minimum. Firing of the Colt AR-15 with complete absence of lubricants in a chemically cleaned condition has in every country where this test has taken place resulted in performance far exceeding any requirements.*

> *The Colt AR-15 rifle will fire longer without cleaning or oiling than any other known rifle. Another condition in which the Colt AR-15 excels is the sub zero temperature test including exposure to icing and freezing. The sand test is one that stops many of the world's best weapons, yet the Colt AR-15 has gone through the most severe of these tests without malfunction.*

THE *NEW* AR-15 COMPLETE OWNER'S GUIDE

(NY5—May 21)PARATROOPERS MAKE FIRST COMBAT MISSION—A U.S. paratrooper with a light new AR15 rifle scans dense jungle as he and fellows members of the 173rd Airborne Brigade take part in first combat mission against the Viet Cong in South Viet Nam. They searched area east of Bien Hoa for the elusive Communist guerrillas. (AP Wirephoto by radio from Saigon) (tvb60600rca)1965

HISTORY

None of the various adverse condition tests including sand have left any ill effects on this weapon. Performance in mud is probably the most difficult of all adverse conditions, the close fitting dust cover makes it possible for the Colt AR-15 to out perform all other automatic weapons in this test.

An occasional simple cleaning will keep the weapon functioning indefinitely. Working parts can be cleaned by wiping with a cloth. The simplicity of field cleaning makes it possible to quickly and easily train a recruit in minimum time.

With this kind of instructional material from Colt, should there be any wonder why M16s were sent to Southeast Asia without cleaning equipment (including cleaning rods), solvents or lubricants? The troops there were burdened by rifles with dirty, corroding chambers that already had extraction difficulties due to their ammunition. Chroming the bore and chamber, loading ammunition with cleaner powder (the Winchester Ball Powder then in use left residue in the gas tube as well as the chamber and upper receiver), changing to a new design recoil buffer (to eliminate carrier bounce) and providing training and equipment for cleaning and lubricating, gradually improved the M16's reliability in the field.

The famous Army "PM-the Preventive Maintenance Monthly" M16 comic book (DA Pam 750-30) was part of this training effort. A sample excerpt: "The big trick to using LSA (on the M16A1) is to get plenty of it on the working parts—like those inside the upper and lower receiver—and very light doses in other places…" Quite a change from "The Colt AR-15 rifle will fire longer without cleaning or oiling than any other known rifle"!

By war's end, the M16 had for the most part redeemed itself and fulfilled the promise seen by Michault, Sullivan, Boutelle and Stoner. Boutelle's reward for his part in the AR-15 story was his firing from Fairchild; the financial rewards of the AR-15 venture as well as the license manufacture of the Fokker F-27 Friendship airliner were never forthcoming, at least as far as Fairchild's Board was concerned.

Grenada to Desert Storm

Both America and the US Army were exhausted by the Vietnam War. The M16 ("M16" is used generically to include both the M16 and the M16A1, the M16 with forward bolt assist) had been perfected, at least to the point of "good enough." GEN S.L.A. Marshall, whose WWII and Korea studies had kicked off the SCHV concept in the first place, validated his precognition with his Vietnam "after-action report."

> **NOTE:**
> COL Hackworth, in his book **About Face**, emphatically repudiates Marshall's conclusions after observing him at work in Vietnam. Makes one wonder if the whole SCHV concept was based on a faulty premise.

The 5.56-MM cartridge had become a second NATO Standard. All seemed right with the world. But new concerns arose, particularly as the Small Arms Weapon System (SAWS) trials of 1964-66 began to explore the utility of the 5.56-MM round in longer-range, support fire roles. Now, the M193 Ball cartridge seemed to be woefully short-ranged. This must have caused Hitchman and Hall no end of heartburn.

THE *NEW* AR-15 COMPLETE OWNER'S GUIDE

The M16A1 in Vietnam... "Doe" Morris moves through heavy grass in a deserted rice paddy while on patrol during operation Kentucky V with A Company, 1st Battalion, 4th Marines. Still Picture Branch, National Archives photograph.

HISTORY

The M16A1 in Vietnam... A member of the 5th Infantry Division (Mechanized) looks out over the fog-shrouded A Shau Valley. Still Picture Branch, National Archives photograph.

US Army M16A1 Operation and Preventative Maintenance manual (DA Pam 750-30, 1 July 1969). The format has caused it to be referred to as the "Comic Book."

The M16A1 in Vietnam... Specialist 4 Richard Champion, squad leader, Company B, 4th Battalion, 21st Infantry, 11th Light Infantry Brigade, shouts instructions to his squad after receiving sniper fire while on patrol on Hill 56, 70 miles southeast of Chu Lai. Still Picture Branch, National Archives photograph.

HISTORY

(NY35)LONG BINH,South Vietnam,Oct.30--'LAST PATROL'--The last official American combat patrol stood down three months ago,but these GIs rate the title of the "really last patrol" as they cross stream on perimeter of Long Binh supply base,15 miles northeast of Saigon,recently. A makeshift unit of GIs at the base has been formed into the "87th Infantry (Provisional)" which patrols the huge base's perimeter against possible attack.Leading GI carries combination M16 and grenade launcher. U.S. forces in Vietnam dropped by another 300 men last week,leaving 33,700. (AP Wirephoto)(See AP AAA Wire Story)(jc21925str) 1972

THE *NEW* AR-15 COMPLETE OWNER'S GUIDE

US Marines armed with M16A1 rifles take cover during a terrorist attack during their deployment to Lebanon as part of an international peacekeeping force, 1 April 1983. USMC Photograph.

A Marine armed with an M16A1 rifle stands guard in a bunker at Beirut International Airport, 10 December 1983. USMC Photograph.

HISTORY

Earlier we briefly alluded to the "marginal stability" afforded the M193 Ball round by the original AR-15's 1-in-14 (one turn in 14 inches) twist (see Chapter 4 for a discussion of rifling twist). This situation was addressed by increasing the twist to 1-in-12. While the bullet's stability in air was enhanced, a good thing, its stability in people was also enhanced. This was considered a bad thing, as the tumbling upon impact of the original metastable bullet significantly increased its wounding effect. Nonetheless, 1-in-12 was considered optimum for the 55-grain M193 bullet. Now, with increased range and terminal energy needed, research began into heavier, longer bullets. Since the 5.56-MM round was now a NATO standard, research in the US was augmented by research in Europe.

The winning NATO bullet, at least in Europe, was a Fabrique Nationale (FN) design of 62 grains weight, incorporating a steel penetrator. FN recommended a twist of 1-in-7 to stabilize this longer "SS109" bullet (actually the L110 tracer version, which was even longer), which became the NATO standard. The US also standardized this 5.56-MM variant as the M855 Ball round. The stage was being set for the next chapter in the M16 saga. This time it was the Marines writing the story.

As the 1970's drew to a close, the USMC combined a desire for a "rifleman's M16" with the plain fact that their M16A1s were simply wearing out. Rather than just buy more of the same, the Corps began a series of studies to create a "product improved" M16. Unimaginatively, perhaps, this was known as the Product Improvement Program (PIP). Colt had been proposing changes in the M16 for some years, and in fact several of the elements of the PIP M16 had been created years before, including new-design handguards and a new fully-adjustable rear sight. The new features and components that comprised the PIP M16 are:

1. The barrel is heavier, with the FN-recommended 1-in-7 twist to accommodate the M855 Ball round. The extra barrel weight is concentrated in front of the handguards so that the existing inventory of M203 grenade launchers could still be attached to the rear part of the barrel.
2. The front sight is a square post, adjustable for elevation (the M16A1 front sight post is round). (Since the rear sight is now adjustable for elevation [the A1 rear sight is adjustable for windage only], the front sight adjustment is used only for initial zeroing.)
3. The flash suppressor is of Canadian design with a solid bottom. This reduces the amount of snow (it originated in Canada, eh?) sand, or dust kicked up by muzzle blast. It also has a slight muzzle compensation effect, moderating muzzle rise. (The Canadian Armed Forces/Forces Armées Canadiennes) adopted a version of the AR-15 as their Rifle, C7. It is a hybrid of the M16A1 and M16A2, with the lower receiver refinements of the A2 but the rear sight of the A1. It retains the full automatic capability of the A1 rather than adopting the A2's three-shot burst.)
4. The handguards are of a new, round configuration, parting horizontally and interchangeable from top to bottom. The A1 handguards are triangular, parting vertically, and handed (left different from right).
5. The handguard slip ring is tapered (and now called the "delta ring"), to afford a better grip when removing the rear ends of the handguards. It's now almost a one-person job to remove the handguards; the A1 required the "buddy system":

THE *NEW* AR-15 COMPLETE OWNER'S GUIDE

A member of a group of visiting French commandos prepares to fire an optical sight-equipped 5.56-MM M16A1 rifle off the stern of the fleet oiler USNS JOSHUA HUMPHREYS (T-AO-188) during a weapons familiarization exercise being conducted by members of Sea-Air-Land (SEAL) Team 8. SEAL Team 8 is providing boarding teams to assist the ships of the Maritime Interception Force in their enforcement of U.N. sanctions against Iraq during Operation Desert Storm. Defense Visual Information Center photograph.

The M16A1 in Operation Desert Storm... Petty Officer 3rd Class Frank Baughman of Naval Mobile Construction Battalion 5 (NMCB-5) takes aim with his M16A1 rifle during a camp defense drill. NMCB-5 was in northern Saudi Arabia to provide engineering support for coalition forces during Operation Desert Storm. Defense Visual Information Center photograph.

HISTORY

one person to hold the slip ring back against its spring, and the other to lift each handguard off.
6. The upper receiver is reinforced at the front pivot pin area, and incorporates an integral case deflector (helpful for left-handed shooters).
7. The rear sight is completely different, adjustable for both elevation and windage.
8. The forward assist plunger is changed from a teardrop shape to a round button. The button is easier to make and less likely to snag on brush or clothing.
9. The pistol grip is made of stronger material, with sharp checkering and a finger swell.
10. The selector's three positions are now "Safe," "Semi" and "(three-shot) Burst."
11. The buttstock is 5/8" longer and of stronger construction: foam-filled nylon (shades of Sullivan and Michault).
12. The butt plate is squared and heavily checkered, with a redesigned, easier-opening door.

The PIP M16 was officially type classified by the USMC in September 1982 as the M16A2, and adopted as Standard "A" in November 1983. The Army had more M16A1s in stock and only began buying 'A2s in 1986.

The M16A2 has indeed proved to be a silk purse made from a sow's ear. In Desert Storm, the A2 simply worked where some of our allies' rifles didn't. There were few if any complaints, a complete reversal from the A1's experience in Vietnam. The only systematic issue seems to have been—would you believe it?—the relatively limited range of the 5.56-MM round compared to the 7.62MM M14. Of course, the limitless sands of the Arabian desert invalidated the 300-yard postulate of Marshall, Hitchman and Hall just as the jungles of Vietnam validated it.

In recent years the M16A2 is being gradually replaced by the M16A4 in USMC service. The M16A4 is distinguished by its Safe-Semi-Auto selector (no more three-shot burst), flattop upper receiver, and four-rail handguard system. The Army, in contrast, is migrating to the M4A1.

THE CARBINE ERA

In 1986 Colt created a new carbine version of the M16, based on the M16A2, for the Emirate of Abu Dhabi. This carbine introduced a sliding buttstock and a 14.5-inch barrel.

> **NOTE:**
> The 14.5-inch length apparently was selected so that a bayonet could be attached if desired, while positioning the gas port as far to the rear as good function permitted. The civilian AR-15 carbines have 16-inch barrels (actually 16.1-inch to account for the occasional "short" BATF ruler; for simplicity we'll just refer to the 16.1-inch barrel as the 16-inch barrel) as mandated by law. The flash suppressor ring of a bayonet affixed to a 16-inch carbine barrel ends up positioned behind the flash suppressor and is thus unsupported.

THE *NEW* AR-15 COMPLETE OWNER'S GUIDE

The M16A2 in Operation Desert Storm... A member of D Co., 1st Light Armored Infantry (LAI) Battalion, 1st Marine Division, checks his 5.56-MM M16A2 rifle during Operation Desert Storm. The rifle is fitted with a telescopic sight.
Defense Visual Information Center photograph.

HISTORY

Wearing a grenadier's vest filled with 40mm grenades, Lance Cpl. Charles E. Blevins stands on watch on the perimeter of a desert camp site following withdrawal of Iraqi troops from Kuwait during Operation Desert Storm. Blevins is armed with an M16A2 rifle equipped with an M203 grenade launcher. Defense Visual Information Center photograph.

THE *NEW* AR-15 COMPLETE OWNER'S GUIDE

A U.S. Marine, 11th Marine Expeditionary Unit (MEU), Special Operations Capable (SOC), armed with an M16A2 rifle, signals to another Marine while securing a position in An Najaf, An Najaf Province, Iraq, on Aug. 12, 2004, during a raid of the Muqtada Militia strong points in the area. USMC photo by Cpl. Daniel J. Fosco.

HISTORY

U.S. Marine Corps Cpl. John D. Hart, from the 2nd Battalion, 3rd Marine Regiment, armed with Colt M16A4 5.56 mm assault rifle, conducts a patrol in Haqlaniyah, Iraq, Dec. 1, 2006, during Operation Iraqi Freedom. U.S. Marine Corps photo by Sgt. Brian M. Henner.

THE *NEW* AR-15 COMPLETE OWNER'S GUIDE

U.S. Army Capt. Monty Hodge, with the Camp Echo operations staff, fires his M4 Carbine during weapons zeroing near Camp Echo, Iraq, June 16, 2006. U.S. Air Force photo by Tech. Sgt. Adrian Cadiz.

HISTORY

What differentiated this carbine version of the AR-15/M16 from immediately earlier Colt efforts was its compatibility with the M203 grenade launcher. The barrel contour under the handguards was similar to the contour of the M16A1 and M16A2 under their rifle handguards; the contour of the new carbine barrel in front of the front sight was somewhat heavier, much as in the manner of the M16A2 barrel. When the M203 was clamped to the rifle barrel, both clamps attached to the barrel behind the front sight. However, the shorter carbine barrel forced the front clamp of the M203 to attach to the carbine barrel in front of the front sight. The need to clamp to the heavier barrel required that an annular notch be carved into the heavier carbine barrel to accept the M203's front clamp, reducing the diameter at that point to the same diameter as the M16A2 barrel's diameter behind the rifle's front sight. This need created the distinctive visual characteristic of what was to be the M4 Carbine: the complex barrel contour in front of the front sight.

The Abu Dhabi carbine first came to the attention of the United States Marine Corps; however, paradoxically, it is the US Army that has decided to go "All-Carbine" while the USMC has remained committed to the rifle, and in fact is equipping with the latest M16 rifle version, the M16A4. The US military was concerned with the logistical issues involved in the adoption of a new weapon; consequently, the military demanded the greatest possible commonality with the M16A2. If Colt engineers had had their way, we might have seen an M4 with more changes to the basic components, e.g., bolt and barrel extension, than were actually approved.

The changes that made the cut included shortening the buffer to allow the bolt carrier its full stroke and replacing one of the steel buffer weights inside with a much heavier tungsten weight. These "H"-marked buffers reduced the velocity of the bolt carrier on counter-recoil, minimizing the "bolt bounce" that hindered full-auto fire with the original buffer. The feed ramps in the barrel extension were deepened and complemented by feed ramp cuts in the upper receiver (M4 upper receivers are marked "M4"), to improve feeding on full-auto. The front sight height was altered to account for the shorter barrel's effect on sight radius and the front sight base marked with an "F." The handguards were made elliptical and fitted with double heat shields. Other minor changes were made to small parts.

One additional and important change that was made not long after the first M4s were produced was to incorporate a flattop upper receiver, fitted with a detachable carrier handle/rear sight assembly. No change in designation accompanied this rather consequential development. The significance of the flattop's receiver rail was that it was a harbinger of the M4 as the Lego® set of the US Military!

NOTE:

When the carrying handle is removed, a Swan/Weaver mounting dovetail is revealed. This is the standardized (Standard NATO Agreement, STANAG, 1913), multiposition "Picatinny" mount base for optical sights. "Picatinny" refers to Picatinny Arsenal, the Department of Defense activity that created STANAG 1913. An upper receiver of this configuration is referred to as a "flattop."

THE *NEW* AR-15 COMPLETE OWNER'S GUIDE

The original SOPMOD M4 kit. Legos®, anyone?

HISTORY

And…here's what can happen when Pandora's—oops, SOPMOD's—box o'goodies is opened up by the unwary. This rig looks to be as heavy as a WWII BAR! Department of Defense Photograph.

THE *NEW* AR-15 COMPLETE OWNER'S GUIDE

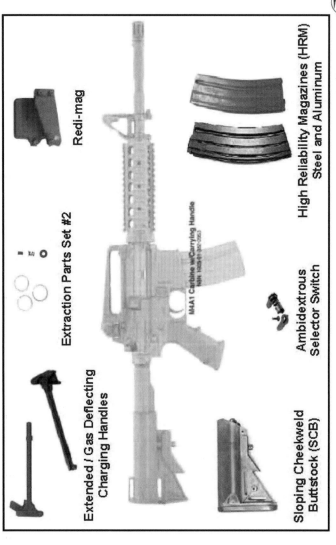

In addition to the parts shown, the M4A1 is fitted with a Safe-Full-Auto selector; ditching the 3-round burst, and a heavier under-the-handguard barrel contour. This new contour requires notches on each side to accommodate the M203's rear clamp.

HISTORY

U.S. Army 1st Lt. John Tilley, a platoon leader for 1st Platoon, Alpha Company, 1st Battalion, 2nd Infantry Regiment, scans the area with his rifle sites, while his Soldiers conduct a traffic checkpoint with members of the Afghan Uniformed Police, near a small village outside Combat Outpost Yosef Khel, Paktika province, Afghanistan, March 9, 2012. U.S. Army photo by Sgt. Ken Scar/Released.

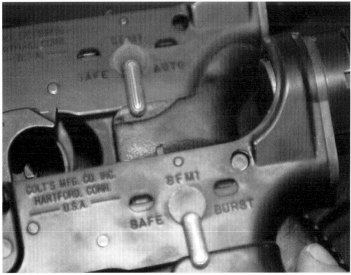

The difference between the new M4 carbine rifle signature, top view, and the previous version, displayed, is the switch goes to fully automatic instead of burst, observed on Joint Base Balad, Iraq, Jan. 18, 2010. U.S. Army photo by Spc. Zane Craig/Released.

Camp Lejeune, N.C. - The M27 Infantry Automatic Rifle looks similar to an M16 rifle and is meant to be operated similarly as well. The IAR will replace the M249 Squad Automatic Weapon, giving Marines a lighter, more precise weapon to use while deployed. USMC Photo by Lance Cpl. Scott W. Whiting, 14 Jan 2013.

HISTORY

The early and enthusiastic adopter of the M4 was the Special Operations community. The M4 quickly became the foundation of what became known as the "SOPMOD" (Special Operations Peculiar Modification) Kit, which began with adding railed handguards and then festooning them with all manner of lights, lasers, sights, grips, and on and on. Over time, the Army as a whole began to reequip with the M4, supplanting the M16A2 with this highly versatile Carbine.

More recently, the M4A1 was further developed to supplant the original M4. The M4A1 designation originally referred to M4 carbines with Safe-Semi-Full selectors. Now, the M4A1 designates an M4 with full-auto capability as before, but also with a heavier barrel under the now-railed handguard. This barrel is notched on the sides to allow the rear clamp of the M203 grenade launcher to be mounted.

The current US military inventory includes the M16A2 (20-inch barrel rifle with safe-semi-burst fire control), M16A3 (as A2, but with safe-semi-auto fire control), M16A4 (as A2, but with detachable carry handle), M4 (14.5-inch barrel carbine with detachable carry handle and safe-semi-burst fire control), M4A1 (as M4 but with safe-semi-auto fire control), and the M27 Infantry Automatic Rifle (IAR) in the USMC.

THE FUTURE BECKONS...

The M27 Infantry Automatic Rifle? The M27 is, in essence, a slightly beefed up M16A4 with a Heckler & Koch gas-piston upper receiver assembly. The complete M27s are, of course, supplied by H&K, incorporating "universal" selector markings, enhanced buffer tube and butt stock assembly, and ambidextrous selector. The M27 replaces the M249 Squad Automatic Weapon (SAW), performing the same function for the Marine rifle squad that the Browning Automatic Rifle did for the WWII infantry squad. While the IAR cannot provide the sustained fire of the SAW, it does have a higher magazine capacity than the BAR, and the Marines seem to have found the limitations of the IAR are outweighed by its lightness and handiness. Outweighed by lightness? You read that first here.

The US military's tilt towards the "AR Carbine" has been reflected in civilian AR-15-type rifle purchases. It appears that many agree "size matters," in this case, shorter and lighter is better.

ArmaLite's Later Years

After Fairchild sold the AR-10 and AR-15 trademarks and the rights to Stoner's gas system patent to Colt, ArmaLite needed new products if it were to maintain in business. Stoner apparently had been working on a sheet-metal version of the AR-10, designated AR-12. The AR-12 that appeared turned out to have a completely different gas system compared to the AR-10. It is often written that Stoner designed this new gas system, a short-stroke piston system, to overcome the deficiencies of his original balanced gas internal piston design. However, this appears not necessarily to have been the case. We can infer this because the bolt carrier of the AR-12 was machined for an internal piston system, and the bolt had provision for a set of gas rings. However, before the AR-12 was finished, Stoner's patent had already passed to Colt. Thus, Stoner was forced into a different direction. The bolt carrier was welded up, closing the gas passage, and the gas rings were omitted from

THE *NEW* AR-15 COMPLETE OWNER'S GUIDE

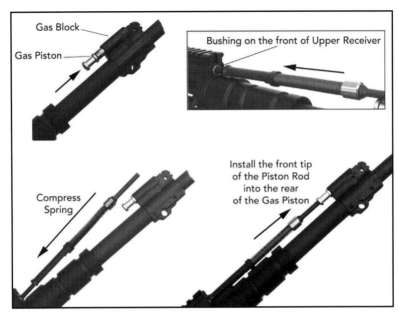

HK gas system as found in the M27. From MR762A1 Operator's Manual.

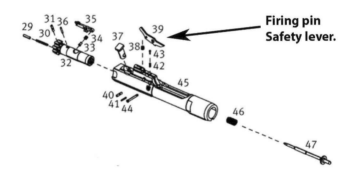

HK 716 bolt diagram. Note the firing pin safety, a diversion from the original AR designs, and found in the M27.

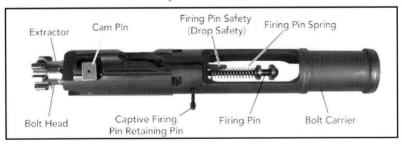

HK 716/M27 bolt carrier group. Note the firing pin safety and captive firing pin retaining pin.

HISTORY

Lance Cpl. Michael Mills, a scout with 2nd Light Armored Reconnaissance Battalion, 2nd Marine Division, fires the M27 Infantry Automatic Rifle on full auto for the first time. The Wytheville, Va., native loves everything about the rifle from its accuracy and smooth trigger pull to its light weight and slim build. Mills said that his favorite feature of the M27 IAR is how easy they are to clean. The rifle is designed so that 95 percent of the carbon is blown out the barrel so that even after dozens of rounds have been shot, as Mills put it, it looks like it hasn't been fired once. USMC Photo by Lance Cpl. James Frazer; 5 April 2012.

THE *NEW* AR-15 COMPLETE OWNER'S GUIDE

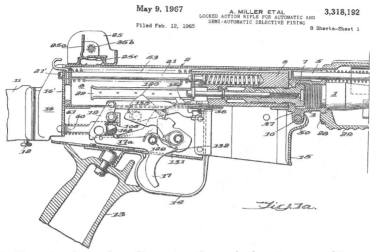

AR-18. Necessity, the mother of invention; Stoner had to circumvent his own patent.

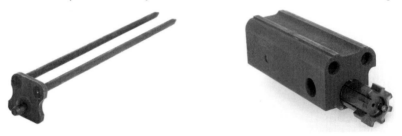

AR-18 guide rods (left); matching bolt carrier (right).

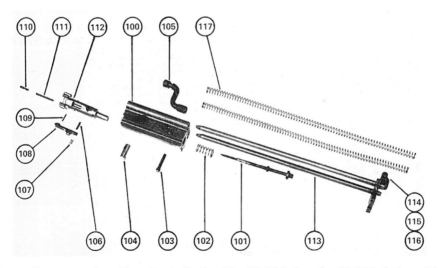

How it all goes together. Note the similarly of the AR-18 bolt to the AR-15 bolt, but without tail and gas rings.

HISTORY

the bolt. Consequently, it is more likely that Stoner's piston system was simply a means of circumventing his then-inaccessible technology, rather than a solution for the original gas system's "drawbacks."

While the AR-12 had a machined aluminum receiver, the receiver was fashioned in such a manner as to represent the characteristics of a sheet metal fabrication. It would seem that a sheet metal receiver would have even more structure and wear issues than an aluminum receiver. Consequently, Stoner stabilized the bolt carrier with the use of two guide rods that incorporated the requisite recoil springs. This design had the very real benefit of taking the recoil system out of the buttstock, allowing the rifle to have a folding buttstock if desired.

The AR-12 begat the AR-16, a true sheet metal .308 that no longer had the vestiges of Stoner's original gas system design. The '16 begat the AR-18, a sheet metal .223. In later years the AR-18 begat the Enfield SA80/L85 bullpup, but that's story to be read in Raw's **The Last Enfield**.

ArmaLite was divested by Fairchild and reacquired by its original principals in 1961. While the AR-18 enjoyed modest commercial success, for a variety of reasons ArmaLite faded from the firearms scene and was sold to the Elisco Tool Manufacturing Company of the Philippines. Sudden changes in Philippine politics eventuated in Elisco abandoning plans to manufacture the AR-18 there, and the US arm of the ArmaLite Division of Elisco Tool was closed in 1987.

HISTORICAL NOTE:

The AR-18 bolt and bolt carrier live on, even though the '18 itself is gone. The UK Government appropriated the AR-18 design from ArmaLite's British licensee, Sterling, including the bullpup version concept that Sterling devised. The purloined design eventually became the SA80/L85, the nominal standard service rifle of the British Army. Alas, the Brits' realization of the AR-18 turned out to be seriously and serially flawed. When Heckler & Koch (H&K) acquired Royal Ordnance, the German firm took on the task of making the rifle right and mostly succeeded.

H&K, in turn, used the Stoner bolt as found in the AR-18 in their G36, as did Steyr in their AUG. It appears that if you don't have a Garand bolt (Kalashnikov), you have to have a Stoner bolt in your modern rifle design!

In 1986 Karl Lewis and Jim Glazier founded Eagle Arms in Illinois Lewis' Lewis Machine and Tool (LMT) had been making parts for the AR-15 and M16 rifles; Eagle Arms was intended to be LMT's retail outlet for parts and complete rifles. Stoner's patent had expired by this time, of course. In 1994, a retired Army Ordnance Officer, Mark Westrom, purchased Eagle Arms. Coincident with his discovery that there were at least seven other US firms named "Eagle Arms," Westrom found that the ArmaLite name was owned by the last President of Elisco's ArmaLite Division, John Ugarti, and that John lived in a modest house in a suburb of Seattle.

Westrom hopped a plane to Washington State, drove up to Ugarte's front door, and knocked. A handshake later and Eagle Arms became ArmaLite, Inc., with a "generic" parts and rifles division, "Eagle Arms." The "new" ArmaLite is a worthy successor to the original.

THE *NEW* AR-15 COMPLETE OWNER'S GUIDE

Stoner's "M-7" rifle in .308, his first to use a Fiberglas stock, includes an aluminum receiver with a multi-lug bolt locking into a steel barrel extension. The gas system is patterned after the M1 Garand. If you peer closely at the bolt carrier assembly, with the exception of the missing carrier gas key it would not look out of place in a pile of AR-15 parts! SANHS Photographs.

HISTORY
AN INTERLUDE...
SULLIVAN'S SURPRISE
—*or, how in Heaven's name did* that *happen?*—

The AR-15 is both a convergence of technologies and a convergence of people. At this far remove we shall never know all of the details and nuances of the personal relationships—although some reminiscences reek of innuendo—but, we may be able to better infer how the technologies came together.

From what we know today, we can reasonably conclude that the multi-lug rotary bolt with enveloping cylindrical bolt carrier locking into a steel barrel extension technology was brought to the party by Gene Stoner. As we can see in his "pre-ArmaLite-era" Stoner M5, M6 and M7 rifles, Stoner incorporated the multi-lug rotary bolt that would later be a part of his carrier-integrated-internal-piston balanced pressure gas system, described below. However, in these three earlier designs, he used a long-stroke direct impingement gas system very reminiscent of the M1 Garand.

Stoner was at this time committed to the idea of the use of an aluminum receiver. He knew, of course, that an aluminum receiver was completely unsuited to withstanding the wear of the locking process, not to mention being far too weak to withstand the bolt thrust on the locking lugs at the moment of firing. Thus, Stoner used a steel barrel extension to allow the bolt to lock directly to the barrel in a very practical fashion.

It's interesting to note that Mikhail Kalashnikov came to a similar conclusion as he pondered how to lock a bolt, in this case his Garand-type bolt, into a sheet steel receiver. Kalashnikov's solution was what we today call the "trunnion" in the AK-47 design. The AK's barrel is pressed and pinned into the trunnion, though the barrel could have just as well been screwed into the trunnion just as the AR's barrel is screwed into its barrel extension. The fact that the AK's trunnion is square while the AR's barrel extension is round is immaterial. They each provide the same function, a steel construct able to withstand the wear and forces applied by the bolt during cycling and firing.

At this point one might wonder why Stoner changed from a conventional Garand-type gas system to his innovative balanced gas pressure system. Stoner's new system, documented in Patent No. 2951424, essentially moved the gas piston from the tip of the operating rod to the inside rear of the bolt carrier, turning the piston inside out in the process. The need for this new concept gas system becomes evident with a close examination of the Stoner M4 rifle: the receiver rail that supports the operating rod is cracked. Stoner noted this deficiency and attempted to correct it by widening the corresponding rail on his M5. However, the strengthened rail of the M5 also cracked.

What was causing the rails to crack? Here is the irony of ironies, when viewed from the 21st century: the force causing the rails to crack was the asymmetry of the force applied to the bolt carrier by the necessarily offset operating rod. In short, Stoner designed a new concept of gas system to eliminate…carrier tilt! Today, of course, we are bombarded with a panoply of gas piston systems to solve the "problems" of the balanced gas pressure system's

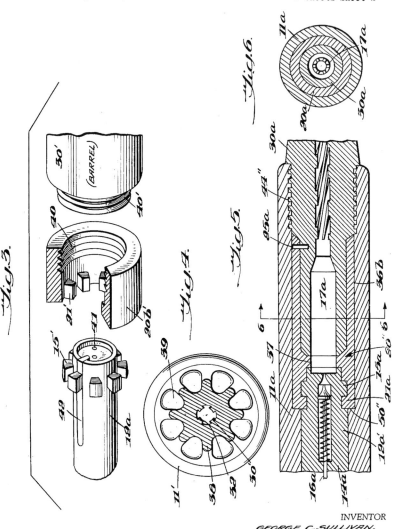

Sullivan's multi-lug bolt patent, allowing the use of an aluminum receiver via the steel barrel extension.

HISTORY

exhaust. We have come full circle, as we seek ways to avoid and ameliorate the "carrier tilt" caused by external piston systems' asymmetric application of force to the bolt carrier. *"Plus ça change, plus c'est la même chose"*—"the more it changes, the more it's the same thing", usually translated as "the more things change, the more they stay the same" (Jean-Baptiste Alphonse Karr, Les Guêpes, January 1849). But, more on external piston systems later.

So, what did George Sullivan bring to the party? The man variously described as Lockheed's patent counsel, a engineer working for Lockheed, or a "patent investigator," was in fact a classic "gun crank." His vision was the use of modern, lightweight materials to create new classes of firearms. Sullivan applied two new technologies to his firearms designs. The first was the use of a foam-filled fiberglass-shell stock. The second was an aluminum barrel with a steel liner. These exercises in adding lightness came together in the ArmaLite Parasniper, also known as the ArmaLite AR-1, a bolt-action .308 rifle that incorporated the fiberglass stock and steel-lined aluminum barrel. A variety of Mauser and commercial bolt actions was used as the bases for these rifles. For example, one of the four Parasnipers in the Springfield Armory National Historic Site (SANHS) collection is built on a Remington 722 receiver, S/N 351553. Perhaps as a consequence of their light weight, several, if not all, of the SANHS Parasnipers is equipped with a commercial "NOSHOC" recoil pad.

While the fiberglass stock proved to be enduring, the aluminum barrel did not fare so well. When the Aberdeen Proving Ground sectioned the barrel of Parasniper S/N 189, they noted a separation between the steel liner and the aluminum jacket in one small area. This "delamination" creates a weak spot that can lead to catastrophic failure, as indeed as it may have done in later Ordnance testing of the early AR-10. That barrel failure essentially ended the chance that the AR-10 could become a serious contender to the T44 and T48 in the quest for a new US service rifle. Sullivan had patented an electroplating process to line an aluminum barrel with a hard, e.g., steel, surface, but this idea does not seem to have gotten anywhere. Today, of course, we have composite barrels by the score, particularly for the Ruger 10/22 rimfire rifle. The pressures involved for a .22 LR barrel are much less than for a typical centerfire cartridge, but the technology and materials have advanced to the point that composite centerfire barrels have been successfully developed. George Sullivan had the right idea, but perhaps the wrong material. Speaking of material, Sullivan developed an aluminum alloy he called "Sullalloy," which skeptics have described as a minor variation on the then-new 7075-T6.

So, what was "Sullivan's Surprise"? Simply this: the patent for the rotary bolt locking into a steel barrel extension to permit the use of an aluminum receiver was awarded to George Sullivan, not Eugene Stoner. How did that happen? I doubt we will ever know.

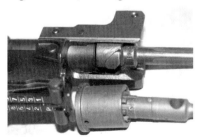

Kalashnikov's two-lug bolt and trunnion (upper), compared to Stoner's multi-lug bolt and barrel extension (lower).

THE *NEW* AR-15 COMPLETE OWNER'S GUIDE

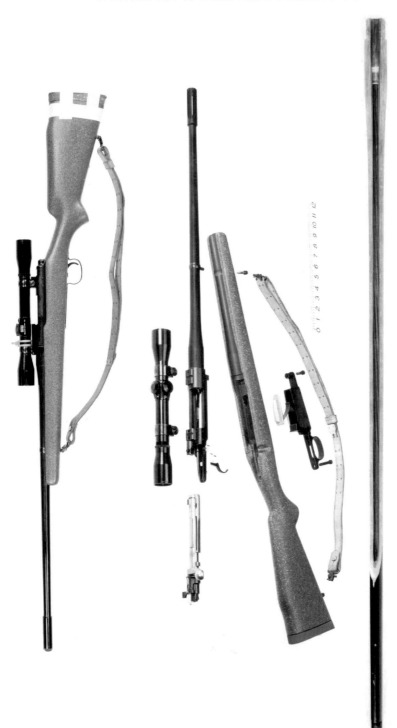

George Sullivan's Parasniper in .308 Winchester. Note that at this time the military 7.62-MM cartridge development was not completed. The stock is foam-filled fiberglass, the barrel is aluminum with a steel liner. The Aberdeen Proving Ground staff sectioned a Parasniper barrel to study its composite construction. SANHS Photographs.

HISTORY

Here is a closeup of the sectioned Parasniper barrel; the light area is aluminum, the darker area is steel, and the black area is the bore. The arrow is pointing to an point where the steel liner is slightly separated from the aluminum jacket. Is that important? See below. SANHS Photograph.

During initial testing by the Ordnance Department, this early AR-10 barrel failed catastrophically, injuring the soldier shooter and knocking the AR-10 out of the Light Rifle competition. The failure may well have been caused by the kind of void seen in the Parasniper barrel in the picture above. SANHS Photograph.

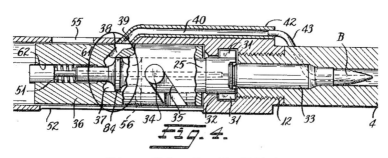

"Figure 4" from Pat. No. 2951424.
Note the circled area. This is the internal chamber #37, here in "contracted" state before the gas of firing enters the chamber. Top view.

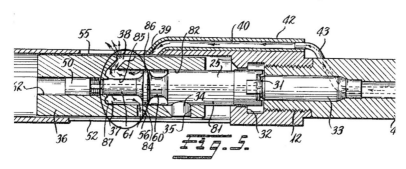

"Figure 5" from Pat. No. 2951424.
Note the circled area. This is the internal chamber #37, here in "expanded" state after the gas of firing has been admitted into the chamber, and just as the gas is being exhausted.

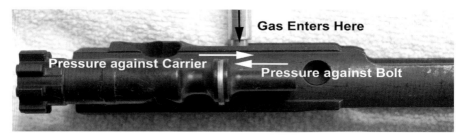

AR-15 Bolt Carrier Assembly.
The eventual AR design differs in detail from the patent, but is similar in principle. The major deviation for the AR bolt carrier is that the gas cut-off feature has been omitted. Michael C. Morris, in his Pat. No. 4765224, offered an extended gas key design that restores the "gas cutoff and expansion" principle found in Stoner's patent. Mr. Morris' purpose was to keep the propellant gas from entering the upper receiver. The AR gas key disengages from the gas tube, allowing the propellant gas an avenue into the upper receiver.

HISTORY

STONER'S SECRET
—or, when everything you know is not exactly the way you thought it was—

When Eugene Stoner created the gas system that became the foundation of ArmaLite's autoloading firearms, he laid the foundation for an ongoing misapprehension about the operating principle of his brainchild. The use of the term "direct gas impingement," in conjunction with citing the Rossignol and Ljungman gas systems as predecessors to the ArmaLite design, has misled many. It is easy to believe that the gas let into the bolt carrier via the gas tube and gas key is used to directly push the bolt carrier rearward. The gas does *not* impart its energy to the bolt carrier by directly impinging on the carrier. To quote from Stoner's Patent No. 2951424:

> *This invention is a true expanding gas system instead of the conventional impinging gas system.*

What, then, is an "impinging gas system"? We can use the Ljungman-derived system of the Hakim Egyptian battle rifle to illustrate:

Bolt carrier from Hakim, license-built Ljungman AG42B rifle. The Ljungman/Hakim, along with the French MAS 44,49, and 49/56 rifles, was designed with a true direct-impingement gas system. Note the blind hole in the face of the bolt carrier. This is where the gas tube "dumps" its gas, pushing the carrier rearward.

So then, how does the Stoner system work? And, how does the Stoner system differ from a "Gas-Piston-Type" (external gas piston) mechanism? Simply put, the Stoner system *is* a gas piston system—but a gas piston system where the piston is inside the bolt carrier assembly. Let's review the components involved in the AR's gas operation, and see how they accomplish the cycling of the rifle, starting with Stoner's patent.

Referring to Figures 4 and 5 to the left, we may recognize the general arrangement found in our AR rifles. Figures 4 and 5 depict the original layout of the AR rifle, but with the gas tube to the left of the receiver. In this initial concept, the gas is taken off below the barrel, with a gas tube wrapping up and around to the left side of the receiver. From there, the gas is admitted into the bolt carrier via a port in the receiver (call-out #39) and a matching port in the bolt carrier (#38). The gas enters an internal chamber (#37) circled in the figures, closed at the rear by the bolt carrier body and closed at the front by the bolt's tail. The tail is sealed via piston rings in our AR rifles; here, the seal is effected by the fit between the outer diameter of the bolt tail and the inner diameter of the bolt carrier.

As the gas pressurizes the bolt carrier's internal chamber, it pushes equally in all directions, most notably on the inside of the bolt carrier at the rear of the chamber, and on the tail of the bolt (bottom picture). Because the bolt carrier body and bolt are free to move relative

THE *NEW* AR-15 COMPLETE OWNER'S GUIDE

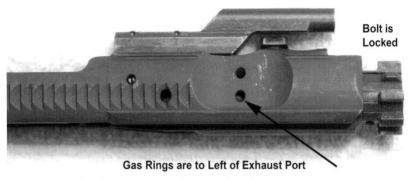

Gas Rings are to Left of Exhaust Port

As the gas begins to enter the bolt carrier via the gas key, the gas pressure acts equally forward on the bolt and rearward on the bolt carrier.

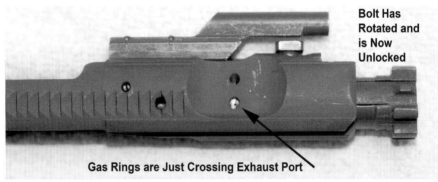

Gas Rings are Just Crossing Exhaust Port

While it appears that the gas pressure is only forcing the bolt carrier rearward, the gas is also pushing the bolt forward. As the gas "expands" the bolt carrier assembly, the initial relative motion of the bolt and bolt carrier rotates and unlocks the bolt. The bolt rotates freely because it is pressed forward against the inside of the barrel extension, not pulled backward and dragging on the extension recesses.

Gas Rings are Just Unmasking Exhaust Port

When the bolt gas rings unmask the bolt carrier exhaust ports, the pressure in the carrier drops to zero. The inertia of the rearward motion of the bolt carrier withdraws the bolt from the barrel extension when the cam pin reaches the end of the cam pin's track in the carrier.

HISTORY

to one another within the limits imposed by the cam pin track found in the bolt body, the bolt carrier begins to move rearward under the push of the gas pressure. However, because the bolt is being pushed forward equally by the same pressure, the bolt is pressed forward against the breech face of the barrel as the bolt carrier moves rearward.

During the rearward motion of the bolt carrier, the first motion imposed on the bolt is its rotation to "unlock" as the cam pin is drawn along the cam track in the bolt carrier. The bolt is still being pressed forward by gas pressure, so as the bolt rotates, the bolt locking lugs have little or no contact with the inside faces of the barrel extension's locking lug recesses. This allows the rifle designer to use a smaller barrel extension and bolt than might otherwise be required. The cam pin doesn't reach the end of the cam track and begin to pull the bolt with the expended cartridge rearward until the bolt is unlocked. Further, in the application of the patent to the AR-15, you can see that the exhaust ports in the bolt carrier body are only unmasked as the bolt cam pin reaches the end of the cam track.

Returning to "Figure 5," a close examination of the diagram reveals that the inlet for the gas to the chamber is cut off when the gas is being permitted to exit from the chamber via the exhaust port. This is described in Patent No. 2951424:

> *It is another object of this invention to utilize the energy of the expanding gas developed by the firing of the weapon for actuating the automatic rifle mechanism directly by use of a metered amount of the gas coming from the barrel. This invention is a true expanding gas system instead of the conventional impinging gas system. By utilization of a metered amount of gas from the barrel, the automatic rifle mechanism is less sensitive to different firing pressures caused by variations in the propelling charge. It is therefore still another object of this invention, to provide a rifle mechanism which is not affected by variations in the propelling charge.*

Essentially what Stoner was describing was an adaptation of the White gas cut-off-and-expansion gas cylinder concept. The White system can be seen in the M14 rifle, wherein the gas piston admits a fixed amount of gas; the piston cuts off the input of gas when "enough" gas has been admitted to function the mechanism. Had Stoner persisted with the controlled

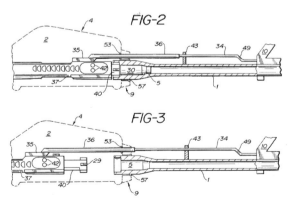

Michael Morris' extended carrier key. Note that in "Fig-3" the extended carrier key never unmasks the gas tube when the bolt carrier is all the way to the rear. This is one way to keep gas out of the receivers; it would seem to be a simpler solution than a full-blown external piston system. However, it's not a cutoff and expansion design.

THE *NEW* AR-15 COMPLETE OWNER'S GUIDE

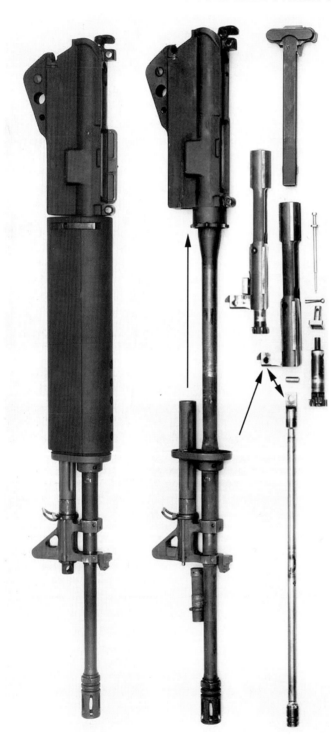

The Colt M16A2 of 1969. This long-stroke piston system is a little reminiscent of the AK, down to the pressed flutes in the gas tube. Colt claimed;
"It is Colt's belief that Colt's M16A2 will demonstrate better performance and superior durability when compared to the M16A1.
"Prototype number 1 features a closed, adjustable gas system which is completely housed in the front sight assembly. This allows the user to optimize his weapon's efficiency according to conditions dictated by climate or ammunition. No gas deposits are permitted to enter the breech mechanism and the result is a cleaner operating weapon.
"In addition, a larger extractor, a failure-free extractor spring and increased dwell before unlocking have been incorporated."

HISTORY

inlet of gas that he describes, many of the problems—real and perceived—resulting from fouling in the receivers and from variations in powder type might have been averted.

Because the AR-15 as it was finally designed allows the carrier key to unmask the gas tube as the carrier moves rearward, gas escapes from the chamber in the bolt carrier through the exhaust ports but also "burps" back out the way it came in and into the receivers. Michael C. Morris, in his Pat No. 4765224, offered an extended carrier key design that keeps the propellant gas from entering the upper receiver via the carrier gas key. However, Morris' is not a cutoff and expansion design.

One might wonder why Gene Stoner went to all the trouble to create his unique system. The reason may be simple: simplicity. The Stoner System is about as simple as a gas operated locked-breech firearm can get. There is another benefit, as described in Patent No. 2981424; all the forces acting on the rifle are along the axis of the rifle bore. There are no mechanisms, no off-center loads to disturb the arm or aim:

> *A further object of this invention is to provide smoother operation and longer life of the working parts of the automatic rifle mechanism. Since in this invention the actuating force is transmitted directly down the center line of the barrel and the bolt mechanism to the shoulder of the shooter, all of the off-center loads found in most other types of gas actuated weapons are eliminated. It will therefore be obvious because of this factor that another object of this invention is to cut down on "climb" which occurs during automatic firing operations.*

It wasn't long before attempts to despoil the purity of the Stoner System emerged. One of the earliest, if not the first, came from Colt itself. In 1969, Colt prototyped and proposed what they called the "M16A2." The M16A2 of '69 is not to be confused with the later, "official" M16A2 of 1982. Evidently, nothing came of the '69 proposal, though to this day Colt continues to design, show and on occasion offer external piston-driven adaptations of the AR-15. Of course, many inventors and entrepreneurs have proposed, designed and offered their own flavors of external gas piston system for the AR.

—*Age cannot wither her, nor custom stale, Her infinite variety.*
Antony and Cleopatra Act 2, scene 2—

Much the same can be said for the external piston AR-15. When we consider the M16's early difficulties in Vietnam, the appeal of a gas system that keeps the interior of the receivers free of propellant gas fouling is undeniable. But, that's not the only benefit perceived stemming from the adaptation of a gas piston system. Gas piston systems with gas flow adjustment can be less sensitive to suppressor use, barrel length, and gas port enlargement caused by erosion.

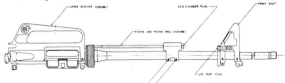

Winchester's little-known piston project of 1967 to solve the problem of gas tube fouling...caused by Winchester ammo?

Gene Stoner's Patent Claims
from Patent No. 2951424

Having thus described my invention, what I (Gene Stoner, not your author!) *claim is:*

1. In a gas operated system for a firearm, the combination of: a receiver; a bolt carrier slidable in said receiver; a bolt movably mounted in said carrier, said bolt having a piston thereupon and locking lug means thereupon engageable with corresponding lug means on said receiver to prevent relative movement between said bolt and said receiver when the lug and lug means are engaged, said bolt piston and bolt carrier defining between them an expandable chamber; and means for carrying the explosive gases resulting from the firing of said firearm to said expandable chamber whereby the gases operate within said chamber directly on said bolt and said bolt carrier to retract said bolt carrier relative to said bolt.

2. In a firearm construction, the combination of: a receiver having an abutment thereupon; a bolt carrier having an axial bore therein terminating intermediate the extremities of said carrier, said carrier being movable in said receiver; a bolt mounted for movement in said bore and having a piston thereupon engageable with the side wall of said bore to define an expandable chamber in said carrier, said bolt and said carrier being movable relative to each other and said bolt having locking lugs thereupon engageable with said abutment on said receiver; and means for carrying explosive gases directly from the barrel of said firearm to said expandable chamber whereby, when said firearm is fired, the gases expand said chamber by sliding said bolt carrier relative to said bolt while simultaneously causing rotation of said bolt to release said lugs from said abutment until said chamber is fully expanded whereupon said bolt is retracted.

3. In a gas operated system for a firearm, the combination of: a receiver having an abutment therein; a barrel mounted in said receiver; a bolt carrier movable in said receiver, said bolt carrier having an axial bore formed therein provided with an end wall terminating intermediate the extremities thereof and said carrier having an intake port and an exhaust port communicating with said bore adjacent said end wall; a bolt slidable in said carrier bore having a portion thereupon defining an expandable chamber in conjunction with said end wall; and a conduit for carrying gases from the bore of the barrel of said firearm to said intake port having sliding engagement with said intake port whereby said intake port communicates with said conduit when said bolt and bolt carrier are in battery position and whereby, upon firing said firearm and ingress of gases into said expandable chamber, communication between said intake port and said conduit is terminated.

HISTORY

4. In a gas operated system for a firearm, the combination of: a bolt carrier having a longitudinal bore therein provided with an end wall intermediate the extremities of said carrier, said carrier having an exhaust port communicating with said bore; a bolt slidable in said bore having a piston portion thereupon engageable with the wall of said bore and defining an expandable chamber in conjunction with said end wall of said bore; and means for carrying the gases resulting from firing of said firearm to said expandable chamber, said piston portion of said bolt being adapted to isolate said exhaust port from communication with said expandable chamber when said bolt is in battery position and to permit said exhaust port to communicate with said chamber when said carrier is slidably reciprocated with reference to said bolt to expand said chamber.

5. In a gas operated system for a firearm, the combination of: a receiver having a barrel and a bolt abutment thereupon; a bolt carrier slidably mounted in said receiver having a first bore extending inwardly from one end thereof and a second bore of lesser diameter than said first bore communicating with said first bore, said carrier having an operating groove therein; a bolt having abutment engaging lugs thereupon and a first portion slidable in said first bore and a second portion slidable in said second bore, said bolt having an operating lug engageable in said operating groove in said carrier and having a piston portion defined at the juncture between said first and second portions thereof and defining an expandable chamber in said carrier in conjunction with the opposed end of said first bore; and means for introducing actuating gas into said expandable chamber whereby said chamber will be expanded to cause relative sliding movement between said bolt and said carrier to cause said lug to move from one extremity of said groove to the other and rotate said bolt relatively to said receiver to release said lugs from said abutment.

6. In a gas operated system for a firearm, the combination of: a receiver having a barrel and a bolt abutment thereupon; a bolt carrier slidably mounted in said receiver having an axially oriented bore with one end located intermediate the extremities of said carrier and the opposite end open to the forward extremity of said carrier, said carrier having intake and exhaust ports adjacent said one end; a bolt slidably mounted in said carrier having abutment engaging lugs thereupon projecting from the open end of said bore and having a piston thereupon located within said bore and defining an expandable chamber in conjunction with said one end thereof; and means for transmitting firing gases from said barrel to said intake port including an elongated tubular member terminating in a gas outlet opening in said receiver engageable with said intake port in said carrier.

THE *NEW* AR-15 COMPLETE OWNER'S GUIDE

But, there are some disadvantages to the external gas piston concept. For one, there are more parts. For another, accuracy can take a hit because free-floating the barrel is, as a rule, impractical. Keep in mind that the balanced pressure in the bolt carrier assembly of the Stoner System "unloads" the bolt as the bolt unlocks, reducing wear and breakage, compared to the typical external gas piston design. And "infinite variety"? No two external piston systems are alike; you have to get your parts from a sole source, trusting that it will be around down the line when you need support.

What if...the external piston design had come first? Would we now be seeing Stoner System retrofit kits to do away with the complexity of external piston systems? We might well herald the simplicity and directness of the Stoner System and race to converting our external gas piston guns to gain all the Stoner System's benefits! Oh, the irony...

We conclude with a Tech Note by Mark Westrom of ArmaLite:

P.O. Box 299 Geneseo Illinois, U.S.A. 61254 Tel 309-944-6939 fax 309-944-6949 info@armalite.com

TECHNICAL NOTE 54:

DIRECT IMPINGEMENT VERSUS PISTON DRIVE

PURPOSE: To compare the merits of internal and external piston drive systems.

FACTS: The AR-15/M16 and the AR-10 family of rifles employ a unique gas powered operating system patented by Eugene Stoner in the 1950's. This gas operating system works by passing high pressure propellant gases tapped from the barrel down a tube and into the carrier group within the upper receiver, and is commonly but incorrectly referred to as a "direct impingement" system.

The gas expands within a donut shaped gas cylinder within the carrier. Because the bolt is prevented from moving forward by the barrel, the carrier is driven to the rear by the expanding gases and thus converts the energy of the gas to movement of the rifle's parts. The bolt bears a piston head and the cavity in the bolt carrier is the piston sleeve. It is more correct to call it an "internal piston" system.

Most previous semiautomatic rifles use an "external piston" system operating in a gas cylinder mounted outside the receiver, but instead attached to the barrel. Propellant gases expand within the cylinder and force the piston to the rear. The piston either contacts a rod that and drives a carrier to the rear (FAL), or are part of, connected to, or strike a rod segment that passed around the action to cam and move the bolt (M1, M14, AK-47, SCAR). In some cases the piston is fixed and the movable cylinder drives the rod (AR-180).

ADVANTAGES AND DISADVANTAGES: The Stoner system provides a very symmetric design that allows straight line movement of the operating components. This allows recoil forces to drive straight to the rear. Instead of connecting or other mechanical parts driving the system, high pressure gas performs this function, reducing the weight of moving parts and the rifle as a whole.

HISTORY

In external piston systems, the path of the operating force is mechanically shifted around the action, resulting in a considerable mass of moving parts moving outside the centerline of the firearm and producing various torques within the system.

There is a common belief that the external piston operated systems are less accurate than the Stoner internal piston system because the operating parts start moving while the bullet is still in the bore. This is not true: Army Ordnance tests conducted in the 1960's revealed that the bullet is 25 feet out of the bore of the M1 and 15 feet out of the bore of the M14 before any operating part begins to move. It is more likely that the imbalances of the external piston, operating rod, cylinder, and other parts hanging on the barrel produce disruptive vibrations as the bullet exits the bore.

Although movement of the operating parts while the bullet is in the bore isn't apparently a culprit in reducing the accuracy of external piston systems, the inherent accuracy of the Stoner internal piston system has been consistently confirmed in competitive shooting. In all events that allow use of any mechanism the shooter wishes, the Stoner internal piston system is prevailing. Few competitive shooters use the Garand or Kalashnikov systems, and none observed now use the FAL system. In American Service Rifle and NRA competition, the external-piston operated rifles are considered a significant disadvantage.

There is a debate about which system remains cleanest. The internal piston system tends to leave propellant residue in the receivers, while the external piston systems keep the residue outside the action in the cylinder. External piston driven systems, however, tend to allow more external dirt into the action because of the openings required for various connecting members (operating rod, bolt lugs, etc). Comparison tests of the M16 and the M14 before Desert Storm confirmed the superiority of the Stoner system in sand and dust tests, and recent testing has proven that proper cleaning of either system provides excellent reliability.

ArmaLite concludes that there is no technical advantage to an external piston system employing current ammunition. It will likely, however, provide external-piston systems to the market as customers demand.

As a last note, misuse of the term "direct impingement" to describe the Stoner system is so common that it has confused the issue. A direct impingement system like that of the AG-42 Ljungman or the French MAS-49 rifle taps gas at the barrel and passes it into the receiver in a way similar to the M16, (the source of the confusion) but deposits it into a small, shallow cup or pocket in the carrier. The gas expands there and drives the carrier to the rear with relatively little pneumatic advantage. The addition of the Stoner internal piston system provides significantly more pneumatic advantage to the rifle and little of the blast of escaping gas at the breech end of the gas tube of the earlier rifles.

MARK A. WESTROM

President

© 2010 ArmaLite, Inc. All rights reserved. Reprinted by permission.

THE *NEW* AR-15 COMPLETE OWNER'S GUIDE

Fosbery's multilug bolt shotgun. Note the six lugs, the lug recesses in the receiver, and the operating rod on the right of the receiver (to the bottom of the picture as shown). Photo courtesy of David J. Baker, coauthor of **Paradox, The Story of Col. G.V. Fosbery, Holland & Holland, and the Paradox**.

A side view of Fosbery's shotgun. In both these pictures the bolt is fully rearward. Photo courtesy of David J. Baker.

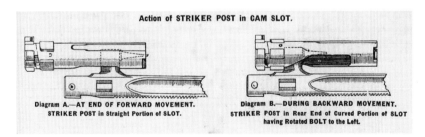

The Lewis Gun mechanism. Note that the four bolt locking lugs are on the left end, or the rear, of the bolt. Note also the early use of a cam slot and stud to rotate the bolt in and out of locking.

HISTORY

JOHNSON'S JEREMIAD
—or, did the prophet finally find honor in his own country?—

In this narrative of the technical roots of the AR-15, you may have noticed the distinct lack of references to Melvin M. Johnson, Jr., the Johnson Rifle, and the Johnson's multilug rotary bolt locking into a barrel extension. Many accounts of the history of the Stoner System point to Johnson's M1941 rifle as the immediate antecedent to the AR-10/AR-15. However, as with so many aspects of the development of the Stoner System and the AR-10/AR-15, things may not be as simple as they seem.

Let's address the multilug rotating bolt, common to the Johnson rifle and Stoner's designs. The first documented use of a multilug bolt appears to be in George V. Fosbery's British Patent #11,339, applied for on 3 July 1891 and accepted on 2 July 1892. Fosbery is better known for his Paradox combination "ball" and shot barrel design, and in this country best known for the Webley-Fosbery revolver of "Maltese Falcon" cinema notoriety.

Fosbery's patent drawing shows a four-lug bolt. However, the sole known example of the use of Fosbery's design, a pump shotgun, has a six-lug bolt. The bolt is turned by an operating rod with an uncanny resemblance to a Garand op rod, albeit a rod actuated by a forend pump rather than a gas piston push. Why six lugs? Perhaps to shorten the cam track in the op rod "hump." The more lugs, the less rotation is needed to unlock the bolt.

One of the next appearances of the multi-lug bolt was in the Lewis machine gun. The Lewis gun used a four-lug bolt, albeit with the lugs at the rear of the bolt rather than the front. Bruce Canfield's account in **Johnson Rifles and Machine Guns** relates that one of Johnson's criticisms of the nascent Garand rifle was its use of the "obsolete" gas operation typified by the Lewis gun. Johnson was intimately familiar with the Lewis gun, and with all the small arms in common use by our military of the day.

Johnson was the scion of a white-shoe Boston lawyer, a prep school and Harvard graduate who had a lifelong love of things that go "Bang!" He was an accomplished shooter with rifle, shotgun and pistol. While at Harvard he became an ROTC cadet, though an illness prevented him from attending the final summer camp that would have led to his commission in the US Army. Mel finally acquiesced to his father's pressure, attending and graduating from Harvard Law and joining his father's Boston law firm. But, when an opportunity to be commissioned in the US Marine Corps arose, he accepted with alacrity. It was in his capacity as a reserve officer in the USMC that he visited Springfield Armory to audit the Garand and Pedersen rifles, and where his disdain for the Garand was formed.

It was around this time that the opportunity arose for Johnson to become involved in the development and promotion of a semiautomatic conversion of the '03 rifle, based on a concept designed and patented by one Franklin K. Young. His patent, #764,513, described what was in effect a primer-actuated automatic bolt. While Young asserted that his invention could be used with any common ammunition, the mechanism would seem to function most plausibly with a cartridge of Young's own design, Patent #624146, a cartridge that contains what is in essence a gas piston.

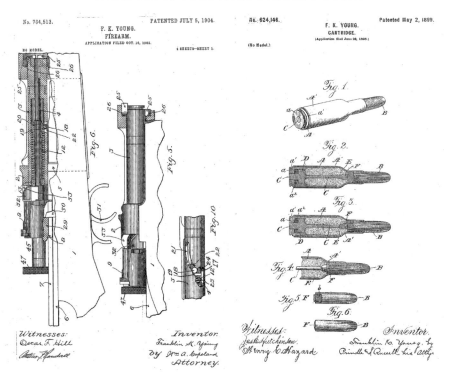

This is Young's patent for a (presumably) primer actuated semiautomatic rifle. Adapting this design to convert M1903 Springfield bolt-action rifles to semiauto was Johnson's first foray into firearms design. Alas, the mechanism could not be made to work with full-power US service ammunition and the project failed.

Young's patent rifle action was originally intended to be paired with his patent cartridge. Rather than depending on the primer to push the firing pin rearward to unlock the bolt, an internal piston is employed to push rearward on the firing pin. Essentially, each cartridge has within it a gas piston! Clearly, this would not be an economic proposition and rendered the concept spectacularly impractical.

The Johnson (upper) and Stoner (lower) bolts and barrel extensions. Brothers from another mother? We report, you decide.

HISTORY

Unfortunately, Young's design proved to be faulty. Its apparent "success" was based on the use of "downloaded" US service ammunition. It's also hard to see how the primer-actuated firing pin, the heart of the concept, could function with crimped-primer ammunition, the adoption of which sidelined Garand's primer-actued designs.

However, the idea of converting bolt action rifles to semiautomatic arms seems to have stuck with Johnson. Canfield relates that Johnson, after pondering the action of his beloved Springfield, visualized that he could use the recoil of the barrel to actuate the unlocking of the bolt from the barrel via an external cam. This approach would require, of course, that the bolt lock directly into the barrel, or to an extension of the barrel, just as found in every recoil-operated firearm with rotating bolt that came before. Examples range from the Remington Model 8 to the much-reviled Gladiator Chauchat light machine gun. Thus, locking a rotating bolt into a barrel extension preceded Johnson's application of it by thirty years or so.

But, what of the multilug configuration Johnson chose for his bolt? To understand that, one must first realize that Johnson's action was not, as is so generally and erroneously described, a "short recoil" action. Johnson was very clear that the barrel and bolt recoiled together just 3/8 inch before the bolt unlocked; the balance of the travel of the bolt was driven by residual chamber pressure, rather than by bolt inertia as in the traditional short-recoil action. This is the classic description of a delayed-blowback action. Johnson pointed to this feature of the design as a major advance on the Garand, because it rendered the action largely insensitive to variations in ammunition. The author's experience with extensive shooting of a reproduction Gas Trap Garand validates the sensitivity of the M1's gas trap to varying gas port pressure.

In order for the residual pressure to be sufficient to cycle the bolt, Johnson felt that a conventional two-lug bolt would absorb too much of the energy in the residual gas by virtue of its need to rotate up to 90 degrees. Canfield describes how Johnson, when contemplating a spoked wheel, realized that a multilug bolt would require far less rotation—in this case, 18 to 20 degrees—than a more conventional bolt, leaving enough energy for the bolt to cycle fully. Thus, for the Johnson rifle, the multilug bolt and barrel extension were a natural evolution in design. One is tempted to say that Mel was reinventing the wheel, but that would be a bit unfair. The Johnson M1941 rifle was a solid design that worked well. Johnson tilted at the windmills that were Rene Studler and the Ordnance Department for a decade, but he really had no chance of unseating the Garand in US service.

Have we answered the question, "Did Stoner adapt the Johnson bolt and barrel extension?" No, and until documentation is found, we may never know the true answer. We suggest that an hypothesis equally plausible to the Johnson connection is that Stoner came to recognize the need of a barrel extension with an aluminum receiver and the usefulness of a multilug bolt to conserve gas system energy by limiting the rotation needed for unlocking.

Early Colt SP1 Model R6000 from the first year of full production, 1964. Walt Kuleck Collection.

Later Colt SP1 Model R6000, circa 1979; note the M16A1 flash suppressor. Walt Kuleck Collection.

Colt AR-15A2 Sporter II Model 6500. Note the forward assist, but the lower remains the early design. Scott Duff Collection.

HISTORY
Back to Colt and the AR-15: the M16 for the Civilian Market

Colt began very quickly to open the civilian and law enforcement markets after winning US military orders. While 25 semi-auto-only "AR-15 SP1s" were built in 1963, production really didn't get underway until the next year. However, production of civilian AR-15s drifted along in a desultory fashion at the rate of only one or two thousand rifles a year. Was this due to production limits during the Vietnam War or a lack of interest in the civilian model? Probably a combination of these two factors obtained. This low rate continued until the early 1970's, the wind-down of US involvement in the war, when production began to leap upward with roughly three thousand in '71, five thousand in '72, eight thousand in '73, eleven thousand in '74, and so on. Perhaps this growth in sales was in part a result of television exposure to the M16 in the nightly news in Vietnam. Many wish to own an example of the current military rifle, and the AR-15 is as close as you can get.

In 1993, in anticipation of the "Assault Weapon Ban," Colt shipped nearly 60,000 AR-15s. By 1996 production was back down to 15,000. While the AR-15 roughly parallels its military cousins, it has been offered by Colt in a bewildering array of variations, subvariations, and deviations for the civilian market starting in 1963. We have documented over thirty-four different "pre-ban" variants (including conversion kits) in .223 Remington, 9x19mm Parabellum and .222 Remington (exported to countries banning "military" calibers, rare to find in the US) as having been offered in the twentieth century. AR-15 aficionados will refer to "Green (box) Label" and "Blue Label" models (with and without bayonet lug, respectively). We have also found "Red Label" and "No Label" boxes! Colt has used model names such as "Sporter" (SP1), "Sporter II" (AR-15A2 Sporter II), "Sporter Match," "Sporter Competition," and more recently "Match Target." Early select-fire AR-15s were marked with both "Colt" and "ArmaLite," including "Colt ArmaLite AR-15 Model 01" S/N 0266 (held by the Ministry of Defence Pattern Room now at Leeds, England), but no AR-15 SP1 was (at least beginning with SP00011, the earliest [1963] examined by the author). Further, it is known that Colt freely substituted components without changing model numbers or names, presumably to deplete excess inventory, particularly military overrun inventory.

We found that while the AR-15 generally paralleled the evolution of the M16/M16A1, the SP1 and the later Sporter II had something of lives of their own. Certainly the earliest SP1s are very nearly semi-automatic versions of the M16. But even in the case of the M16, running changes took place. Dating these changes for the M16 series is difficult enough; doing so for the SP1 is very challenging indeed. A case in point is the trapdoor buttstock. While this newer buttstock was patented by Henry Into in 1971, when did it actually come into use? The M16/M16A1 Technical Manual (TM) of August 1966 shows the plain buttstock only. By the TM of Sept. '71 both early and late buttstocks are shown, but the plain buttstock is "obsolete, unavailable." Similarly, the pinned receiver extension (buffer tube) is found on early M16/M16A1 and SP1 rifles, but at some point hand-tightening and pinning the tube was abandoned in favor of the current style of tube with wrench flats at its rear. While the TM of August 1966 shows the pin and how to install it, by the TM of August 1968 (available in reprint from ArmaLite, Inc.) the pin is missing, never to return. The author's SP1 (S/N 01468) from 1964 is pinned; SP1 S/N 12495 from 1968 is not pinned. In contrast, the change from the three-prong flash suppressor to the birdcage type can be more closely

M16, M16A1 and M16A2 Comparisons

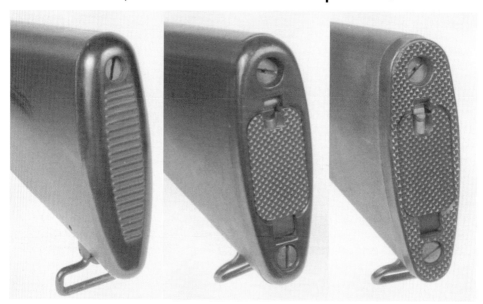

Left to right: M16 "no-trap" butt plate, M16A1 butt plate with trap, M16A2 butt plate. Walt Kuleck Collection.

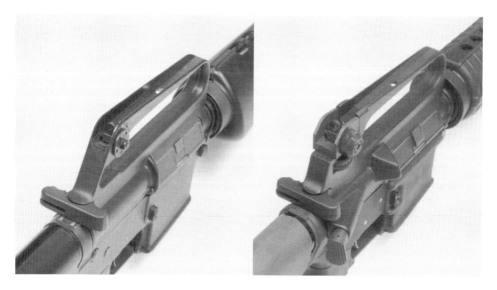

Left, M16 Upper, no forward assist, no case deflector, rear sight windage adjustable only. Right, M16A2 Upper, with forward assist, case deflector, and rear sight adjustable for both windage and elevation. Walt Kuleck Collection.

HISTORY

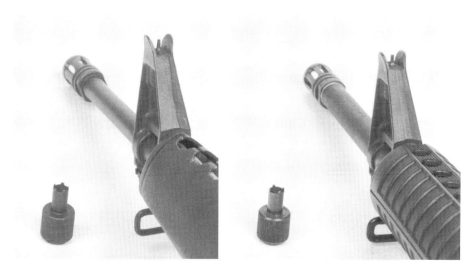

Left, M16/M16A1 Front Sight, round post, five detent positions for elevation adjustment. Right, M16A2 Front Sight, square post, four detent positions. Walt Kuleck Collection.

Left, M16 Upper Receiver, no forward assist. Right, M16A1 Upper Receiver, w/forward assist. Walt Kuleck Collection.

Left, M16A2 Upper Receiver, with forward assist and case deflector.. Right, M16A4 flat top Upper Receiver, with forward assist, case deflector, and detachable carry handle. Walt Kuleck Collection.

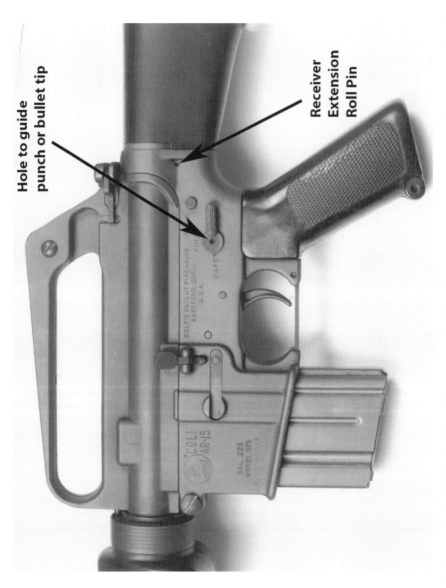

Early Colt AR-15 Sporter Rifle (SP1) Model R6000, circa 1964. Note the lower receiver extension roll pin and shallow hole drilled in the end of selector switch shaft.

HISTORY

dated; it was adopted for M16A1 production starting in January 1967; however, we have S/N 12495 from 1968, which has the three-prong flash suppressor!

Here's a mystery for you: why did early AR-15s and very early SP1s have small, shallow holes drilled in the ends of their takedown, pivot, trigger and hammer pins, and the selector switch shaft? Clint McKee of Fulton Armory originally suggested that this was done to keep a bullet tip from slipping off the pin and damaging the finish of the lower receiver. Subsequent research confirmed that the purpose of the holes was to facilitate the use of a cartridge's bullet for disassembly. However, the holes seem to have disappeared from SP1s by the late 1960's or early 1970's. It's likely that production stocks of "with hole" and "without hole" pins and selectors were intermixed in their respective supply bins well after the holes were no longer being drilled; thus a firm cut-off date cannot be established.

We know that early Colt (pre-M16, but select-fire) "Colt ArmaLite AR-15"s had green furniture; by the time of the SP1, the furniture has turned black. However, the early flat-ended machined firing pin retainer found in S/N 0266 at the MoD Pattern Room is still found in SP1 production into at least 1965. It was replaced by the now-familiar "cotter-pin" style retainer at some point in that time frame (we have found evidence that the retainer was changed in mid-1965). Likewise, the early delta-shaped charging handle found on S/N 0266 lingered on through very early SP1s. Early M16s and SP1s had chromed bolt carrier groups, as did the antecedent S/N 0266 at the Pattern Room. At some point the chroming was dropped, except for the inside of the bolt carrier.

The original SP1s were very similar to the original M16 (without forward assist), but with an oversize front pivot pin of screw-together design (rather than the military-style push pin), presumably to discourage using military upper receiver assemblies on civilian lower receivers.

> **NOTE:**
> This feature led to the following witticism, "How can you tell a Colt (SP1) shooter in the field? He has two screwdrivers sticking out of his pocket!"

Speaking of the forward assist, the original M16 buy for the Air Force occurred prior to the invention and adoption of the forward assist by the Army. Consequently, for some years bolt carriers with and without forward assist serrations (the notches milled into the side of the carrier engaged by the forward assist plunger) were to be found in the Defense Supply system. By the TM of August 1966, non-serrated bolt carriers were no longer supported because the serrated carriers work fine in upper receivers without forward assists. However, civilian SP1s continued to feature the non-serrated bolt carriers right through the 1980's.

With the introduction of the M16A2, Colt began to phase in the A2-type lower receiver, but with A1 (forward assist) uppers. You will find original Colt civilian AR-15s with A2 lowers and A1 uppers, A2 lowers with A2 uppers, and quite likely A1 lowers with A2 uppers! Speaking of uppers, we have found three different ejection cover latches: on an early SP1, a late SP1, and an AR-15A2, respectively!

How important is it to know the ins and outs of early Colts? It's probably more of academic than practical interest. Nonetheless, you should know some of the features and

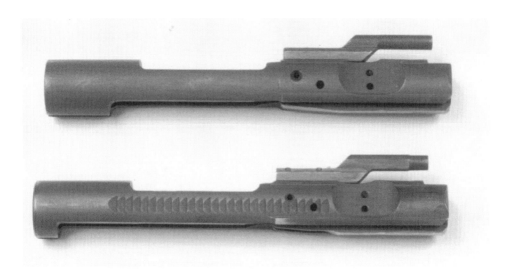

Bolt carrier assemblies. Top: early without serrations for use without a forward assist, Bottom: later with serrations for use with a forward assist.

Firing pin retaining pins. Top: early machined type, Bottom: later "cotter pin" type.

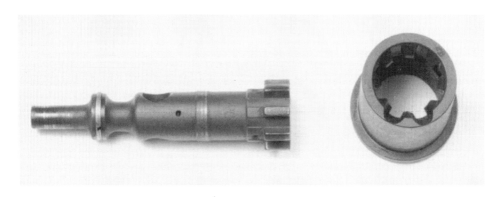

The AR-15 bolt locking lugs and corresponding inside of the barrel extension.

configuration variances that you'll find in older Colt AR-15s you'll see in the market. We've already mentioned the oversize front pivot pin. Many older Colts also have oversize trigger and hammer pins; the practical effect here is that fire control parts (both original type and aftermarket enhanced) you purchase must be compatible with the pin size you find in your lower. The purpose of using oversize pins seems to be to make installing "full-auto" M16 parts difficult or impossible. Colt lowers have had a "sear block" in the rear of the inside of the lower receiver. The purpose of this block is to prevent the installation of an automatic-fire sear. It can make the installation and adjustment of an aftermarket match trigger somewhat inconvenient, but has no effect on everyday function. The very latest Colt lowers seem to lack the sear block.

Contemporary, that is to say 21st Century, Colts now conform to what has become the *de facto* standard, that is, as close to the military M16 and M4 as the various laws permit. The days of seemingly capricious and annoying incompatibilities are over.

Others Enter the Market; Lots and Lots of Others!

As noted earlier, Colt AR-15 production was limited early on. After the popularity of military-style weapons exploded in the 1980's and the patents had expired, the demand for AR-15-type rifles was great enough that others began to enter the market. Of course, none could use the "AR-15" name, as Colt vigorously defended its trademark (and continues to do so). However, the patent on Stoner's gas system had expired on 6 September, 1977, and the clones began to proliferate. Olympic Arms, Nesard/Sendra, and Springfield, Inc. were among the AR-15 pioneers. You will see lowers and complete rifles from them as well as ArmaLite, Bushmaster, Dalphon, DPMS (Defense Procurement Manufacturing Services), Eagle Arms, Essential Arms, PWA (Pacific Western Arms/PacWest Arms), and others from the early "clone" era. Fabrique Nationale (FN, of Herstal, Belgium) opened a US plant and wrested a production contract for M16s away from Colt. Further, entrepreneurs such as John Norell welded demilled M16 receivers back together again. One subject to note is that most cloners position their offerings as "mil-spec" compared to Colt AR-15s. Of course, none are truly and completely "mil-spec"; the cloners are really referring to Colt's use of non-standard pins and the inclusion of their lower receiver sear block. Today there are likely millions of AR-15s in the civilian market. Not only can you purchase from a vast array of new and used guns, you can also acquire all the parts needed to build an AR from a wide range of sources. In that sense, life in the AR-15 world is better than ever.

In the Selecting chapter we will discuss the alternatives available to buyers and builders of AR-15-type rifles. The companies offering AR rifles, uppers, lowers, parts, accessories and upgrades are nearly too many to count. The market has literally exploded!

The AR-15: an Engineering Perspective

The AR-15 (and the AR-10 before it) broke new ground with its blend of features and principles combined with the use of materials new to arms manufacture. To review, a key element is the multi-lugged bolt and barrel extension combination. If we were to describe the bolt/barrel combination in traditional terms, the barrel extension performs the function of the usual "receiver." The forces of firing are held completely within that interface and not transmitted to any other part of the rifle's structure. Further, the innovative gas system uses

THE *NEW* AR-15 COMPLETE OWNER'S GUIDE

A Sidebar on Legislation

One of the absolute worst things to happen to modern American firearms ownership was the popularization of the term "Assault Rifle." The author early on predicted (and hoped against hope his prediction would prove wrong) that the hoplophobic anti-gunners on the American political scene would grab that term and run with it—and they did. "Saturday Night Special" didn't work very well for them, but "Assault Rifle" sure did! After all, who needs a rifle whose purpose is "Assault"? No right-minded person, that's certain! And who will stand up and defend such evil, ugly, death-dealing tools of the Devil? Not any politician interested in reelection! In October, 1988 Josh Sugerman, formerly communications director for the National Coalition to Ban Handguns, published a strategy paper, "Assault Weapons and Accessories in America." He wrote that because military-style semiautomatic firearms were commonly called "assault rifles," they were ideally suited for a public relations campaign along the lines of "Cop Killer Bullets." If even a few weapons could be banned using the "assault weapons" label, the door was then wide open to broaden the definition of banned guns or to simply widen the ban itself.

Then, on 17 January 1989, a disturbed individual carried a Chinese Type 56 (semiauto version of the AK-47) rifle into a crowded schoolyard in Stockton, California. In minutes he had killed five students and wounded 25 others before laying his rifle down and taking his own life with a Taurus PT-92 pistol. California Attorney General John Van de Kamp had despaired of getting "assault weapon" legislation through California's State Assembly; Purdy's despicable act made "assault weapon" legislation a done deal. The result was California's 1989 "Roberti-Roos" bill that registered a wide range of "assault weapons," including the "Colt AR-15." Colt responded by removing the bayonet lug from their AR-15s and assiduously avoiding any mention of "AR-15." Similar legislation harassed military look-alike rifle owners in New York City.

The second major event to affect the AR-15 world was the signing by Clinton of the so-called "assault weapons ban," which declared that "Semiautomatic pistols and rifles assembled after September 13, 1994, and possessing two or more of the features listed in [Section 921 (a) (30), Title 18 U.S.C.] are semiautomatic assault weapons as defined. The fact that the receiver may have been manufactured prior to September 13, 1994, was immaterial to classification of a weapon as a semiautomatic assault weapon." Such weapons were banned from manufacture after 13 September 1994. The features listed in Section 921 (a) (30), Title 18 U.S.C. included a prominent pistol grip, a bayonet lug, and a flash suppressor *or* a threaded barrel capable of mounting a flash suppressor. Clearly the AR-15 has a prominent pistol grip; thus AR-15s built after 13 September 1994 may not have had any other "ugly gun" feature, so the bayonet lug (already eliminated by Colt as a sop to Roberti-Roos) and flash suppressor were history. So was the "AR-15" name, as that was specifically declared an "assault weapon" in the bill. Fortunately for the Nation, the "assault weapons ban" failed renewal in 2004 and "sunset," or expired.

Sadly, On December 14, 2012, a mentally ill youth fatally shot twenty children and six adult staff members in a mass murder at Sandy Hook Elementary School in the village of Sandy Hook in Newtown, Connecticut, culminating a series of high-profile mass shootings. This atrocity revived calls for "assault weapon" and "high capacity magazine" bans on the national level, and used the spectre of dead children as emotional fodder. While these efforts failed on a national level, opportunistic state politicians did not let this tragedy go to waste, and rushed through draconian anti-AR measures in several states. While American ingenuity went to work on creating ARs that conformed to these laws, citizens of those states have had their rights significantly infringed. We hope for the best and fear for the worst. Join the NRA and get involved in the fight for our rights!

the bolt carrier as the "piston," thus the forces of unlocking are along the bore axis as well! The recoil spring is also in line with the bore. There is no moment arm in either case to be resisted by receiver structure. Thus, the only purpose of the upper and lower "receivers" is to permit conventional firearm function. The strength required of them to "keep it all (the rifle) together" is quite limited. Therefore, the usual concerns of receiver strength simply do not apply and the receivers can be made from very lightweight materials. Indeed, Colt has made experimental receivers from injection-molded plastic. Professional Ordnance, later acquired by Bushmaster, pioneered an AR-15-like rifle and pistol made from carbon fiber composite. Both Bushmaster and Wyndham Weaponry offer "plastic ARs." Keep in mind that because the integrity of the AR's lockup does not depend on the fit of the upper and lower receivers to each other, a tight fit between them is not important.

Further, the eight lugs (actually seven, one is the extractor) of the AR's rotary bolt provide more than the needed lockup strength to withstand the chamber pressure of the cartridge being fired. These multiple lugs also provide nearly-symmetric stiffness to the bolt/barrel extension coupling. More conventional bolts, e.g., the two-lug M1/M14-type bolt, provide stiffness in the horizontal plane but not the vertical plane. Thus, the lockup will not be as consistent as with the eight-lug AR bolt.

NOTE:
> Yes, we know that the Stoner bolt is really a seven-lug bolt, with the extractor in place of the eighth lug. Thus, the radial symmetry is not complete. Designers continue to develop means by which to gain the complete symmetry of eight lugs while retaining an extractor. We would submit that seven lugs provide more stability than two, even if the solution is less than perfect.

The down side to the AR's bolt design is that it does not provide primary extraction, i.e., the "leverage" afforded by the helix angle of the bolt lugs of the M1/M14. If the gas system is not balanced and timed precisely, it may attempt to open the bolt while the chamber pressure is still high enough to cause the cartridge case to be still obturated, that is, expanded and firmly gripping the chamber walls. This type of extraction failure was common during the Vietnam War period. Savvy sergeants, when handed a rifle with this sort of extraction failure, simply waited a moment; when the case cooled, it would often drop out by its own weight when the rifle was tilted muzzle up with the bolt open! At the very least, cycling the bolt would then nearly always extract the case.

The straight-line stock arrangement has two major benefits. First, the recoil vector is taken straight back into the shooter's shoulder; the vector is not offset as is the case with conventional dropped stocks. Therefore, the recoil has no moment arm to cause muzzle rise. This is particularly significant during automatic fire, but even in semiauto mode the rifle may be brought back on target very quickly after firing. However, it is very easy to "cant" an AR-15 because the pistol grip forces a somewhat unnatural angle to the shooter's right (if right-handed) arm; with its high-offset-to-the-bore sights, the effects of canting may be more severe than for a rifle whose sights are closer to the bore.

Care should be taken when shooting an AR over a barricade. With the relatively large sight-line-to-bore-axis offset, you can find yourself sighted on your target but shooting into

The early "duck bill" type flash suppressor on Colt ArmaLite AR-15 Model 01, S/N 0266 at the Ministry of Defence Pattern Room at Nottingham, England.

An early Colt AR-15 (SP1) 3-prong flash suppressor.

A later Colt AR-15 (SP1) birdcage flash suppressor.

A Colt AR-15A2 closed-bottom birdcage flash suppressor.

HISTORY

the barricade! As for canting, G. David Tubbs (several-time National Champion) says to not worry about it; just cant the rifle the same every time!

The second benefit from the stock configuration is that the recoil spring can be mounted in the buttstock. While the buttstock mounting of the spring precludes a conventional folding stock (which is why the carbine versions of the AR-15 have a "collapsible" sliding buttstock), it takes the recoil spring as far from the heat of firing as is physically possible. This gives the recoil spring a potentially longer operating life. In contrast, for example, the first prototype Savage-Lewis Gun had its recoil spring mounted around its gas system's operating rod, leading to spring endurance problems. Lewis switched to a clock-type mainspring mounted in the front of the trigger guard to get the recoil spring away from the heat of the gas system. The Lewis Gun then went on to a long and successful service life.

The ergonomics of the AR-15 are excellent for right-handed shooters. For lefties, ambidextrous safeties and magazine catches as well as extended bolt releases are available from AR-15 suppliers including Brownells and MidwayUSA. For those who are emphatically left-handed, complete mirror image rifles are available. The aperture rear sight continues the superiority of US military rifle sighting systems established by the Garand in 1936. The thumb of the shooting hand easily and conveniently manipulates the safety; in contrast, that of the AK, for example, is a human factors horror. While the Garand safety is arguably superior ergonomically, the Garand safety is not readily adaptable to a safe/semi/auto configuration, a requirement for the parent M16, of course. Unlike the AK series or even the Garand-actioned M14, the magazine goes straight into the magazine well rather than being cammed in to lock, *i.e.*, "rock 'n lock." Simply pressing the magazine release with the trigger finger of the right hand drops the magazine free. A replacement magazine may be immediately inserted using the left hand, which then drops the bolt by pressing the bolt release with the thumb. In contrast, removing the cammed-lock-type magazine is usually a two-hand operation. Nothing reciprocates outside the body of the rifle, preventing injury to the operator or malfunctions due to the snagging of external moving parts.

The Stoner design used in the AR gas system eliminates components required by other systems, whether they be the long and somewhat awkward operating rod of the M1 Rifle or the occasionally troublesome gas piston of the M14. A simple tube brings high-pressure gas from the barrel back to the bolt carrier. The gas scrubs the tube to the point that the greater part of the tube is self-cleaning. Fouling, when it occurs, is generally found at the front end of the gas tube. The combination of bolt and carrier acts much like a gas cut off-and-expansion system. Unfortunately, the simplicity of the design results in the exhausted gas (the gas that is not vented out the carrier's gas ports) being discharged more-or-less directly into the upper and lower receiver cavities, liberally coating them with combustion residues. The many crooks and crannies of the bolt carrier and the upper receiver ensure that the gas will "stagnate" and precipitate carbon and other combustion products liberally inside them. This is the source of the AR's reputation of being a "dirty gun." Many believe that it is important to keep the interior of the AR clean, another lesson learned the hard way in Vietnam.

The use of molded plastics and forged aluminum reduces the number of machining operations and the machining time to produce the stock, handguards, receivers and the like. Small pins and springs, easy to make, replace the complex interlocking parts found in the

A twenty-first century Colt: Model LE6920.

HISTORY

Garand-type action. The bolt and carrier require complex milling to be sure, but they are cylindrical in shape and in many respects easier to make (with CNC machining centers) than the Garand, or even the '03 Springfield, bolt. The author has been advised by manufacturing specialists that the most difficult AR-15 part to make is the extractor, while the carrier is probably the most complex. However, the investment to produce the forge dies, and to program and tool up machining centers, is significant. Once the tooling is amortized, though, production can be very economical indeed.

TRIVIA
For the complete opposite in manufacturing complexity, see the C96 ("Broomhandle") Mauser. It has no pins or screws (less the grip screw) and goes together like a Chinese puzzle. You wouldn't want to try making one at home, unless, of course, you're a Pathan in Peshawar!

Some Comments on the "Flat Top"

The original design of the AR-15 did not lend itself to optical sights, or indeed any sighting system intended to supplement or supplant the AR-15's original fixed, iron sights. Colt's initial solution was its series of carry-handle-mounted scopes, each having an integral carry handle mount. This arrangement fell short of perfection, as the already high sight line of the iron sights was made even higher by a scope mounted over them! Clearly this was an unsatisfactory solution. The obvious remedy was to remove the carry handle, and mount optical or match iron sights directly to the upper surface of the receiver. This course of action provides roughly the same sight line as provided by the original iron sights.

The Black Rifle by Stevens and Ezell illustrates experiments in the US and Canada in which the carry handle of an A1 or A2 upper receiver was milled off, and various sorts of mounting blocks, notches and bases were formed or attached to the now "flattop" upper for mounting optical or match iron sights. However, with this approach, versatility was lacking. The ability to mount one sort, or even one brand of sight, did not necessarily permit the mounting of another make or model of sight.

The answer proved to be providing a dovetail surface with transverse slots that would accept Weaver-type sight rings and mounts. After at least one aborted attempt at creating their own dovetail design (examined by the author at the MoD Pattern Room), Colt on 8 August 1990 resorted to the Swan/Weaver dovetail. This configuration was formalized as NATO Standards Agreement #1913, or STANAG 1913. The Canadian Armed Forces/ Forces Armee Canadien standardized on the Swan/Weaver system at about the same time. Subsequently this mounting arrangement has been mischaracterized as the "Picatinny Rail," after the Army arsenal responsible for much of US small arms development of late. Regardless, it is the Swan/Weaver dovetail!

In Conclusion

In conclusion, the AR-15 is a brilliant design in its combination of function and manufacturability. Does it fall short of "perfection"? Many would argue that the AR-15 does, but over time the AR has proven to be "good enough!"

From the simple... One of my very favorite AR types, a Fulton Armory flattop carbine with Lucid wood furniture courtesy of Clem Boyd. You have to see it in color to really appreciate the beauty of the walnut. Thanks, Clem! Walt Kuleck Collection.

...to the complex. A Brownells Dream Rifle, a long range sniper/hunter. Photograph Courtesy of Brownells.

SELECTING

CHAPTER 3

UNDERSTANDING, EVALUATING AND SELECTING YOUR AR-15

The Infinitely Variable AR-15

The AR-15 is one of the most versatile rifle systems available today, or in any time in history. True, other rifles, and pistols for that matter, have been adaptable to a wide range of roles. The US Army's M14, M1 Garand, and M1903 Springfield have all been turned into sniper rifles, for instance. In contrast with the AR-15, the changes required of these three for that new role were at the very least "semi-permanent." One is hard-pressed to recall a third role played by any of these three—save experimental "shorty" versions. None was readily adapted to a different caliber. When such an adaptation was made, it was a permanent conversion. For each of these rifles, changing caliber, barrel length or barrel contour requires not just a different barrel but the services of an armorer with his special tools. There was no going back except via a corresponding re-conversion.

Turning to non-military bolt action rifles, historically only a very few specialist models have permitted changing from one purpose to another. More recently there have been hunting bolt actions at a popular price that permit caliber changes via a barrel swap. However, these limited examples fall far short of the scope of the AR's modularity. Perhaps only the Thompson-Center "Contender®" series provides the versatility afforded the shooter by the AR-15. But the Contender is a single-shot break-open, not an autoloader nor even a bolt-action repeater. Its appeal is sincere to its aficionados, but limited in scope.

What gives the Contender its versatility is the same fundamental characteristic that gives the AR-15 its characteristic adaptability: modularity. The AR-15 is one rifle, and many rifles. With one "lower," or complete lower receiver assembly (the serial number is on the lower, thus legally the lower receiver is the "firearm"), one may affix any number of "uppers," or complete upper assemblies. These "uppers" can have different physical characteristics (A1, A2, flattop, high-riser, tri-mount, slick side, forward assist, etc., etc.) as well as different barrel assemblies (lightweight, HBAR, A2, M4, etc.) of differing lengths (from the legal 16" minimum to 24" and more), with different handguards and front sight arrangements including no front sight at all. With Brownells and MidwayUSA catalogs and a copy of ***The AR-15 Complete Assembly Guide***, you, the AR-15 owner, can truly "have it your way!"

Fewer variations of "lowers" are extant. In addition to cosmetic variations, there are lower receivers made of lightweight magnesium/aluminum alloy or polymers. "Upmarket" lowers may feature an integral trigger guard or various reinforcements. But, the real sizzle comes from the selection of butt stock, pistol grip, fire control group, and so on.

Many of the modifications or accessories one might add to a lower receiver are generally reversible, but those adaptations are more typically optimized for a particular range of purposes. For example, a "defense rifle" is not likely to have fitted to it a bulky, four-degree-

THE *NEW* AR-15 COMPLETE OWNER'S GUIDE

Brownells Dream Gun. Take particular note of the EOTech sight and the one-piece lower receiver/butt stock. Photograph Courtesy of Brownells.

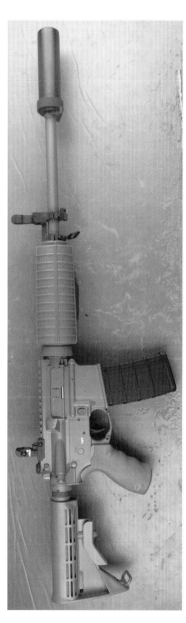

Nothing too unusual about this carbine in GunKote Desert Tan. However, the carbine does sport an excellent accessory for home defense: a sound suppressor. Worth the $200 transfer stamp and the paperwork hassle if your state permits you to have a suppressor. No sense in losing your hearing in a gunfight if you don't have to. Greg King Collection.

SELECTING

of-freedom match rifle butt plate, as a varmint or target AR-15 might have. Changing butt plates or butt stocks is quite straightforward, but doing so on a regular basis might prove to become tedious in short order. The same principle applies to extended bolt releases, ambidextrous magazine latches, and the like. But, within a broad range of applications, one lower assembly can serve admirably as a basis for a selection of upper assemblies for different uses.

There are many ways to categorize the potential uses of the AR-15. The following taxonomy, we believe, gives as good a basis as any for discussing the appropriate options and accessories one might specify on his or her AR-15:

General Purpose	Specific Application		
Defensive Rifle	Close Quarters	"Out There"	
Hunting	Varmint	Small Game	Boar and Deer-size
Competition	Service Rifle	Match Rifle	3-Gun/ IPSC/ Action Games
Just Plain Fun	"Plinking"		

Defining Your Purpose
Defensive Rifle: Close Quarters

Let's start with the Short Range Defensive Rifle. While the AR-15 was originally designed as a relatively short-range battle rifle, many think of it first as a Close Quarter Battle (CQB) rifle, particularly in carbine form. As a short-range defensive rifle, the AR-15 has no peer. With proper ammunition, the AR can even serve as a "house gun."

A typical short-range defensive rifle configuration will emphasize compactness. A 16-inch barrel provides the legal minimum "front-end" length, while a collapsible stock minimizes the "back-end" length. The shortest practical overall length is usually considered a "good thing" in this application, as "close quarters" imply confined spaces. Full-length rifles are awkward under these conditions.

> **TIP:**
> A collapsible butt stock will also adjust to fit a given rifle to both a short-armed small person and a long-armed big person, making the AR platform accessible to persons of all statures. Furthermore, a collapsible stock will allow the rifle to "grow" with a boy or girl from youth through adulthood.

> **TIP:**
> Those who are willing to submit a Form 1 and pay the $200 tax may choose to go with the 14.5-inch "M4" barrel. A barrel of this length will properly mount a

THE *NEW* AR-15 COMPLETE OWNER'S GUIDE

Fulton Armory lower receiver with Adams Arms gas piston conversion kit on a flattop upper with M4 barrel, Yankee Hill folding sights and GI three-prong flash suppressor. Fitted with Magpul MOE furniture with Blue Force Vickers Tactical Sling. Walt Kuleck Collection.

Brownells Dream Gun. Here we have a carbine with all the "mod cons": extended quad rail, enhanced collapsible stock, forward grip with integral weaponlight, and Trijicon ACOG. Photograph Courtesy of Brownells.

SELECTING

bayonet (with bayonet lug and flash hider, of course). This may be important if a bayonet figures in to your defense plans.

Barrel weight becomes a matter of taste. For quick handling, a lightweight barrel is indicated. However, there are those who feel the need for the rifle's balance to be further forward than will result from a lightweight barrel. The shorter the barrel, the more the need for an effective flash suppressor. The light recoil of the .223 cartridge, combined with the straight-line stock design of the AR-15, makes a muzzle brake or compensator less helpful in home-defense situations. A muzzle brake *will* direct the sound and pressure pulse of firing more in your direction and towards anyone to your side; this may not be a good thing. To allow the mounting of desired sights and ancillaries, handguard float tubes with rails on all four sides are nearly a standard today.

When the AR-15 is to be used in CQB situations, besides the implication of short range there is also the implication of "built-up" spaces, including habitations. In that case, penetration can quickly become "over-penetration." One way to avoid perforating the neighbor's home as well as one's own is to use lightweight, frangible, "varmint-style" bullets. Forty- or 45-grain hollowpoint bullets will offer sufficient energy dump on the initial target to provide the desired effect while limiting secondary penetration. Thus, a 1 in 12 twist could be a good choice for these conditions. Faster twists, particularly 1 in 7, have been known to cause light, thin-jacketed bullets to disintegrate in flight due to centrifugal forces in excess of the bullet's design specifications.

TIP:
> Ammunition companies are now offering "defensive" ammo that is designed to function well in an anti-personnel mode while not unduly over-penetrating. Check the recommendations from Cor-Bon, Federal, Hornady and so on for their current offerings for home defense purposes.

Once the barrel configuration has been determined, the sighting systems to be used must be considered. Here there are many variations from which to choose. As we are considering a defensive rifle, we must be prepared to use it properly in a wide range of situations. Thus a degree of redundancy is advised if one chooses to use an optical sight.

Let's start with iron sights. Factory AR-15 models are now only rarely equipped with A1 sights (adjustable for windage only), A2 sights (adjustable for both windage and elevation), and detachable carry handles with the A2 sight. The standard today appears to be a "flat-top" upper receiver configuration, with a Swan/Weaver Picatinny rail able to accept a wide variety of rear sights, of both fixed and foldable types, in addition to red dot sights, holographic sights, telescopic sights, and so on. Most users of this type of rifle will opt for foldable rear and front sights, most commonly called "Back Up Iron Sights" (BUISs) when an optic is used as the primary sighting system.

TIP:
> Some authorities suggest leaving the sights up, selecting and mounting an optic such that the optic can be used while sighting through the iron sights. They assert that if the optic goes down, one will be sufficiently discomfited that flipping up the iron sights may be too readily fumbled under stress. Your call.

The lead author's home defense rifle, a Fulton Armory "Millennial" with full-length gas system. The optic is a C-More Scout with integral forward mount that attaches to the A2 carry handle. The light is a Surefire M600 with upgraded aftermarket LED module. The laser and mount are from ALPEC. The butt stock is a Fulton Armory "Shorty" A2-type, with an adjustable butt plate also from Fulton Armory. It may not be au courant, but it's been with me for way over a decade, and I'm comfortable with it! Walt Kuleck Collection. Postscript: My publisher Scott Duff points out that I may want to rethink that sling; it's too easy for a sling to catch on doorknobs, flower vases, small pets, and so on, while moving through the house. Point well taken.

SELECTING

TIP:
To avoid excessive occlusion of the field of view, modern thinking is that the iron sights should appear only in the lower third of the optic. This "lower third" or "SOCOM" co-witness supersedes the old "center the irons in the optic" approach.

NOTE:
It would seem intuitive that one would want "absolute," or centered co-witness, putting the red dot on top of the front sight post. However, a decade or more of combat experience has taught special operations troops that an absolute co-witness can put an potential adversary's hands out of view behind the front sight post. Because it's the hands that can hold the weapon that will kill you, a lower third co-witness where the front sight is well below the centered red dot allows the viewer to better recognize an opponent's intentions.

Useful supplements to the CQB rifle's sighting systems include lights and lasers. High intensity flashlights provide illumination of a suspected target. These lighting systems can rise to the level of intensity that the person "caught in the headlights" is literally blinded and disoriented. These lights are generally provided with momentary switches so that the user does not become a gratuitous target, but can "flash on" quite briefly to identify a shadow in the darkness.

TIP:
A weaponlight on your defensive rifle may help you avoid shooting an intruder that legally poses no threat, or even a loved one. Many training authorities insist that a defensive rifle is not a "defensive" rifle unless it has an illumination system. Why? The legal system generally frowns on shooting unarmed persons. Check your local laws and justice system predilections.

PITFALL:
Weaponlights can be "too" bright in the experience of some. Most homes, for example, have light-colored walls, which will reflect a large percentage of the emitted lumens back into the eyes of wielder of the light. This does night vision no good whatsoever when the light blinks off.

While lasers are "sexy," and some believe that a laser dot can intimidate an adversary to the point of surrender, others find the laser dot's "wobble" to be distracting. Vendors now offer light/laser combination units, some of which are integrated into a vertical forward hand grip. If your tactical doctrine includes a sighting laser, many offerings are available to you.

The handguard arrangement for a short range rifle can be simply the standard-type AR-15 handguards, "railed" handguards that attach in the same manner as the GI handguards, or one of the various "floating" handguard tubes. As the short range application will require neither tight slinging-up nor bipod use (as a rule), the accuracy advantages of a floating handguard assembly will not apply as emphatically. There may be aesthetic or preferential reasons for the use of one handguard style or another, or a given style of handguard may more readily accept some needed or desired equipment or accessory.

THE *NEW* AR-15 COMPLETE OWNER'S GUIDE

Brownells Long Range Dream Gun. Note the Magpul PRS buttstock; this allows adjustment of comb height and length of pull to get the perfect cheek weld—and with that big scope, you want your eye in the same place for every shot. Photograph Courtesy of Brownells.

The lead author's long-range rifle nicknamed "The Desert Cruiser." Best seen in color; the Cruiser is based on a Fulton Armory lower receiver; with walnut butt stock and pistol grip with palm rest. The Magpul PMAG and rail covers are in desert tan. Walt Kuleck Collection.

SELECTING

But what of the lower receiver assembly? In a short-range defensive rifle, the argument can be made that simpler is better. Being able to handle and operate one's rifle safely and effectively argues against a plethora of gadgets. One option that may prove valuable is a collapsible stock, which permits the user to adjust its length to suit individual physiognomy and can make stowage a bit simpler.

PITFALL:
The "GI-style" collapsible butt stock generally does not afford a good cheek weld for sighting with optics. One of the newer aftermarket stocks may fit your face, or be adjustable to fit your face, as well as your length of pull, giving you a solid cheek weld.

TIP:
An ambidextrous (specifically helpful for the sinistrous among us) charging handle may make readying the rifle a bit easier and more certain. Unless an extended firefight is anticipated requiring rapid and frequent magazine changes, an extended bolt catch is just one more projection to catch on clothing or brush. Southpaws may want to install an ambidextrous safety and ambidextrous magazine catch, but that's about it.

Remember, please, that as in other aspects of life (e.g., wine, women and song), the AR-15 is as much a matter of taste as of objectivity. Further, the AR-15 may be adapted to suit your fancy, fancifully if that's your preference.

Defensive Rifle: Long Range

The Long Range Defensive Rifle presents a somewhat different set of requirements compared to the short range rifle, while sharing some characteristics. For example, whereas with the short range rifle we might well dispense with optical sights as an unnecessary complication, on a long range rifle a telescopic sight will be needed by most users. A red-dot sight or occluded-eye sight may be preferred by some, but their optimum applications would seem to be at shorter ranges than that implied by "long range."

While excellent work can be performed with aperture sights, the scope provides an edge for those with ageing eyes or just a desire for higher perceived precision. More generally, a scope facilitates target identification. When you are off the "square range" with its obvious bulls-eye, one brown blob at 600 meters looks much like another. That blob might be a bear, or a cow, or an innocent passer-by. In this case, the flattop receiver provides the best mounting arrangement for a conventional scope. Supplemental iron sights are optional for a sporting application, though for a military shooter they might be a lifesaver if the scope goes down.

Since the optimum in interior ballistics is desired in a long range rifle, a 20 inch or even 24 inch barrel would be appropriate. Likewise, a heavier barrel will give more predictable accuracy, particularly after being heated by repetitive shots. However, more is not always better; a very heavy match barrel would possibly be more weight than one would care to hump for any distance. If the rifle is intended to be carried on foot for considerable distances, an 18 inch barrel, possibly fluted to reduce weight while minimally reducing stiffness, might

THE *NEW* AR-15 COMPLETE OWNER'S GUIDE

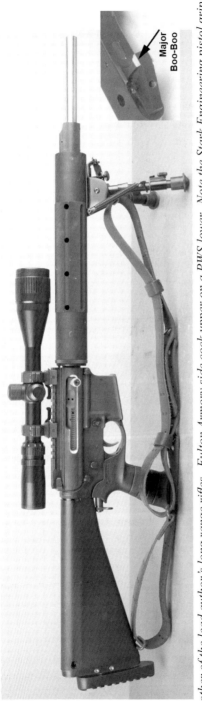

Another of the lead author's long range rifles. Fulton Armory side cock upper on a PWS lower. Note the Stark Engineering pistol grip. Many years ago I broke the trigger guard ears clean off the lower; this Stark grip, with its integral trigger guard, allowed me to rescue the lower from my recycle bin. Walt Kuleck Collection.

Brownells Long Range Dream Gun. The PRS stock is evident again. Photograph Courtesy of Brownells.

SELECTING

be appreciated. Validation for this approach can be found in the "Mk 12" M16 SOCOM upper of the '00's, which had a medium-weight 18 inch barrel. The Mk 12 was intended by the US military to be used for precision shots by a "designated marksman." Since long range is the mission, heavy bullets (e.g., 62-grain and up) are required. The faster twists of 1 in 9 or 1 in 7 are needed to stabilize these bullets. The heavier you go, bullet-wise, the faster the twist you'll want. We will go into twist in more detail in the Details chapter.

The long-range rifle requires a handguard float tube, if only to keep the stress applied by the use of a bipod from changing the point of impact, an important consideration at long ranges. Because the long range rifle generally does not benefit from a light or laser, a simple round handguard generally suffices. Full-length rails, or even rails on all four sides, are not needed as a rule. However, in military settings there may be exceptions to this "rule."

As for the lower receiver, an adjustable butt stock to properly fit the scope's sight line is generally required.

PITFALL:
> Many scopes used for long range work have large objective lenses (the big one at the front of the scope), which must be mounted higher than the usual AR sight line. Thus, unless provisions are made via the butt stock, one may find oneself lifting one's head to peer through the scope and lose one's cheek weld.

Because in a long range defensive situation, e.g., on a Western plain, one may have the opportunity to go through several magazines worth of ammunition in an encounter, features to facilitate quick and sure magazine changes might be contemplated. But, as with the short range rifle, simpler is probably better.

Hunting Rifle: Varmint

The Varmint Rifle may start out looking something like the long range defensive rifle, but its character is quite different. For one, sight redundancy is not only unnecessary, it is superfluous. One will not be shifting to iron sights if one's scope goes bad whilst plinking groundhogs at 300 yards. One will, as a rule, simply go home, or hike back to the pickup for the backup rifle. Yes, there are those who enjoy the challenge of the stalk. For them, reversion to iron sights might just add to the pleasure of their hunt. I would imagine them to be in the minority. Thus, iron sights will be generally entirely omitted. The front sight will be supplanted by a simple gas block with no provision for sight mounting. The barrel will be of 20, 24 or even 26 inches in length, and of "bull" configuration: very, very heavy. A handguard float tube will provide a convenient place to mount a bipod without affecting the barrel and shifting the point of impact. As the eyepiece "bell" of a long-range scope interferes with access to the charging handle, a "tactical" or extended charging handle latch will make bolt cycling trouble-free.

The varmint rifle "lower" may be more elaborate than those used for defensive rifles. A contoured pistol grip can provide more comfort and control during long periods of searching and sighting. An adjustable butt plate can likewise tailor the rifle's fit to the user without fear of overcomplication. However, a "tricked-out" lower is less suited to defensive ap-

THE *NEW* AR-15 COMPLETE OWNER'S GUIDE

A–Hunting we will go…with apologies to Jeff Cooper. A "Pseudo-Scout" based on a Ruger SR-556 in 6.8 SPC, a worthy successor to the Winchester 94 for whitetail, if the Ruger didn't weigh so much. Leatherwood scope, Ching Sling by Andy Langlois. Walt Kuleck Collection.

A classic CMP/NRA Service Rifle. Looks just like an M16, doesn't it? Looks can be so deceiving. Photograph Courtesy of Fulton Armory.

SELECTING

plications than a more conservatively equipped one might be. Thus the effect on a given lower's adaptability to the range of uppers contemplated must be considered.

Note:
> The varmint—and match rifle, for that matter—application is more tolerant of components and accessories liable to get out of adjustment. Further, there is no danger of "hanging up" on "environmental hazards" such as clothing and car doors. On the whole, failure in this arena is embarrassing rather than life-threatening.

Hunting Rifle: Small Game

The AR-15 may not be the tool that first comes to mind when considering small-game (e.g. squirrels, rabbits and other less-than-deer-size legal game) hunting, but it certainly qualifies by virtue of its potential for lightness and quick handling. One approach to this application might blend features of the short range defensive rifle with that of the varmint rifle. For this use, a red-dot or long-eye-relief sight might be just the ticket, as long range is not required.

The Short Range Defensive Rifle would seem to include most of the requisite features, with one exception: as with the varmint rifle, iron sight redundancy is not required. Because a small game hunter is typically "walking the woods" (or fields), light weight would be a virtue. If iron sights are desired, the longer sight radius of a 20 inch barrel would be advised (albeit in lightweight form to keep the rifle's weight down). A 1 in 12 twist would be optimum for the light bullets typical of this kind of hunting. For the small game rifle's lower, the short range defensive rifle's assembly would appear to be equally suited to this application. In sum, the small game rifle boils down to a short range defensive rifle with a 20 inch barrel!

Hunting Rifle: Deer-Size Game

The AR-15's .223 Remington cartridge is not recommended for deer-size game. In many states the .223 does not meet the caliber or power requirements set forth by state authorities for deer hunting rifles. However, the AR-15 may be fitted with any one of a number of alternative-caliber uppers, among them 6.5 Grendel, 6.8 SPC, .300 Blackout, .450 Bushmaster, 7.62x39mm (.30 Russian Short) and others. These cartridges range in power from the equivalent of the .30/30 Winchester, which has been the most popular short-range deer cartridge almost since its inception in the late 19th century, to a "short .45-70."

NOTE:
> The "big block," or AR-10-type rifle, is available in calibers from .243 on up...to pretty much any caliber based on the .308 cartridge case, for which the AR-10 was originally designed.

The major difference between the .223 and the "alternative caliber" AR-15s is the barrel, though many alternative calibers will also require a specific bolt and/or magazine. Thus, the comments found here regarding the small game rifle will generally apply if deer-size game are the quarry, with the exception of caliber.

THE *NEW* AR-15 COMPLETE OWNER'S GUIDE

Another Service Rifle Match Rifle, this a .308 M110 clone, allowed under NRA Service Rifle rules. Photograph Courtesy of Fulton Armory.

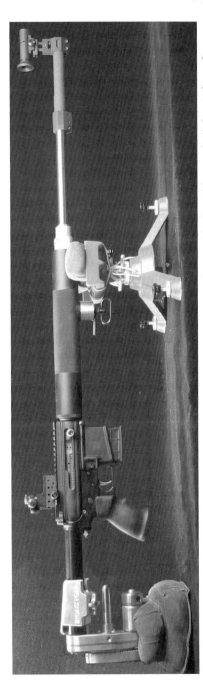

Here we have a full-tilt NRA Match Rifle from Fulton Armory. Note the exotic butt stock, the "bloop tube" for sight radius extension and the Redfield Olympic sights. Photo by Walt Kuleck for Fulton Armory.

SELECTING

Target Rifle: CMP/NRA Service Rifle Competition

The Civilian Marksmanship Program (CMP, formerly the DCM, Director of Civilian Marksmanship) sanctions competitions in cooperation with the National Rifle Association (NRA) for US Service Rifles. Currently accepted rifles for this popular competition include the US Rifle Cal..30, M1 (Garand), the US Rifle Cal. 7.62MM, M14, the US Rifle Cal. 5.56-MM, M16, and the US Rifle, Cal. 7.62MM, M110 (AR-10-type). Alas, true M14s and M16s are capable of full-automatic fire. Civilian ownership is restricted to the few that were entered into the National Firearms Act (NFA) registry prior to 1986. However, CMP/NRA rules permit the use of "commercial equivalents" to the true US Service Rifles. Thus, the AR-15 qualifies as a Service Rifle for the purposes of Service Rifle competition.

But, for the purposes of Service Rifle competition, not just any AR-15 will do. The AR-15 you use must duplicate the configuration of the M16A2 Service Rifle. It may not have any external modifications. Thus, detachable carry handles are out. Muzzle brakes are out, though "A2" flash hiders (when legal) are in. A plain muzzle is allowed. The barrel must be 20 inches in length, though twist is optional. Its visible contour, that is, the portion of the barrel in front of the front sight, must be .75" or less in diameter. Standard "A2" buttstocks and pistol grips must be used. A two-stage trigger of 4.5 pounds pull weight is specified. A hidden float tube is permitted and necessary for an M16A2 counterpart, as Service Rifle shooters sling up very, very tightly.

A Sidebar on Why the M16/AR-15 superseded the M14/M1A

The AR-15/M16 is a fine rifle, as we've seen. However, after the M16 was approved by the National Board for the Promotion of Rifle Practice (NBPRP) for Service Rifle competition in 1971, it was not competitive against the M1 and M14/M1A. Slinging-up would unpredictably change its point of impact. The M16's service bullets and barrel twist were ineffective past 300 yards, far short of the 600 yards that is the longest-range stage of Service Rifle. Heavy barrels helped, but not enough. The situation was sufficiently discouraging that in 1974 the NBPRP proposed an altered course of fire for Service Rifle, "Course B," whose maximum range stage was limited to 300 yards.

The solution, as developed by U.S. Army Marksmanship Training Unit armorers, turned out to be two-fold. First, the "no-external-modifications" rule was relaxed to the extent that float tubes hidden under the standard "A2" handguards were permitted. Why did this require a rule change, if the float tube was hidden? Because in order to take the strain of slinging-up off the barrel, the front sling swivel could then be attached to the float tube, rather than the front sight/gas block as on the standard rifle. Strictly speaking, this was an "external modification."

Second, the use of "handloads" with heavy, non-military-specification bullets was allowed and the barrel twist "quickened" to suit. Thus, the AR-15 is becoming the rifle of choice in Service Rifle competition. Its light recoil makes recovery in rapid fire much simpler, but more importantly, it's what the Service teams are using—and for many shooters, that makes all the difference!

THE *NEW* AR-15 COMPLETE OWNER'S GUIDE

One of Colt's Competition Three-Gun Match Rifles. Photograph Courtesy of Colt's Manufacturing LLC.

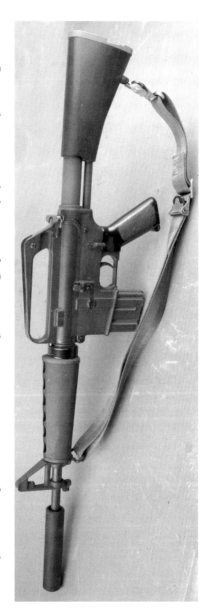

The definition of "fun." A Colt Model 607 clone on a Colt SP1 lower. Note the original design collapsible two-position stock. No, that's not a real suppressor; it's a slip-over muzzle brake. Someday perhaps it will have two tax stamps, one for the suppressor and one for a 10 inch barrel. Walt Kuleck Collection.

SELECTING

Returning to the CMP/NRA Service Rifle

Consequently, the CMP/NRA Service Rifle (Service Rifle) is much like the original NHRA "Super Stock" drag racers: outside, "box-stock." Inside, blueprinted and massaged right to the ragged edge of the rules (and beyond, when it could be gotten away with)! One has little wiggle room for modifications. The secret to a good match rifle is—that there are no secrets! Use the best barrel and other components you can find, have it assembled by the most meticulous armorer, ensure that the devil is exorcised from the details, and you'll have a rifle that will shoot well enough to win. You must do your part with proper maintenance and the best ammunition you can make or buy.

Target Rifle: NRA Match Rifle Competition

NRA Match Rifle competition allows caliber variations, action variations, and a wide variety of modifications. It is truly the "unlimited" class. Suitable ARs would have uppers fitted with 24- or 26-inch bull barrels, full-length float tubes, precision aperture iron sights front and rear, all of course on a flat-top upper receiver.

The lower receiver is also an "anything goes" playing field. Contoured pistol grips, adjustable butt plates, extended bolt releases and the like are commonplace.

In sum, the match rifle is much like the varmint rifle, with the exceptions of the sight arrangements and the barrel twist. The match rifle will be used with a sling and hand stop, the varmint rifle with a bipod or rest.

Action Shooting/Three Gun/IPSC Competition

As personalized and idiosyncratic as AR-15 configurations are, this category may stimulate the widest range of variations to suit personal taste. Action shooting is intended to simulate various kinds of combat scenarios, some short range, some long range. Speed of target acquisition, rifle handling and rapid accurate fire are critical. This is the arena where extended/ambidextrous magazine catches, extended bolt releases and ambidextrous safeties have merit in the eyes of many. Fanciful color schemes have been fashionable, and aesthetic oddities such as octagonal upper receivers (and lowers to match!) have been offered to the competing public.

Since the basic rationale of the action gun is that of defensive rifle, most competitors seem to blend characteristics of the short and long range defensive rifles described above, to suit personal taste or the current en vogue styling.

Fun Shooting

For many, there's nothing more relaxing than spending a day at the range or other safe area informally shooting impromptu targets, i.e., "plinking." This is truly a setting where you can "run what ya brung." Shoot whichever AR-15 configuration you want! Here is definitely a place for the Cal..22 rimfire conversion units. Note that you'll want to have a slow (1 in 12 or 1 in 14) twist if you want those stubby "Long Rifle" bullets to grab the rifling.

Speaking of .22 LR ARs, today one can choose from a variety of dedicated .22LR uppers with the proper chamber, bore diameter and twist for the rimfire cartridge to assure

More fun, this on a budget. Ruger SR22 Rifle, essentially a Ruger 10/22 in a Nordic Design chassis with Ruger enhancements and a few Ruger-branded accessories that were briefly available. The magazine is a Ruger BX-25. Walt Kuleck Collection.

SELECTING

optimum function and accuracy. In addition, there are a variety of "AR-15" lookalikes that are completely dedicated .22LR rifles. Some of these cost little more than a .22LR upper with its magazines, so it may make sense for the shooter to consider them.

Understanding, Evaluating and Selecting Your AR-15: Conclusions

Perhaps we can summarize the selection process best by resorting to some basic principles; ask yourself the following questions:

- Are there rules or limits that will apply to my configuration's intended application?
- What bullets do I want to shoot?
- What type of sights do I want to use?
- What handling characteristics would suit my needs?
- What are my ergonomic considerations?
- Is weight or length an issue?
- What accessories might I wish for which I should make provisions?

The versatility of the AR-15 may seem bewildering at first; but, if you think through your needs and the best way to fill them, you'll lessen your waste of time, effort and money acquiring or assembling a configuration that falls short of its intended purpose.

In this chapter we've discussed AR-15 components in general terms, in the context to which they might be used. In the next chapter, we'll detail the major components and systems, to further guide your selection and evaluation process.

Ever wonder how we get those rifle pictures? Here's the secret: a pair of photo lights, a cream-colored backdrop, a workbench and a pair of Canon cameras: an EOS Rebel T3i and a T4i. Mostly we use the workaday 18-55 Canon zoom, but for close-ups we have an EF-S 60mm Canon macro. Faithful readers of the **Complete Guide** *books will recognize the shop and bench from* **The M1911 Complete Assembly Guide**, *and the fellow in the background as Eric.*

The heart of the AR-15: the Stoner bolt and barrel extension. Federal definitions aside, this *is the AR-15 rifle. All the rest, the upper receiver, the lower receiver, the handguards, the butt stock, the pistol grip—all the rest of it is simply to make it convenient to hold, easy to shoot, and semiautomatically function as a repeater. Walt Kuleck Collection.*

DETAILS

CHAPTER 4

AR-15 COMPONENTS IN DETAIL

The Barrel

AR-15 barrels are fairly simple to make. Unlike an M1 Garand barrel, for instance, they have no asymmetric contours and require little complicated machining. Even the locking lug recesses are incorporated in a separate component, the barrel extension. This component is threaded onto the breech end of the AR barrel and pinned in place with the same locating pin used to align the barrel radially in the upper receiver. The most critical operations in making an AR barrel are properly aligning the threads for the barrel extension and properly locating the gas port.

Thus, it is a fairly straightforward process to lathe turn an AR-15 barrel from a barrel blank. Almost anyone can do it, and almost everyone does. You will find barrels available from a large number of sources, though the barrel blanks come from a smaller number of sources, e.g., Douglas. In general, however, you will not know the original source of a vendor's barrel, whether as a separate component or a barreled upper. You may not even care, as you should keep in mind one very important point:

It is the _inside_ of the barrel that matters!

You will have to depend on the reputation and integrity of the barrel vendor to ensure, as best you can, the quality of that critically important bore.

Other features of the barrel are important, of course. If the locating pin is not properly indexed with respect to the gas port, for example, the front sight may end up tilted to one side or the other. The high sight line of the AR design will magnify even a slight tilt to the point that you may end up using all your sight's windage adjustment to get on target! But, given adherence to the design specifications of the rifle, the barrel's performance will be most affected by its bore. The bore must be uniform in diameter along its length for maximum accuracy.

AR-15 barrels are offered in chrome-moly (Chromium/Molybdenum, CM) steel, stainless steel (SS), and chrome-lined chrome-moly steel. Stainless is more difficult to machine compared to chrome-moly, but the results can be equally satisfactory. Stainless steel is reputed to be somewhat easier to clean and is far more corrosion-resistant compared to CM, but those qualities come at a higher price compared to CM. The third variation, chrome lining, was initially adopted by the military in response to the harsh tropical conditions faced by the M16 in Southeast Asia. Chrome-lined barrels are CM barrels fashioned with oversize chambers and bores. Chrome is then plated inside, on the chamber and bore, bringing their dimensions back to nominal.

There are several ways to form the rifling in a rifle barrel. These include hammer-forging, buttoning, and cutting. In hammer forging, a mandrel with "rifling" in relief or reverse is inserted into the bore. The barrel is then hammered on the outside until the bore inside

THE *NEW* AR-15 COMPLETE OWNER'S GUIDE

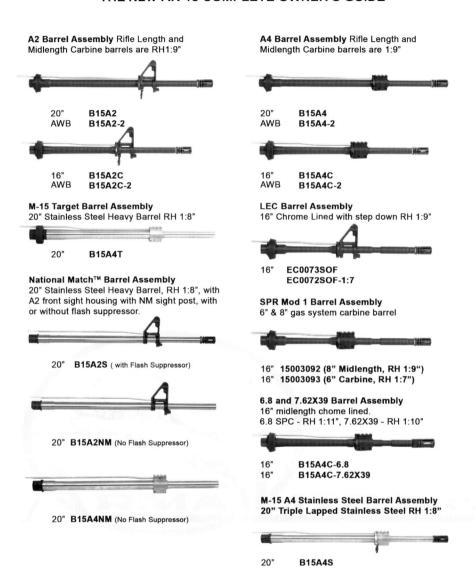

Barrels, barrels, barrels. In the bad old days, we had just five barrel contours: "A1," "A2", "M4," "HBAR" and "Bull." Now, we have every conceivable permutation of light, heavy, fluted, you name it. Ever wonder what the purpose of the groove in front of the gas block on the M4 barrel is (see EA1C0073SOF above)? It's to allow the attachment of the M203 grenade launcher. The newer M4A1 carbine's barrel looks the same as the M4 in front of the gas block, but heavy behind it. The heavy part of the M4A1 barrel has a flat on each side to accommodate the M203's barrel clamps.

Photograph Courtesy of ArmaLite, Inc.

DETAILS

takes on the rifling formed on the mandrel. This process is becoming more common in the manufacture of AR-15 barrels; for example, Ruger SR-556 barrels are hammer-forged. "Button" rifling is formed by forcing a shape down the barrel in a spiral path, displacing the metal such that the desired form and depth of all the grooves are achieved. "Cut" rifling is formed by removing metal rather than reshaping it as in button rifling. Single-point cut rifling cuts the grooves one at a time, one shallow pass at a time. There is also broach-cut rifling, which cuts all the grooves full-depth in one pass by means of a series of cutters, each a smidgen larger than the next, which cut the groove in tandem. Each of the cutters makes the groove a little deeper, until the last cutter creates the final desired depth of groove.

A Note on "National Match" Barrels:

Clint McKee of Fulton Armory reports that sometime in the '80's or so a contract was let for an official Army "National Match" AR-15 barrel, but that the contractor defaulted and no barrels were actually made. It would be interesting if the drawing for that barrel could be found (if it still exists), if only for historical purposes.

Many believe that the required uniformity is best achieved via single-point cut rifling rather than button rifling. This is because single-point rifling forms the rifling grooves comparatively gently, adding little or no stress to the barrel. Hammer forging has its advocates, too. The best quality barrels, such as Kriegers, are almost always made with cut rifling. However, whatever method is used, it's the uniformity of the bore that counts.

A Note on the Term "National Match" as Applied to AR-15s

There no such thing as a "National Match" AR-15, nor any AR-15 component that can be termed "National Match." "National Match" (NM) is a term that was devised for rifles and rifle components that met Army-set specifications for National Match-type target competition. Components such as barrels and sights were designed for the M1 and M14, and new-made replicas are available that conform to their official Army-produced drawings. No such designs or drawings were made for the AR-15. In the main, accuracy and marksmanship enhancements for the M16 have been devised by Service Marksmanship Units, and emulated for the AR-15 by civilian providers. Be aware that the label "National Match" has no intrinsic meaning in the AR-15 world. At best it indicates a good-faith effort to provide the vendor's best product for use in National Match competition. At worst, it is a meaningless marketing ploy.

Once upon a time, AR-15 barrels came in five basic configurations. These forms follow the history of the AR-15, from the original lightweight A1 rifle with its skinny "pencil barrel" through the "light under the handguards, heavy in front of the gas block" A2, the HBAR heavy barrel, the M4 with its M203 Grenade Launcher groove, to the bull-barreled match and varmint variants of the present day. As the figure to the left hints, today the permutations of AR barrels are legion. Because it's the inside of the barrel that really counts, if you don't have an air gauge you must depend on the integrity of the vendor to assure a barrel's bore quality.

RIFLE RELOADS

Charles Houseman

STABILITY

THE AVERAGE RELOADER probably thinks he needs to know very little about the factors which affect projectile stability. This is in direct contrast with the average target rifleman, who is convinced he knows all about the subject! If the reloader is going to use long and heavy bullets for the calibre he is dealing with, it is possible he will meet problems which are difficult to understand unless he recognises the symptoms of under-stabilisation.

Sporting bullets are usually shorter and blunter than target bullets in the same calibre and are easier to stabilise by the application of spin; those familiar with children's tops will be aware of the superiority of the short, fat type over those of tall and thin configuration. Most of the following discussion will therefore be slanted towards the effects of stability on accuracy, which is of more concern to the target rifleman than to the sportsman, as the effects tend to increase with range. Fortunately, some of the major effects of spin stabilisation upon the trajectory of projectiles do not affect even the long range target shot, since the angle of departure for 1,000 yards with 7.62 mm. and similar cartridges is comfortably under one degree. It might be as well to mention here that with normal military full-bore cartridges the lateral displacement (drift) of the bullet caused by gyroscopic effects is about one minute of angle at 1,000 yards and perhaps as much as ten minutes at 2,000 yards, although it depends on so many factors that it is difficult to give more than a rough idea of its value. With right hand twist rifling the drift is to the right.

In the nineteenth century, Sir George Greenhill, professor of mathematics at the Royal Military Academy Woolwich, carried out a great deal of research into spin stabilisation and its effects, mainly with respect to Artillery. For small arms he evolved an empirical rule which is as useful today as it was when he defined it. To assess if a projectile will be sufficiently well stabilised Greenhill's formula states:

$$\text{Required twist (in calibres)} = \frac{150}{\text{Bullet length (in calibres)}}$$

The formula is dependent upon the bullet having a specific gravity of 10.9; most modern jacketed bullets are close to this value. The factor of 150 can be increased to 200 without without de-stabilising the bullet; the original factor is applicable to military weapons, while target rifles can usually stand a slower twist without degrading accuracy and consistency. The unfired diameter of the bullet should be taken as the calibre for calculation. The formula can also be used to assess the stability factor (written as "S") of a given bullet in an existing barrel; if a factor of 200 is used the results will be acceptably close to measured values of "S". Testing for stability is a long and tedious process requiring a good deal of specialised equipment; the modern version of Greenhill's rule provides a simple, accurate and reliable method of avoiding stability problems by choice of an unsuitable projectile.

Those wishing to study the subject of spin stabilisation as it applies to small arms should try to read two articles in the American Rifleman (References 1 and 2). Although they contain one or two small errors these articles give a clear idea of the basic problem, together with data on actual projectiles, at much greater length than is possible here.

Because all modern bullets are long and (relatively) thin, it is necessary not only to keep them "point on" after discharge but to reduce yawing movements which increase drag and produce "lift" in an inconsistent manner, greatly increasing dispersion. All bullets yaw to some extent as they leave the muzzle; uneven muzzle blast caused by a faulty barrel crown can accentuate the yaw. This initial yaw must be brought under control early in flight, to ensure that dispersion is minimised. The direction and extent of the initial yaw is heavily dependent upon in-bore yaw. All projectiles yaw to some extent while in the bore; with rifle bullets the effect can be minimised by ensuring that the bullet closely matches the groove diameter of the barrel, which will thus align its axis with that of the bore more efficiently than is the case when undersized bullets are used. The centre of gravity of bullets with jackets of uneven thickness does not lie on the axis of the bullet; in the barrel the bullet is constrained about its centre of form, thus producing a small force which deflects it as it emerges from the muzzle. In the atmosphere the bullet rotates about its centre of gravity; the importance of concentricity in bullet manufacture is obvious, since the effect increases with rapidity of rotation. It is not generally realised that a 7.62 mm. NATO bullet is rotating at about 180,000 r.p.m. at the muzzle and that this rate of rotation decays relatively slowly during flight.

The relationship between the forces trying to deflect or overturn the bullet and the gyroscopic forces which keep it point on are called stability factor ("S"), as has been mentioned. It can be calculated from the basic equation:

$$S = \frac{A^2 N^2}{4B\mu}$$

where
- A = longitudinal moment of inertia
- B = transverse moment of inertia
- N = spin rate
- μ = is a complex factor encompassing air density, velocity and other quantities.

The moments of inertia of a bullet can be obtained (with difficulty) by use of a specialised torsion pendulum, as is used in some so-called 400-day clocks. Instructions for the manufacture and use of such a pendulum will be found in References 1 and 2.

"S" must exceed unity, i.e. the stabilising forces must be greater than the overturning forces if the bullet is to remain point foremost. In practice it is necessary to arrange a margin of safety by making "S" appreciably more than unity. For military rifle cartridges it is usual to design for a value of "S" of approximately 2; for target shooting with bullets of high quality which have little or no static or dynamic imbalance the initial value of "S" can be reduced to a minimum of 1.3 or so. When low values of "S" are used, the magnitude and direction of the initial yawing movements outside the barrel become particularly important to accuracy of shooting. Contrary to popular opinion, very high values of "S", of the order of 5 or even 10, do not significantly degrade accuracy provided that bullets of high quality are used, and the angle of departure does not exceed one degree. The most satisfactory value of "S" for sporting or target use is about 1.4 to 2, with accuracy of shooting being relatively unaffected where high quality components are used.

The causes and remedies for dispersion due to spin stabilisation can be tabulated as:

Cause of dispersion	Remedy
1. Static imbalance of bullet	Slower twist
2. Dynamic imbalance of bullet	Slower twist
3. Yaw in the bore	Slower twist
4. Insufficiently rapid rotation	Faster twist

Of these the fourth is by far the most important, but the others indicate the desirability of maintaining "S" at the minimum practical level where bullets and their dimensional match with the barrel in use are less than perfect.

The basic stability formula indicates that the value of "S" for a given projectile varies as the square of the steepness of the twist; for instance a 10" twist has almost twice the stabilising effect of a 14" twist ($10^2 = 100$; $14^2 = 196$). Once the stability of a bullet in a given twist is known or has been calculated, the equivalent value of "S" for any desired twist can be found by a comparison of the squares of the steepness of twist.

Some measured values of representative 7.62 mm. target bullets are shown below; also shown are the values calculated by Greenhill's rule using a factor of 200 for those and other bullets.

Bullet	Twist	Measured "S"	Calculated "S"
144 grain NATO	1 in 12"	1.85	1.95
144 grain NATO	1 in 14"	—	1.46
173 grain US M118	1 in 10"	1.9	2.1
185 grain Raufoss	1 in 10"	1.4	1.4
220 grain Sierra	1 in 10"	—	1.67
190 grain Sierra	1 in 10"	—	1.94
190 grain Sierra	1 in 12"	—	1.34
190 grain Hornady	1 in 12"	—	1.29
185 grain Lapua	1 in 12"	—	1.44

It will be seen that a twist of 1 in 14" is about ideal for the 7.62 mm. NATO bullet but that heavier bullets need a 10" or 12" twist for adequate stability.

References:
1. "American Rifleman" July 1962 pages 50-56.
2. "American Rifleman" November 1965 pages 52-56.

GUNS REVIEW, March 1982

One of the best succinct explanations of rifling twist we've seen, from the now-defunct **Guns Review** *of the UK.*

DETAILS
A Note on Fluting
(Or, The Grooves on the Outside of the Barrel):

No, we're not referring to the musical instrument, but rather to the technique of grooving the outside of a rifle barrel to "increase stiffness." Fluting cannot "increase stiffness." It is a well-known engineering principle that the major diameter of a column is the biggest contributor to its stiffness, all other things (e.g., material) being equal. Thus, one may take a large diameter barrel and flute it without significantly reducing the barrel's stiffness. However, the fluting process does reduce the barrel's weight. The confusion arises from the fact that for a given weight, a fluted barrel is stiffer than an unfluted barrel. This is because the fluted barrel will be larger in diameter than an unfluted barrel of the same weight. So fluting does not increase stiffness, but it does allow a barrel of a given stiffness to be of less weight, or a barrel of a given weight to be made as to be stiffer (through its larger, fluted, diameter). *Ist alles klar?*

A Note on Barrel Twist
(Or, The Grooves on the Inside of the Barrel):

Not to be confused with the dance craze started by Chubby Checker (younger readers will have to Google "The Twist"), barrel twist is a primary consideration in barrel selection. The twist, or the number of inches for a bullet to be rotated completely through 360 degrees as it travels down the bore, is the characteristic of the barrel that gives the bullet gyroscopic stability during its flight. Historians are not clear about exactly when or why barrels were grooved and (presumably later) the grooves were given a "twist" or spiral down the bore.

How much twist is required to stabilize a given bullet in a given caliber depends on the length of the bullet. Charles Houseman in the adjacent article relates how Dr. George Greenhill, "professor of mathematics at the Royal Military Academy Woolwich," performed extensive empirical testing to support the development of a rule of thumb for twist and stability now known as "The Greenhill Formula." We need not belabor the mathematics involved, but despite the nearly 150 years since Greenhill did his pioneering work the Greenhill Formula remains a useful tool for determining the twist rate required to stabilize a given bullet.

For a given caliber, the critical bullet dimension for determining the twist required for stability is determined by the bullet's length. Because in general longer bullets in a given caliber are heavier, we customarily use bullet weight as a surrogate for bullet length. Of course, there can be exceptions, for example "Very Low Drag" (VLD) bullets often used by long range marksmanship competitors. VLD drag bullets have a very long, shallow "ogive"; the ogive is the part of the bullet in front that tapers to the tip, which latter is called the "meplat."

One might wonder why the solution to the twist question is not simply to use the fastest twist offered, *e.g.,* 1 in 7, one rotation in seven inches of bullet travel, for all bullet weights not just heavy (long) bullets. As Houseman notes, "overstabilization," rotating the bullet "too fast," can hurt accuracy if the bullet is not balanced both statically and dynamically. While

THE *NEW* AR-15 COMPLETE OWNER'S GUIDE

(C) Colt, (MP) Magnetic Particle, Chrome Bore; Colt 1 in 12 barrel.

(FA) Fulton Armory, NM, 5.56-MM, 1 in 8, (H-BAR) Heavy Barrel

(FA) Fulton Armory, MP, 5.56-MM, Chrome Bore, 1 in 9 barrel.

White Oak Armory, July 2012, 1 in 7 barrel.

Ruger 5.56 NATO 1 in 9 barrel for SR-556.

(C) Colt, (MP) Magnetic Particle, 5.56 NATO 1 in 9 barrel.

(FA) Fulton Armory, (MP) Magnetic Particle, 5.56-MM 1 in 8 barrel.

(FA) Fulton Armory, MP, 5.56-MM Match, 1 in 9 barrel.

(FA) Fulton Armory, MP, 5.56-MM Match, 1 in 9 barrel.

Just making sure you're paying attention. ArmaLite 6.8 SPC II, Chrome-Molybdenum-Vanadium, Chrome Lined, 1 in 11 barrel.

DETAILS

bullets today are manufactured to near-perfection, any imbalance in a bullet is magnified the faster it is spun. Overstabilization can be too much of a good thing.

Further, very light bullets are often intended for such tasks as varmint hunting and as such are designed with very thin jackets to assure expansion in a small target and to avoid ricochets via disintegrating upon striking a hard object in the event the bullet misses its mark. Spin a thin-jacketed bullet too fast and it may come apart and literally vaporize on its way downrange.

So, what is the "perfect" twist for the common bullets used in the .223/5.56-MM AR? Not only will authorities differ on the subject, rifles will too. Some rifles will shoot a bullet that's seemingly ill-matched to the rifle barrel's twist very, very well.

TIP:
For very light bullets, that is, bullets of 50 grains or less, the original AR twist rates of 1 in 14 and 1 in 12 should work well. However, go above 55 grains and even 1 in 12 might be a bit "slow." For the typical military-analogue 55 and 62 grain bullets, 1 in 9 would likely be adequate. While very heavy match bullets would be understabilized, and very light varmint bullets overstabilized, some authorities recommend 1 in 8 as an "all-around" twist rate suitable for nearly all commonly-used bullet weights. So, now we see why 1 in 8 and 1 in 9 are the most commonly found and recommended "universal" twist rates. Oh, and good luck finding a "1 in 14" barrel!

PITFALL:
In the matter of twist rates, as in most things, your mileage *will* vary. If your rifle doesn't shoot Brand X bullets of yy grains well, try Brand Z and Brand W before giving up on that particular weight.

NOTE:
The standard twist rate for USGI M16A2/A4 and M4/M4A1 rifles is 1 in 7. This choice was made necessary by the adoption of the NATO-standard 62-gr SS109 "semi-armor-piercing" bullet and its even-longer L110 tracer counterpart.

PITFALL:
Keep in mind that, all things being equal, faster twists mean faster barrel wear. Also keep in mind that you'll have to shoot a powerful lot to see that increased wear.

TIP:
If you have settled on a specific cartridge or bullet, the manufacturer should be able to provide you with their recommended twist for that bullet. Might as well let CorBon or Federal or Hornady invest in all that testing for you.

5.56, .223, Wylde...What's Up with That?

While the bore of the barrel is very important to the proper function and performance, the chamber is very important to function, performance—and safety. To understand that, we must review the distinction between the military 5.56-MM and commercial .223 Remington

THE *NEW* AR-15 COMPLETE OWNER'S GUIDE

 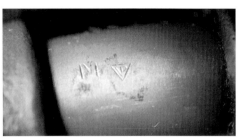

Let's see what we have; the number "12," for 1 in 12, on the bottom of the barrel behind the front sight base.

Then, an "M" and a Colt "VP" Verified Proof Mark at the front sight base. So, from what rifle cometh this barrel?

From this first (full) year production Colt AR-15; it's an M16 barrel. The rifle is marked ".223," but the .223/5.56? Gage (below) verifies it's actually 5.56-MM.

Unfortunately, some barrels don't have any markings on them at all. Sigh.

For those barrels where there's a question, of .223 or 5.56-MM chambering of course, here's the answer: the .223/5.56? Gage. Hold the upper muzzle down, drop the tool into the chamber. Turn the upper muzzle up; if the gage falls out, it's a 5.56 chamber. If the gage sticks, it's a .223 chamber. Simple, effective; M-Guns.net. Tell Ned we sent ya.

DETAILS

cartridges. The cartridges are to all appearances physically identical. And, for all practical purposes, they are. But, they are not interchangeable. Why? The Devil is in the details.

The 5.56-MM cartridge was designed as a military round for a full-automatic rifle and later adapted to belt-fed machine guns. Consequently, the 5.56-MM chamber was designed for reliable function under the less-than-ideal environmental conditions found in combat. Specifically, the throat, or "leade," was provided with a longer, more generous taper than that found in the .223 Remington chamber. The .223 Remington's varmint cartridge heritage is betrayed by its comparatively snug—with respect to the 5.56—chamber and short, steep leade. The consequence of these chamber differences is that it's more important than ever to respect the caliber marking on your rifle's barrel. If it says ".223," by all means use only .223 Remington ammunition in that rifle. If it says "5.56," you can safely use ammunition designated "5.56."

PITFALL:
Except...because it's the 5.56-MM throat and chamber that's "larger" than the .223 chamber, you *can* use .223 ammo in a 5.56 chamber. But, *you can't go the other way.*

CATCH-22:
A dirty little secret in the AR community is that not all barrels marked "5.56" have 5.56-MM chambers! Why? Perhaps the manufacturer wants their product to appear "tactical" or "military." For whatever reason, if you have a 5.56-marked barrel and want to use true 5.56-MM cartridges, you should definitely confirm that the barrel has a 5.56 chamber.

TIP:
There is a handy little tool available to confirm that a 5.56-marked barrel has a 5.56-MM chamber: the .223/5.56? Gage. Follow the instructions, and you will quickly validate—or, invalidate—your barrel's cartridge marking. There is a special reamer available from the same source to convert .223 chambers to 5.56; this reamer slightly enlarges the neck area of the chamber while lengthening the leade. This special reamer stops on the barrel shoulder so using the reamer has no effect on headspace. Use on a chrome-lined barrel is hard on the reamer, but if the rifle has been fired a lot the chrome is likely to be pretty thin anyway.

NOTE:
The reason that a 5.56-MM cartridge in a .223 chamber is so dangerous is that the 5.56-MM cartridge's powder charge is regulated so as to not exceed its maximum chamber pressure with the generous neck diameter and long leade of the 5.56-MM. That long leade gives the bullet a running start—often called "freebore"—before it enters the rifling and momentarily slows down, creating the pressure spike that we call "maximum chamber pressure." Put that same cartridge in a .223 chamber with its snug neck and short leade, and pop goes the primer from excessive chamber pressure. At some point, assuming that a case doesn't rupture along the way, the popped-out primers get into the hammer and trigger, the rifle stops, and the shooter's puzzlement begins.

THE *NEW* AR-15 COMPLETE OWNER'S GUIDE

A sample of the vast array of muzzle devices for the AR-15. Pick your poison. Photograph Courtesy of MidwayUSA.

AR-15 Flash Hiders, Compensators and Muzzle Brakes

DETAILS
But, What About the Wylde?

Glad you asked. The Wylde chamber is one of several chamber designs that combines the .223 chamber's snug case body area while opening up the throat and lengthening the leade. Thus, it combines the accuracy-enhancing .223 chamber's body dimension with the neck and leade required to prevent overpressure from the use of 5.56-MM cartridges. Fulton Armory has a similar chamber, their 5.56-MM Match.

An allied consideration, particularly for those intending to use very heavy bullets, for example, is the barrel's chamber shape. Match barrel vendors often offer chambers intended for specific types of bullets or even specific bullets. These may not shoot well with bullets for which they were not intended. Serious match shooters will have their own specific ideas as to what works for them, but their needs are beyond the scope of this book. Your barrel vendor should specify if any but the standard SAAMI chamber is incorporated in a barrel he offers.

Fortunately for most shooters, who will not be seriously competing at 600 yards at Camp Perry, even the most basic AR barrel may well suffice for punching tin cans at 100 yards. A good chrome-lined barrel can be a one-MOA barrel or better. As with most things in life, you get what you pay for—if you're lucky!

Muzzle Devices

Muzzle devices do nothing to enhance accuracy. Compensators, which divert muzzle gases upward, can help keep the muzzle down in rapid-fire, which is why action shooters are partial to them. The value in muzzle brakes, which divert the gases rearward, in reducing recoil would seem to be marginal as the .223/5.56-MM cartridge has no recoil worth mentioning. Muzzle brakes are generally not permitted in bull's-eye competition, for the simple reason that the redirected muzzle gases (muzzle blast) are seriously annoying to those on the firing line adjacent to the brake.

Flash suppressors would seem to have more general utility than brakes, particularly for low-light or indoor shooting, e.g., home defense. Those who expect to do much shooting in reduced light conditions should select their ammunition carefully to minimize flash, and seek out the most effective flash suppressor currently on the market.

A modern trend in muzzle devices is the muzzle brake or flash suppressor that doubles as a sound suppressor quick detach mount. The devices on the third row of the illustration to the left are examples of double-duty devices.

> **TIP:**
> In general, open-face flash suppressors seem to be more effective in reducing flash than devices with closed ends. However, the open face makes the device more prone to snagging on brush and equipment than those with a closed face. Keep in mind that the choice of ammunition will influence flash at least as much as the flash suppressor.

Handguards and Float Tubes

The AR-15's furniture, its stock, pistol grip and handguards, have evolved on the military M16 side from the A1 through the A2 style to various types of four-rail systems. The solid

THE *NEW* AR-15 COMPLETE OWNER'S GUIDE

There's that early AR-15 SP1 again, this time to illustrate the triangular handguards and short butt stock without "trap." Walt Kuleck Collection.

This Colt "Match Target" illustrates the A2 round handguards and longer butt stock with trap. Walt Kuleck Collection.

DETAILS

buttstock of the early M16 evolved to the A2 with a trapdoor butt plate and recess, and 5/8" greater length. The early pistol grip, which had provision for a sling swivel, was replaced with the A2 style incorporating a finger ridge. The early triangular "handed" handguards were replaced with the A2's interchangeable upper and lower symmetric round handguards. More recently, the M4A1 and M16A4 are provided with four-rail handguards, that is, handguards with Swan/Weaver (Picatinny) rails on top, bottom and each side.

While the variety of handguards pales in comparison to the variety of float tubes now available, there are a number of alternatives to the original triangular or round handguards. Most mimic the "official" aforementioned four-rail M4A1/M16A4 handguards, but some take a road less traveled. These tend to be polymer, smooth, ergonomically contoured and configurable with optional rail panels of the user's choice in length and placement. For those seeking a balance between handiness and utility, these new approaches may appeal to those unwilling or unable to move to a full floating handguard tube. However, handguards cannot isolate the barrel from the bending stresses resulting from the weight of accessories or the pull of sling tension. To isolate the barrel from these loads, you need a handguard float tube.

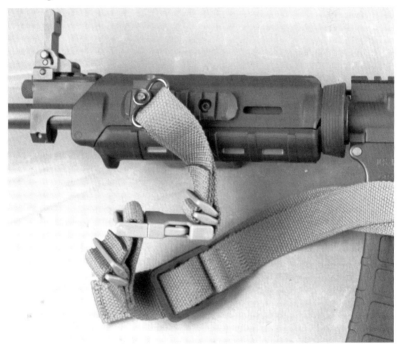

Here's an example of the "new breed" of lightweight polymer handguards, the Magpul MOE handguard. Magpul offers rail sections that can be attached to the side or bottom of the assembly. In this case, the user has attached a rail section to the left side in order to install a Blue Force Gear Vickers Tactical sling on a QD swivel. Walt Kuleck Collection.

THE *NEW* AR-15 COMPLETE OWNER'S GUIDE

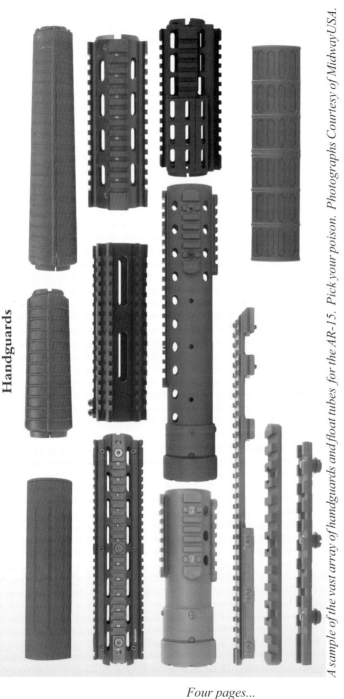

A sample of the vast array of handguards and float tubes for the AR-15. Pick your poison. Photographs Courtesy of MidwayUSA.

CMP/DCM-Legal Hidden Float Tube. Walt Kuleck Collection.

Four pages...

DETAILS

Float Tubes: First, "DCM/CMP Legal"; Then, The Dam Broke

One design deficiency of the AR-15 is its mounting of the front sling swivel directly to the barrel. M1 and M14 sling swivels mount to the forend of these rifles' stocks, thereby absorbing the pull of tight "slinging up" without putting bending stress directly on the barrel. Because the AR-15 does not have a conventional stock, the conventional design approach was not available to Gene Stoner. Despite the adoption of heavy target barrels, tight "slinging-up" still caused unpredictable shifts in the AR-15's point of impact. As the AR-15 platform continued to evolve, the number of accessories available to mount on the AR-15-type rifle—lights, lasers, front sights, hand stops, forward grips, and of course slings—exploded. Adding this weight, often in addition to sling tension, could wreak havoc with Point of Impact (POI) repeatability.

The solution to this challenge was ingenious. Because the Service Rifle match rifles were the first to really need load isolation, the front sling swivel was cantilevered out from the upper receiver via a "float tube" that did not contact the barrel anywhere along its length. This allows tight slinging-up as well as benchrest or bipod use without bending the barrel. Because these "hidden" float tubes are, well, hidden under the conventional handguards, they were deemed DCM/CPM-legal because alterations to Service Rifle match rifles must not be visible externally. Of course, close inspection reveals the front sling swivel attached to the handguard, leaving a gap between the swivel and the base of the front sight, to which the swivel "should" be attached. Expedience triumphed; absent the "hidden float tube," the current US Service Rifle can not compete with the venerable M14!

While the chronology is not entirely clear, the "exposed" handguard float tube may have actually preceded its hidden counterpart. The intent was the same as for the hidden version, to free-float the barrel to isolate it from external influences. "Free-floating" was in fact the source of the term, "handguard float tube." The only external influence on the barrel is the flimsy and flexible gas tube, which has very little influence indeed.

A float tube is actually a replacement for the barrel nut. That is, it is a really, really long barrel nut. For any given shooter's particular functional requirements, there are several considerations in selecting a float tube. Primary among them are the means by which the float tube is secured, and the allied means by which the tube may be properly aligned.

Early in the history of float tubes, a simpler time indeed, the major distinction was between two- and three-piece tubes. Two-piece tubes consist of an extended, threaded "barrel nut" that is screwed into the upper to retain the barrel, and a float tube that is in turn screwed onto the extended barrel nut. The tube can be indexed in rotation, should there be some asymmetry to consider. LockTite® secures the tube itself to the extended barrel nut. However, there is no mechanical means of taking up thread clearances or securing the tube coaxially with the barrel; thus they can sag at the free end. A variation on this theme uses setscrews to supplement the LockTite®. This type of tube permits indexing but still is not optimally stable. Two-piece tubes have all but disappeared from the scene, though several manufacturers still offer them and possibly will into the future.

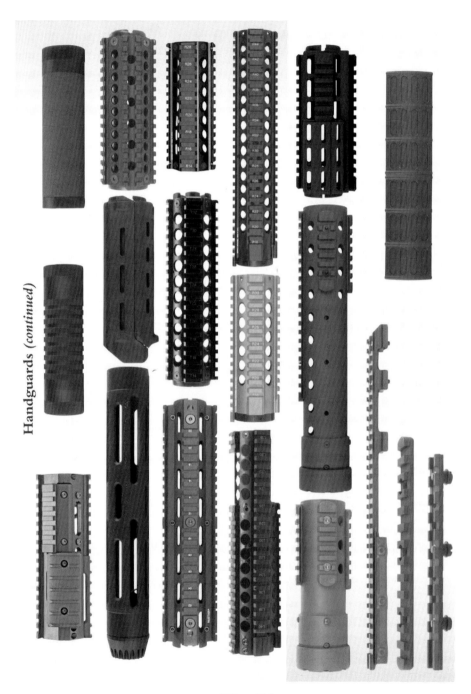

...of Float Tubes...

DETAILS

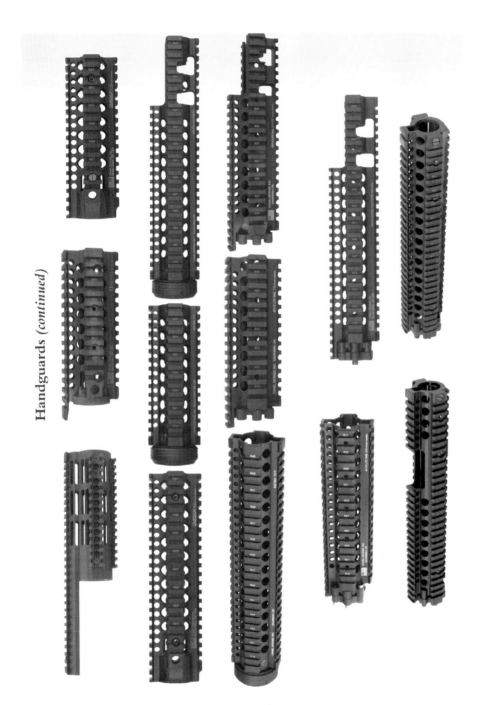

...and Handguards.

THE *NEW* AR-15 COMPLETE OWNER'S GUIDE

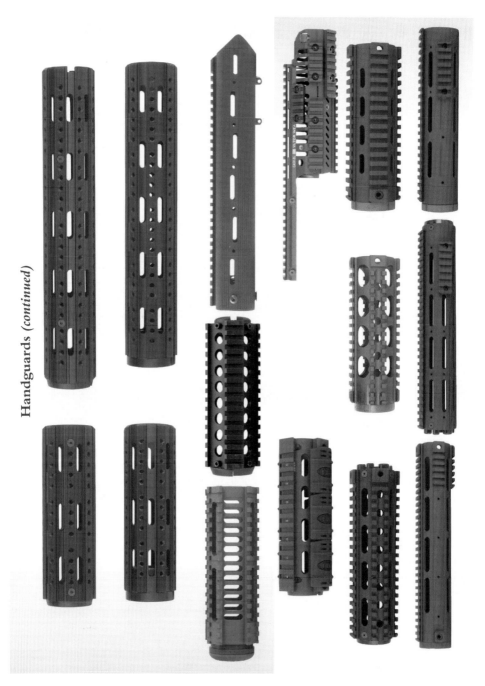

Handguards (continued)

Photograph Courtesy of MidwayUSA.

DETAILS

More sophisticated are the three piece tubes, where the tube is secured by means of a lock nut to the "extended barrel nut" after it is indexed. LockTite® is often used as a supplement here also. This arrangement provides both indexing and security.

Handguard float tubes have become a major segment of the AR industry all on their own. We now have round tubes, square tubes, elliptical tubes, tubes whose cross-section defies description. Float tubes can be found with integral rails, optional attachable rails, or no rails at all. How does one choose from among this bewildering array of alternatives?

As with all the alternatives in the AR world, the key is defining your purpose. Is weight important? Do you want slim, unencumbered, or fat, full length with four rails? Aluminum or carbon fiber or G10 composite? Flat bottom for bags or rests, or round for the "thumb over the top" support hand hold? Page through the catalogs and the Internet and you'll find what you need; you'll even likely be able to find what you want!

NOTE:
Float tube length has become an important parameter for AR users. Traditionally, float tube length was determined by gas system length. If you had a carbine-length gas system, you had a carbine-length float tube, a rifle-length system, a rifle-length tube, if a mid-length system, a mid-length tube. Today, though, the old rules are gone, and float tube manufacturers have created tubes that overlap gas blocks or even wrap around them. Why? To create more space for mounting stuff and to allow the user to get the support hand out as near the muzzle as possible.

PITFALL:
It's very easy to load up an AR with what may be irrelevancies, and to choose a float tube that's bigger and heavier than need be. Carefully consider just what you should have on your rifle. The AR is supposed to be lighter than the ten-pound Garand!

TIP:
As you peruse the accompanying pictures, take note of the variants that have a rail that extends rearward to integrate with the rail on a flattop receiver. This arrangement further stiffens both the rail interface and the upper receiver. It also makes certain that if it is necessary to mount an optic with one ring over the receiver and one over the rail, both rings will be aligned and not stressing the scope's tube.

The Upper Receiver

AR-15 upper receivers fall into three major categories: the variants with rear sights and carry handle, those without rear sights and carry handle, i.e., flattop uppers, and finally those with no military counterpart, intended for match, varmint or specialized tactical rifle use.

TIP:
If you wish to have your cake and eat it too, detachable carry handles for the military-style flattop receiver are available, and were indeed included on all but the very first military M4 carbines, which had A2-style upper receivers marked "M4."

AR-15 Upper Receivers

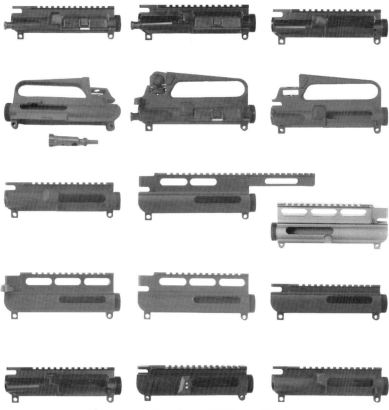

Photograph Courtesy of Midway USA.

Colt M4 Upper Receiver. Note the "C" for Colt. Walt Kuleck Collection.

More on the Colt M4 upper. "M4" means M4.

Note the feed cuts on the Colt M4 upper; check that your barrel has the matching, deeper cuts.

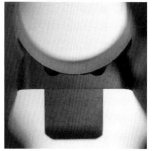

DETAILS

Upper receiver selection is to a great extent determined by the purpose intended for the rifle. Today, it's quite uncommon to find rifles with fixed carry handles. One might venture to say that 90% or more of the rifles on offer have a flattop receiver of some sort, whether the military M4/A4 pattern or one of a particular vendor's specific design. If an optical sight is to be the primary sighting device, then a flattop receiver is more practical than one with a carry handle. As we discussed above in the Selecting chapter, varmint rifles, for example, will generally not have backup sights. For such a rifle a high-riser upper may be just the ticket, allowing mounting a powerful scope sight without the need for excessively high rings to accommodate the AR's high sight line.

However, varmint rifles are not the only application for flattop receivers. The default configuration in self-defense carbines is one with a flattop upper, a red-dot or reflex sight, a short M4-contour barrel and a handguard float tube with one or more rails, depending on the accessory fitment selected. If backup iron sights are desired, flip-up or detachable front and rear sights may be included.

The newer, more exotic upper receivers are a complete break from the military heritage of the AR-15. For example, side-charging receivers make bolt cycling more convenient for match shooters. The ejection port cover, while a valuable military feature to exclude dirt, sand and mud from the action, is an unnecessary complication for a rifle that sees only known-distance target ranges or prairie-dog colonies and is often omitted. For the more "tactical" bent, there are now "monolithic" uppers which incorporate at the least the upper portion of an integrated handguard float tube.

PITFALL:
In the early days of the AR an important consideration in selecting upper receivers and upper receiver assemblies was the pivot pin boss. Two diameters of pin, .250" and .315", were to be found. Non-Colt uppers were invariably configured with a .250" pivot pin boss to accept the military-style "small" pin. The .315" size was used by Colt to hamper the use of M16 upper assemblies on AR-15s; thus Colt SP1s, for example, have a large-pin lower receiver.

TIP:
For those of you with an earlier Colt lower, use of a small, .250" pivot pin upper with a large, .315" lower will require a readily available adapter pin to mate the large-pin lower with the small-pin upper. Conversely, using a large-pin upper on a small-pin lower will require the corresponding adapter bushing for the upper's pin boss.

PSSST: YOU WANNA M4, MISTER?
A special flattop upper receiver is the Colt Genuine M4 Upper. Considered the Holy Grail by M4gers, that is, those interested in recreating the M4 in semi-auto non-Short-Barreled-Rifle (the M4 has a too-short-for-you-and-me 14.5" barrel) guise, this "M4" and "C" marked upper is the same as used in the military M4 and M4A1. Of course, you could just buy a Colt LE6920 SOCOM and have done with it. But, in any case, it won't be select fire and won't have government inspector approval, so it's not a real M4 anyway. Just sayin'.

THE *NEW* AR-15 COMPLETE OWNER'S GUIDE

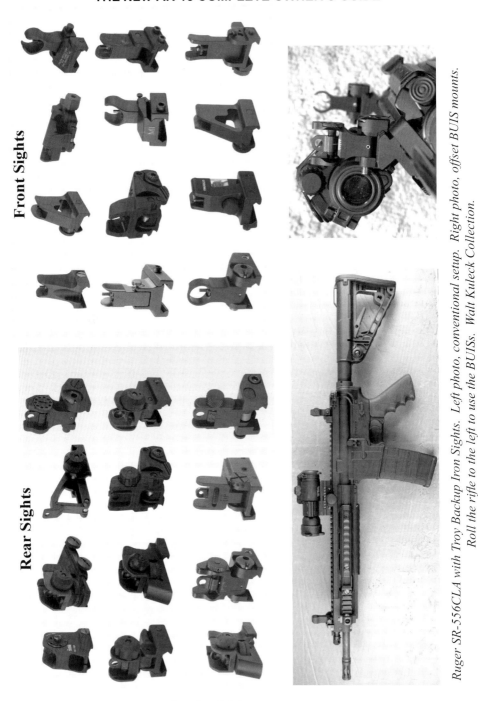

Front Sights and Rear Sights. Photographs Courtesy of MidwayUSA.

Ruger SR-556CLA with Troy Backup Iron Sights. Left photo, conventional setup. Right photo, offset BUIS mounts. Roll the rifle to the left to use the BUISs. Walt Kuleck Collection.

DETAILS

Sight Options

In the early days of the AR, the A1 and A2 carry handle iron sights, along with, in today's eyes, primitive red dot sights and conventional scope sights comprised the totality of the shooter's options. Today, as with nearly all things AR, that situation has not just changed, it has been transformed.

With the contemporary emphasis on flattop upper receivers and handguard float tubes with top rail, the original integrated iron sights found on the semiauto M16 and M4 derivatives have been largely supplanted by rear and front sights that attach to the upper receiver rail and handguard float tube top rail, respectively. You will see some gas blocks with rails on top; there are front sights made for these rails for those who might wish to have a float tube without rail but wish to retain the ability to affix a front sight. These detachable front sights can be fixed or, as in the case of the vast majority, folding.

TIP:
> Regardless of the optic chosen for your AR, it would be prudent, if at all possible, to also have a set of back up iron sights (BUISs). Folded, BUISs can stay out of the way of the optic and out of the shooter's field of view until such time as they might be needed. On offset mounts, you simply tilt the rifle to view the BUISs. Scopes break or lose their zero, red dots fail, batteries die, you get the point. With a set of BUISs you can remain in the game or in the fight, if necessary.

TIP:
> Most authorities will suggest that a short AR-15, for example, an M4 semiauto analog, should have some sort of optic sight suitable for short-range shooting. The US military has wholeheartedly embraced this concept. It is very difficult to find a picture of an M16A4 or M4/M4A1 in the field and in anger without an optic.

So, which optic to choose? Setting aside for the moment conventional scopes, short- to medium-range optics generally have low or no magnification. The optic presents a parallax-free dot, often red, or other reticule such as a chevron to the shooter.

DEFINITION:
> "Parallax" in simple terms is the optical phenomenon that gives the shooter the perception that the aiming point of an optic moves in relation to the target as the shooter peers into the optic from sightly different angles. Conventional scopes are typically designed so that parallax is minimum at some predetermined range, e.g., 200 yards for a hunting scope. Some scopes have a parallax adjustment, that is, a dial with yardage markings allowing the shooter to set the scope for minimum parallax at his or her desired range. "Red dot" optics do not have any parallax at any range, as a rule. Thus, it matters not if the shooter's eye is a bit off-axis with respect to the optic when the shooter takes the shot.

New optics are coming to market every day. At the time of writing, the major forces in the market are Aimpoint, EOTech and Trijicon. Basically, you pays your money and you takes your choice. In the case of these three brands, a not-insignificant amount of money!

THE *NEW* AR-15 COMPLETE OWNER'S GUIDE

A Collage of Favored Optics

EOTech 512.A65. The EOTech is an example of an optic eminently suitable for short range shooting, aka Close Quarters Battle (CQB). You'll see a lot of these on M16s and M4s in the battle zones. This model uses AA batteries, more convenient to have on hand than the more common CR123s Walt Kuleck Collection.

Aimpoint T1, a popular "Micro" red dot. This type of optic is an unobtrusive CQB option. Photograph Courtesy of Aimpoint.

DETAILS

Trijicon ACOG. The ACOG comes in a number of flavors, most of which are magnified to one degree or another. The ACOGs are a good choice for short, 50 to 75 yards, to medium, 100 to 200 yards, ranges. This bright, clear optic is a revelation for those accustomed to inexpensive alternatives. Walt Kuleck Collection.

Aimpoint CompML2. The Aimpoints are unmagnified CQB optics often coupled with 3 power magnifiers. Walt Kuleck Collection.

Aimpoint Patrol Rifle Optic (PRO). This unmagnified sight is marketed to law enforcement for their patrol rifle AR variants. Walt Kuleck Collection.

THE *NEW* AR-15 COMPLETE OWNER'S GUIDE

Traditional AR lowers; Left, M16 analogue, Right, M16A2 analogue. Walt Kuleck Collection.

New shapes and forms. Seekins Precision lower with integrated ambidextrous bolt stop. Note the enlarged trigger guard and reshaped mag well with finger serrations. Be sure you find the instructions in the box, and have the correct teeny tiny Allen wrenches on hand before proceeding to build it! Walt Kuleck Collection.

New materials. Mag Tactical Systems magnesium/aluminum alloy receiver, 35% lighter than 7076T6 aluminum. Note the enlarged trigger guard and Geissele trigger. For strength, the hammer and trigger pin holes have reinforcing bosses, requiring elongated pins. Walt Kuleck Collection.

DETAILS

For the hunter of varmints or big game, the same scopes one would find on a bolt gun for hunting are equally suitable for the AR platform. The varmint hunter may well eschew BUISs, but the big game hunter might be prudent to include them in his rifle setup.

The Lower Receiver

The lower receiver is the serial numbered part, and thus is the one component controlled according to the legislation known as the Gun Control Act of 1968 (GCA '68). Therefore, while one may purchase by mail order every other AR-15 component, the stripped lower receiver is considered to be a "firearm" per GCA '68.

AR-15 lower receivers are found in fewer permutations than upper receivers, at least in mechanical configurations. Lowers have been made from aluminum forgings, aluminum castings and steel castings, and machined from an aluminum billet. In the early days, Colt even experimented with plastic. Alas, the polymers of the day weren't up to the task.

The AR-15's design, as we have seen, places very little structural strength demand on either the upper or lower receivers. The material from which they are made is far less important than is the fidelity of their dimensional characteristics. This is particularly true of the lower receiver, where the take down and pivot pin locations must be accurate in order to permit easy attachment of upper receiver assemblies. Further, the location of the pin holes for the hammer and trigger pins must be correct for consistent trigger function and feel. If the hammer and trigger pins are not parallel, the hammer-trigger interface will be skewed, causing premature wear and change of trigger performance. Some manufacturers tout their practice of "matching" upper and lower receivers to eliminate any perception of looseness between the two. Thankfully, the days of poorly made AR receivers seem to be behind us.

Contemporary lowers will usually be of the A2 pattern, with its comprehensive structural reinforcements. A1 lowers are occasionally encountered, generally sourced from Colt SP1s. NoDak Spud has been making "retro" lowers for some time now, to facilitate the efforts of those seeking to replicate the original '60's AR-15/M16 look or recreate one of the early carbines.

A number of companies are now offering lower receivers with different shapes and forms, and from materials other than aluminum or steel. Often the new forms include integral, enlarged trigger guards. While polymer lowers have been on and off the market for decades, a magnesium/aluminum alloy receiver is something new: lighter weight with the perceived durability of metal. So, as with all things AR, the years continue to broaden our choices.

Model 607 Recreation on SP1 Lower. Walt Kuleck Collection.

THE *NEW* AR-15 COMPLETE OWNER'S GUIDE

Examples of aftermarket AR triggers. Note the fourth from the left on the first row: this is an example of a "Cassette-Style" trigger assembly that installs as an assembled unit. The third from the left on the second row is the Jewell, until the introduction of Geissele triggers the author's preferred choice. Photograph Courtesy MidwayUSA.

DETAILS

Triggers

NOTE:
What we call the "trigger" is actually a fire control assembly comprised of the trigger, hammer, disconnector and selector. Because our AR-15s are semiauto only, the selector is limited to "SAFE" and "FIRE"; so, you'll sometimes see the selector called the "safety."

ACKNOWLEDGEMENT:
This description of AR triggers is based in large part on discussions with Bill Geissele, "Mr. AR Trigger." Thanks, Bill.

The standard AR-15 trigger is a simple design, single-stage trigger. Single-stage means the shooter feels one level of resistance before the rifle fires. We describe this resistance as "weight of pull." For the standard M16, the military requires a weight of pull of between 5.5 and 9.5 pounds. A generally accepted minimum weight of pull for military-type semiauto rifles, and the weight of pull specified in Service Rifle Match Rifle rules, is 4.5 pounds.

However, there is more to the feel of the trigger than weight of pull. The movement of the trigger and the sensation at the "break," the point when the hammer is released, is as if not more important. What the shooter seeks is a trigger that does not move, or "creep," when the shooter begins to apply force to it, and which breaks crisply when the hammer is released and the gun fires.

For single-stage triggers, creating an assembly with a light, 4.5 pound trigger pull, and no creep, is generally not a realistic goal. For example, ALG Defense, manufacturers of very impressive military-type "blueprinted" single-stage triggers, will not attempt to go below about 6.0 pounds even with their high-tech coated trigger. If you break open an AR with a standard single-stage trigger, you can observe the hammer being cammed back as the trigger is pulled. The feel is thus one of serious creep. If you modify or redesign the trigger/hammer interface to eliminate this camming motion, two things happen, neither of them good.

PITFALL:

First, because the AR trigger spring is quite weak, the trigger will be reluctant to "relax" if the shooter, while pulling the trigger, decides not to take the shot and releases the trigger. The trigger can and will stand "on the sear." Then, any little jarring or bumping of the rifle can release the hammer unexpectedly. However, when the trigger cams the hammer back, abandoning a shot in the middle of pulling the trigger results in the hammer camming the trigger back. So, if you have a standard trigger, embrace the creep. The aforementioned ALG triggers are made so as to minimize creep to near imperceptibility, but it's there nonetheless.

Second, all the force holding the hammer back at cock is concentrated on a very small part of the sear. Thus, expect that really nice trigger pull to deteriorate faster than you would like. Every mating surface has to be "hard fit" "just so," or the trigger wouldn't release the hammer, or alternatively, *would* release the hammer autonomously!

QUESTION:
So, why do you want a single-stage trigger in the AR?

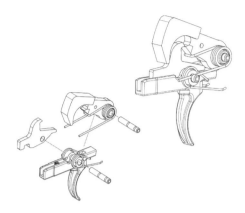

Military-style AR single-stage trigger. Drawing Courtesy ALG Defense.

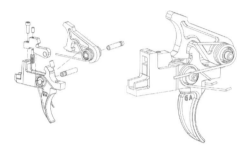

AR two-stage match trigger. Drawing Courtesy Geissele Automatics.

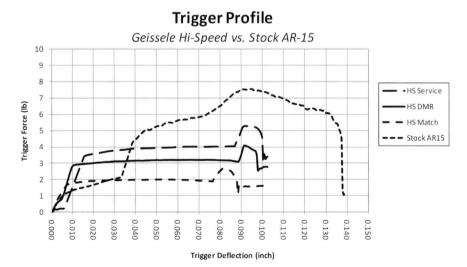

Three Geissele two-stage AR triggers compared to the standard military AR trigger. Do you really, really want a single-stage trigger? Chart Courtesy Geissele Automatics.

DETAILS

ANSWER:
You don't. But, see next note:

NOTE FOR U.S. MILITARY VETERANS:
Thank you for your service. If you were in the military from the mid-'60's on, you trained and fought with a single-stage trigger in your M16 or M4. You may be so accustomed to the single-stage trigger that the suggestion you need a two-stage trigger is either puzzling or presumptuous. Or both. If you can shoot a single-stage trigger well, more power to you; carry on.

The AR trigger was not designed for precision shooting. Keep in mind that the original AR-15 was a select-fire rifle, which raises the already high stakes for safety. A semi-auto rifle is a violent platform for a trigger; uncontrolled full-auto fire due to a failed trigger would be catastrophic. For a light, crisp trigger it is necessary to turn to a two-stage trigger.

NOTE:
Some "Three Gun" or Action Shooting competitors may well disagree with the admonition that one should have a two-stage trigger to make it possible to get the full inherent accuracy from an AR-type rifle. They argue that two-stage triggers are distracting in the sort of dynamic shooting involved in their sport. If you are a serious Three Gun competitor, you're not likely to be reading this anyway, so the author will refrain from gratuitous evangelism. The author comes to ARs from the M1 Garand and M14 world, and has become terminally spoiled by the quintessentially fine triggers that can be tuned into John Garand's interpretation of John Browning's 1901 trigger design. Besides, the AR is the first US Service Rifle to have a single-stage trigger since the days of the Trapdoor Springfield!

So, what's a "two-stage" trigger, anyway? A two-stage trigger has two distinct pull phases; for the AR-15, typical two-stage triggers have a 2.5-pound initial pull followed, as you continue to pull the trigger, by a two pound incremental addition to the pull. The result is that a 4.5-pound trigger feels like a two-pound trigger: the second phase of the pull is what the shooter actually feels before the break.

QUIBBLE:
But, isn't that first stage really "creep"? I thought we didn't want creep in the trigger!

RIPOSTE:
Yes, to some the first stage sounds like creep. However, the first stage doesn't *feel* like creep! If you have no experience with two-stage triggers, the first time you try one you may well experience an epiphany.

You have a wide variety of two-stage triggers from which to choose. As you do so, keep in mind Geissele's Law: a trigger must provide safety, reliability, forgiveness and performance. From modular, "cassette" triggers that install as an assembled unit, to simple military trigger replacements, there is a trigger out there for you. Just make sure that when all is said and done you have a trigger that allows you to wring the best out of your rifle without putting yourself and those around you in danger.

THE *NEW* AR-15 COMPLETE OWNER'S GUIDE

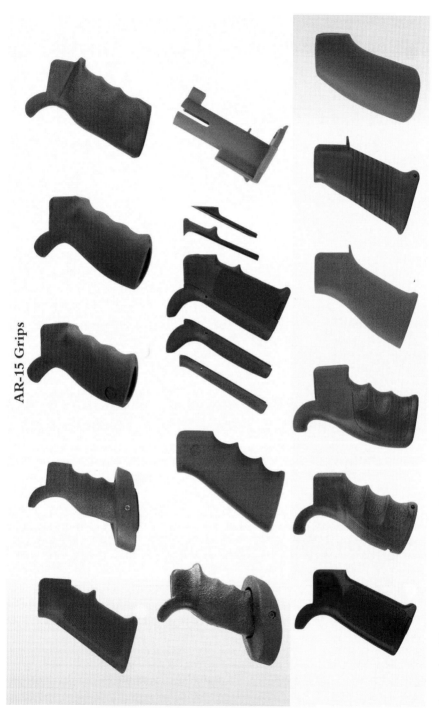

A sample of the vast array of pistol grips for the AR-15. Note the configurable Magpul MAID, second row, third from left, and the Magpul storage insert for Magpul grips. Photographs Courtesy of MidwayUSA.

DETAILS

Pistol Grips and Trigger Guards

There are three points of physical contact between you, the shooter, and your AR: the butt stock, the handguard(s), and the pistol grip. Of the three, possibly the most intimate is the pistol grip. The pistol grip is not merely a handle; it is the foundation and basis for the trigger finger's important work. The pistol grip should be hand-filling without feeling bulky. It should fully support the palm and the three supporting fingers without cramping them. However, it should not get in the way of the efficient use of the rifle. For example, a pistol grip with palm rest might not be the best option for an AR-type carbine used in home defense, or in a situation where you may have to rapidly transition from the long gun to a handgun. The palm rest can just plain get in the way.

In any case, you want to be able to reach the trigger in a relaxed fashion without strain to the trigger finger. Most folks will be using the distal joint rather than the ball of the finger on the trigger, so be sure you have a comfortable fit. A fat grip can put the trigger out of reach of said joint.

Closely allied to the pistol grip is the trigger guard. The original design trigger guard is designed to unlatch at the front and swing down out of the way of a heavily-gloved trigger finger. There are enlarged trigger guards available to replace the original straight trigger guard. This design makes it unnecessary to swing the guard down out of the way to gain freer access to the trigger.

QUERY:
Have you ever seen someone swing down a trigger guard? We haven't.

PITFALL:
If you are building a lower receiver, or removing a straight trigger guard to install one of the newer, enlarged variety, it is very easy to break the tabs off the receiver when installing or removing the roll pin from the rear of the trigger guard. When you do, you have now ruined the receiver. Be sure you support the tabs when installing or removing the pin.

TIP #1:
OK, you've now broken the tabs. You can reclaim the receiver by installing a Stark Enterprises pistol grip. This grip has an integral trigger guard that does not require the tabs.

TIP #2:
Afraid of breaking the tabs on a new build or reinstall? Get a Dead On Arms enlarged trigger guard. It has spring loaded pins at the aft end that avoid roll pin heartbreak.

CAVEAT:
We have mentioned some specific brand names. There is no guarantee that these brands will be available indefinitely into the future, or that there will not be other vendors offering similar products. Do your research.

THE *NEW* AR-15 COMPLETE OWNER'S GUIDE

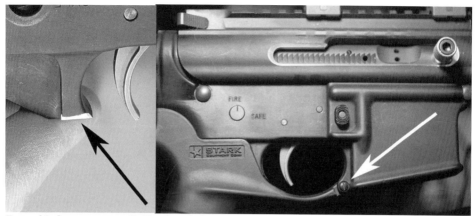

Does this happen to you? You break the trigger guard tabs off the lower receiver trying to pound that trigger guard roll pin in? Well, relief is spelled "S-T-A-R-K." It's a pistol grip with an integral trigger guard. Walt Kuleck Collection (including the boo-boo on the left).

You can avoid the heartbreak. This "enlarged" trigger guard by Dead On Arms uses spring-loaded pins to retain the rear of the guard. No need to risk breaking the tabs. If you want a larger guard, this might be the ticket for you.

An example of a modular pistol grip for the AR, with a choice of three front straps and three back straps. It replaces the original equipment grip on the left, which is pretty comfortable in its own right. The replacement grip also has inserts available for storing CR123 batteries or a spare bolt. Walt Kuleck Collection.

DETAILS

So, you've tried a box full of pistol grips that just don't fit the bill, or your hand. All is not lost.

TIP:

There are a number of modular pistol grips on the market. These typically have a basic body or framework with a selection of front and back straps from which to choose. It should be possible to find a combination of front and back straps that fit the bill for you.

In addition to filling the hand without stuffing it, some pistol grips have what in the M1911 world we would call a "beavertail." This upper rear extension covers what to some is an annoying seam between the top of the pistol grip and the bottom of the receiver. Furthermore, If you find the gap between the front of the grip and the rear end of the trigger guard distracting, there's a little plastic plug called "The Gapper," which fills the gap.

We've come a long way from the days of choosing between A1 and A2 pistol grips. You have a vast array of grips on offer; somewhere out there there's the one that's perfect for you.

On the left, we see the seam between the top of a standard-pattern pistol grip and the bottom of the receiver's pistol grip boss. On the right, a pistol grip with a beavertail covers the seam, making the grip just a bit more comfortable. Just make sure that your trigger finger can reach the trigger comfortably.

Mind the Gap! On the left we see the gap between the front edge of the pistol grip and the rear end of the trigger guard. On the right, we see "The Gapper," a little plastic plug that...fills that annoying gap.

Six Butt Stocks

Two fixed "rifle-length" butt stocks. On the left, an "A2" stock with a literal twist: an adjustable butt plate that adjusts up and down, in and out, and "twists" for cant. On the right, a modern fixed stock. The latter is also available for a carbine-length adjustable stock buffer tube. Hmm...a fixed stock on an adjustable tube... Walt Kuleck Collection.

Two adjustable stocks for carbine-length adjustable stock buffer tubes. On the left, a relatively conventional replacement for the standard military-style collapsible butt stock. On the right, a similar stock but with a swing-away comb piece, allowing a quick transition from an optic to backup iron sights. Walt Kuleck Collection.

There are times when the height of a scope, generally driven by objective lens diameter, requires a high comb. On the left, the multi-adjustable Magpul PRS, destined to be a classic. On the right, a simpler solution; a conventional-style collapsible buttstock with optional height-adjustable cheek piece. Walt Kuleck Collection.

DETAILS

Butt Stocks

From the muzzle device we've traveled down the rifle where our journey ends at the butt stock. The butt stock is the second most intimate "interface" (pun intended) between the shooter and the rifle. The butt stock has two important dimensions that will determine the suitability of a given stock for a given shooter and rifle: the length of pull (LOP) and the comb height. The LOP is the distance between the trigger and the butt plate and the end of the butt stock. The comb height is the distance between the top of the stock where your face goes and the centerline of the buffer tube within the stock. The butt stock has other dimensions too, but for the shooter the LOP and comb height are literally the foundational parameters.

The LOP should be such that the rifle is held comfortably with the butt plate in the "pocket" formed by the strong side arm at the shoulder, with the eye of the shooter a comfortable distance behind the rear sight or optic. The Army's experience with the M16 and M16A1 led to the decision to lengthen the butt stock by 5/8" when the M16A2 was introduced.

Then, came the AR carbines. Once upon a time the AR carbine collapsible stock was primarily a means to make the rifle more compact before deployment. The stock would be collapsed fully during storage or carriage, then extended when readying to fire. The original Colt collapsible butt stock had but two positions: open and closed. Later, the carbine butt stocks had four positions; now, six is the norm. The concept is that the shooter can find a desired length of pull when wearing a T-shirt, but also when wearing a heavy winter parka or body armor simply by collapsing the stock to a shorter position.

The original Colt collapsible stock. A Model 607 recreation of the first Colt AR carbine, with stock collapsed. Walt Kuleck Collection.

Model 607 recreation with stock extended.

THE *NEW* AR-15 COMPLETE OWNER'S GUIDE

No discussion of AR "furniture" is complete without mentioning the magnificent walnut offered by Lucid Manufacturing via Brownells. If you want the most striking AR on the block, you need to give these woods sets strong consideration. Thanks, Clem! Walt Kuleck Collection.

DETAILS

NOTE:
Your author prefers a startlingly short length of pull compared to many shooters. Blame his long experience with the relatively short LOP of the M1 Garand. Keep in mind that Jeff Cooper wrote that a long-armed shooter can adapt to a "too-short" LOP, but that a short-armed shooter will have difficulty with a "too long" LOP. This is a case where longer is not necessarily better.

TIP:
Buffer tubes for carbine-length collapsible butt stocks come in two sizes: "Commercial," 1.17" in diameter, and "Military," 1.15" in diameter. Be sure the collapsible stock you acquire fits the tube on your rifle.

PITFALL:
Alas, diameter is not the only difference between Military and Commercial adjustable-carbine-stock buffer tubes. Commercial tubes are often longer, with a slanted back. So, also be sure that your stock will fit your tube.

While the AR carbine stock can provide a range of adjustment, by and large AR butt stocks do not provide a range of comb heights for the shooter. However, there are butt stocks available with adjustable combs, from simple add-on risers to sophisticated multi-adjustable butt stocks intended for long-range shooters.

Butt stock designers have created a vast panoply of choices. You can find butt stocks that are absolutely minimal, or that incorporate storage for everything from spare batteries to a spare magazine. There are designs that take up the clearance between stock and buffer tube, so that the wobbly fit of the original military-pattern collapsible stock is a thing of the past.

HISTORICAL NOTE;
During the civil war, a model of the Sharps carbine was fitted with a coffee grinder in the butt stock. The idea was that one of every so many men would be equipped with grinder to serve the caffeine needs of his fellow soldiers. If such a thing is attempted today, you can count on the coffee grinder to be battery powered!

No discussion of AR handguards, pistol grips and butt stocks is complete without mentioning the beautiful walnut sets available from Lucid Manufacturing via Brownells. We hope that this wood is available when you read this, because it turns the "Black Rifle" into something approaching a thing of beauty.

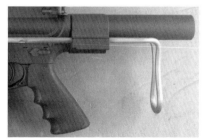

From the sublime, Lucid walnut, to the ridiculous. Check out this M3 Grease Gun collapsible stock on an AR from the Dark Ages of Black Rifles. Greg King Collection.

Carbine Comparison, from left: AR-15A2 Rifle, Carbine with fixed rifle-length stock, Carbine with collapsible stock, extended, Carbine with Magpul carbine-length fixed stock, and Carbine with collapsible stock, collapsed. Hmm...that rifle stock on a 16"-barreled Carbine is pretty handy, an interesting choice albeit with a rifle length-of-pull.

CHAPTER 5

THE RIFLE, COMPLETE

So...You Want A Carbine?

Why not? Everybody does. Check the product offerings from AR rifle vendors; we'll wait. Done? Certainly you noticed the proportion of Carbines vs. Rifles. So, why are Carbines so popular? Is the juice worth the squeeze?

From the early days of the M16, users have been seeking a short AR. In response, Colt began to develop short ARs beginning with the Colt Model 605. The 605 had a 15" barrel, but with a full-length rifle handguard and gas system. This approach was apparently a developmental dead-end, although an uncataloged Colt model of similar design surfaced in 2013.

Evidently 15" wasn't as short as desired by users; the next Carbine version from Colt was the Model 607, referred to by some as a "submachine gun" despite its chambering in a rifle caliber. A 607 recreation is illustrated in the previous chapter. The original 607 had a 10" barrel with a muzzle booster to improve function. The muzzle booster looks like a sound suppressor, and in fact has been classified as such by the US Bureau of Alcohol, Tobacco and Firearms (ATF). However, its true purpose was to increase back pressure in the gas system.

Colt persisted with the 10"-barreled approach with muzzle booster through the models 609 and 610; the 609 gained some Vietnam War combat use and notoriety as the XM177. The 609 and its commercial counterpart, the Model 619, introduced the sliding collapsible stock which has become the standard for AR Carbines. Closing out this line of development were the Models 639 and 649, respectively military and commercial 11.5" Carbines with a "moderator" or muzzle booster masquerading as a flash suppressor. The 11.5" barrel lives on in the modern Models R0933 and R0935, SAFE-SEMI-AUTO and SAFE-SEMI-BURST respectively, marked "Colt M4 Commando."

Finally, Colt hit upon what has proved to be an optimum barrel and gas system length for their Carbine with the 14.5"-barrel Model 650. As has been related in the History chapter, the 14.5" barrel carried through to the M4 and M4A1 military Carbines of today. It took a fair amount of time and effort to develop a short rifle system that approaches the reliability of Stoner's original balance of barrel and gas tube length, without major changes in the rest of the rifle system. For civilians, the barrel is stretched to 16", the US-legal minimum,

That doesn't mean that there didn't have to be some "minor" changes. In order to get a shorter total package, a sliding collapsible butt stock was combined with a shorter buffer tube. In turn, the buffer spring and buffer had to be shortened. What wasn't shortened, though, was the 45mm case length of the 5.56x45/.223 cartridge. That means the bolt carrier stroke is unchanged despite the shorter buffer tube. Consequently, the same energy developed in the rifle has to be absorbed in the shorter buffer (or recoil) system of the Carbine. There's even more, as discussed in the following ArmaLite Tech Note:

P.O. Box 299 Geneseo Illinois, U.S.A. 61254 Tel 309-944-6939 fax 309-944-6949 info@armalite.com

TECHNICAL NOTE 104:

SOME THOUGHTS ON DESIGN AND RELIABILITY OF AR-STYLE FIREARMS

All self-powered firearms are dynamic systems. Dynamic movement and relative timing of various components of the mechanism during the firearm's cycle of operation are critical to the firearm's reliability.

The original AR-15 Rifle design was dynamically well balanced. The AR-15 was designed to assure that all components were given enough time, and enough power, and enough space, and enough strength to perform their functions.

Subsequent variants of the AR-15 (particularly carbines) required design tradeoffs that caused some loss of that dynamic balance.

The U.S. military's M4 Series Carbines have developed a reputation for reduced reliability compared to the excellent reliability of the full length M16 Series Rifles. The somewhat higher malfunction rate of the M4 Carbine is due to dynamic imbalances in the mechanism itself, exacerbated by heat. The dynamic imbalances are a result of the desire for a shorter, lighter firearm. Consciously, or unconsciously, the requirement for more compactness inevitably resulted in a reduction in reliability.

A complete, detailed explanation of all dynamic considerations in firearm design is far beyond the scope of this Technical Note. However, some basic considerations can be presented.

The dynamic cycle of self-powered firearms is typically powered by two forces. Recoil is powered by the cartridge. Counterrecoil is powered by a spring.

In order for the firearm to cycle reliably in recoil, the cartridge must provide enough energy to push the bolt and bolt carrier assembly and empty cartridge case fully to the rear of its stroke without overpowering the bolt, thereby causing collateral wear and damage to the mechanism. And, the firearm must "time" the recoil cycle after the gas pressure in the barrel has subsided enough that the cartridge case can be freed from the chamber walls and successfully extracted. During recoil, the cartridge's energy will be expended unlocking the bolt, extracting and ejecting the empty cartridge case, recocking the hammer, and pushing the bolt and bolt carrier to the rear. The amount of power needed to accomplish these tasks varies somewhat from shot to shot, and varies even more depending on the environment and cleanliness/lubrication of the firearm.

In order for the firearm to cycle reliably in counterrecoil, the cartridge must provide enough energy to fully compress the recoil spring to give the spring its maximum potential energy. That full compression also gives the bolt maximum dwell time behind the feed position so that a new cartridge has time to be raised up in the magazine to the feed position. Then the recoil spring must have enough energy to feed the new cartridge into the chamber, lock the bolt, and (with assistance from the buffer) resist the natural tendency for the bolt carrier to bounce out of battery.

Let's explore why the requirement for a more compact carbine forced tradeoffs that were detrimental to reliability.

DURING RECOIL:

Analysis of carbine reliability issues during recoil requires a good understanding of the bolt carrier group and barrel of the rifle, and the functions of the cartridge case.

The distance from the chamber to the gas port, the length of barrel beyond the port, and the pressure of the propellant gasses determine the amount of energy provided to the action of the M16 series rifle.

The heart of the M16 operating system, the bolt carrier group, was designed to function well with the original 20 inch long barrel of that rifle. The bolt carrier group and the location of the gas port were carefully balanced to provide outstanding reliability with the ammunition that was designed for the M16.

A change in the cartridge (bullet weight or powder), the length of the barrel, or the location of the gas port along the barrel can substantially change the pulse of gas that enters the carrier group and drives the rifle action. Short versions of the M16 (including the M4) suffer from relocation of the gas port and changes in barrel length. The shorter the barrel, and the nearer the gas port to the chamber, the more sensitive the firearm is to variations in ammunition.

The below U.S. Army graph of gas pressure in various locations for the M16 Rifle and M4 Carbine is very instructive. Let's see what we can learn from it (color version available at http://www.Armalite.com/):

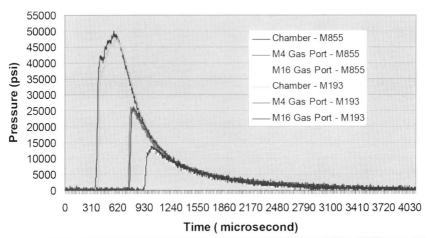

(Note: The timeline of the government-generated chart above is measured in millionths of a second)

The early 5.56mm cartridge was designated the M193. Years ago, the M193 was replaced by the M855 which contained a heavier projectile. The Army changed propellants to assure that the pressure that powered the firearm didn't change. Note that the chamber pressure and gas port pressures of the M855 are nearly identical to those of the M193. The Army was well aware of the need for consistency in these pressures.

However, note the difference in the pressure and timing of the gas port pressures in the M4 versus those in the M16. The gas port pressure of the M4 is approximately twice as high as that of the M16, and the projectile reaches the gas port in the M4 much sooner than it reaches the gas port in the M16.

Also note the slope of the curves at the M4 and M16 port locations. The slope of the curve for the M4 is much steeper than that of the M16. The slope shows how rapidly the gas pressure is changing. So, the gas pressure at the M4 port location is changing much more quickly than at the M16 location. What this means is that small variations in propellant will have much more effect on port pressure of the M4 than on port pressure of the M16. And increased variation implies decreased reliability.

The carbine gas port is located closer to the chamber than the gas port of the rifle: 7.5 inches instead of the 13 inch distance on the rifle. The gas pulse therefore enters the gas tube sooner and reaches the carrier group earlier than it does in the rifle length barrel. In addition to reaching the carrier sooner, it reaches it at higher pressure. The gas pressure at the carbine's gas port is double that of the rifle: 26,000 psi vs. 13,000 pounds per square inch.

To compensate for the higher pressure, the carbine's gas port must be smaller in diameter than the rifle's port. The smaller port is naturally more sensitive to variations in pressure as well as to contamination than the larger port. The higher pressure and temperature at the carbine port also causes more erosion of the barrel at the port.

The early pressurization of the carrier causes the carbine to begin to extract earlier than the rifle does. At the same time, the gas in the carbine's carrier is of higher pressure than it is in the rifle, and it forces the carrier to move the rear at a higher velocity than it moves in the rifle. Because of the earlier extraction, the cartridge case has less time to transfer heat to the chamber wall and shrink away from it before extraction begins. The cartridge case has a tendency to adhere to the chamber wall, and resistance to rearward movement can be high.

When the bolt, drawn rearward by the high velocity bolt carrier, tries to pull this stuck case to the rear, both the extractor and cartridge case are heavily stressed. The resistance can cause the whole mechanism to become sluggish or stop, or to cause early failure of the extractor or bolt.

As discussed above, the distance from the chamber to the gas port is important. So too is the length of the barrel past the gas port.

That's because the bullet serves as a plug to keep the gas pressure trapped in the barrel so that some of it can pass into the gas tube and back to the carrier. If the length of barrel beyond the gas port is too short, so is the "dwell" of the plug in the barrel. The gas pulse supplied to the carrier can be too short to deliver all of the energy that the carrier group needs. Too long a section of barrel beyond the gas port can cause too long a gas pulse.

Carbines with very short barrels (less than 12 inches) have a very short segment of barrel beyond the gas port; and the gas pulse is thus shorter than the carrier group needs. This problem combines with the carbine problems already described resulting in reliability of carbines with short barrels to be significantly poorer than carbines with longer barrels.

Efforts to adjust for the short length of barrel beyond the gas port by enlarging the gas port produce a firearm that is extremely sensitive to differences in ammunition. Efforts to correct the problem by using different springs or buffers or by changing the volume of the gas used are only partially successful.

The faster movement of the carrier group in carbines also creates an interesting and largely unknown problem with the extractor. During extraction, the extractor opens for a very short period, and then recovers to complete extraction. The faster movement of the carbine bolt increase the time that the extractor is open. This tends to decrease extractor efficiency and increase extraction trouble.

And, to exacerbate the problem, the propellant has not burned as completely when the gas reaches the carbine's port, so the firearm's internal mechanism gets dirtier, increasing the need for cleaning and potentially causing malfunctions if a stringent cleaning regimen isn't followed.

DURING COUNTERRECOIL:

The effect on reliability of shortening the rear end of the rifle is, perhaps, more subtle than the effect of shortening the front end. In order to reduce the length of the rear half of the M16, the buffer tube, the recoil spring, and the buffer all had to be redesigned. The redesign changes the nature of the power stroke provided by the recoil spring. In addition, one purpose of the buffer is to inhibit the bolt carrier from "bouncing" back out of battery. A bolt carrier slightly out of battery can absorb the blow of the hammer, causing failures to fire. The shorter carbine buffer simply isn't as efficient at preventing bolt carrier bounce as is the rifle buffer.

OTHER SYSTEM EFFECTS OF REDUCING BARREL LENGTHS:

Remember that the only purpose of the firearm is to project a bullet to it a target. Reducing barrel length has consequences beyond the firearm itself. Negative "system" impacts of reducing barrel length include:

1. Reducing muzzle velocity;
2. Increasing the arch of the bullet's trajectory;
3. Increasing muzzle blast and muzzle flash;
4. Reducing the effectiveness of terminal ballistics (damage) to the target.

The shorter the barrel, the worse the consequences. So, wise customers do not purchase barrels shorter than absolutely necessary for their tactical situations.

EFFECT OF HEAT ON FIREARM FUNCTION:

Heat increases the carbine problems listed above. Understanding the effect of heat requires a firm understanding of the purpose and action of a component of the firearm system that is often overlooked: the cartridge case. The cartridge case is a highly sophisticated component that performs a number of functions:

1. The case holds components (bullet, primer, powder) together precisely.
2. It engages key surfaces of the magazine and rifle to transport the cartridge's components into the chamber.

3. Upon firing, it expands into intimate contact with the chamber wall to seal high pressure gas in the barrel.
4. It contracts from the chamber wall when pressures lower to an acceptable level.
5. It transfers some of the heat within the case to the chamber wall.
6. It transports heat out of the weapon when extracted.

When the weapon heats up from extended firing, it is harder for the cartridge case to transfer heat to the hot chamber wall and shrink away from it. Adhesion of the cartridge case to the chamber wall results in increased resistance to extraction.

Heat affects carbines more than it affects rifles because of the carbine's earlier extraction at higher pressures and temperatures. Because heat affects a carbine, let's discuss heating in more detail.

EFFECTS OF HEAT ON THE BARREL:
BARREL STRUCTURAL FAILURES: In addition to increasing the malfunction rate, excess heat weakens the material of the barrel. The barrel of the M4 carbine is made of chrome-molybdenum-vanadium steel, and is chrome lined. It is a high quality grade of steel capable of long service. This steel tolerates high temperatures well. At a temperature of approximately 1100 degrees, however, the structure of this alloy (and most alloys) undergoes a permanent transformation that substantially, and permanently, alters it. The steel becomes prone to rupture under high pressure. It may not fail at the time of overheating, but instead may fail at a later date and far lower temperature. Thus, the cause of the failure may not be apparent to the user.

USEFUL BARREL LIFE: In actuality, very few barrels reach the end of their useful life via catastrophic failure. Most of them become inaccurate before they physically fail.

The higher the rate of fire, the hotter the barrel gets. The hotter the barrel gets, the more erosion eats away at the bore's surface. Eventually, the bore surface is so eroded that it can't adequately spin the projectile to stabilize it. So, to maximize barrel life, minimize rate of fire.

COOKOFFS: If too many rounds are fired too rapidly, the firearm's barrel can become so hot that a live round left in the chamber will ignite. This is called a "cookoff". If a firearm is often fired at such a high rate that a cartridge will cook off, the barrel life will certainly be adversely affected. In addition, cookoff can be a serious safety hazard. Typically, the cartridge will cookoff unexpectedly. If the firearm happens to be pointed in an unsafe direction at the time, unintended casualties and/or damage can result. Cookoff is taken so seriously by the military that military manuals contain maximum advisable rates to avoid it. For the M16, maximum sustained rate to avoid cookoff is 12-15 rounds per minute. Firing an M16 as rapidly as possible for less than 150 rounds can also cause a cookoff.

ELIMINATING BARREL FAILURE:
Design efforts to reduce barrel failure have taken at least three approaches: 1 different materials or coatings; 2. adding mass to serve as a heat sink; and 3. providing other features like cooling fins or water jackets to cool the barrel. All of these techniques provide either little benefit or result in serious disadvantages like increased weight and/or cost.

There is a novel design effort underway to avoid heat by designing ammunition that will reduce the amount of heat that the case transfers to the barrel in the first place. This effort is in its early stages and, even if successful, would not result in a change to service ammunition for some years to come.

Users can prevent barrel failures by limiting their rates of fire to the minimum necessary.

SUMMARY:
Tradeoffs in AR-style carbine design are more subtle than they appear.

Performance of the M4 Carbine has been repeatedly reviewed by Service authorities.

The tradeoffs summarized above have been deemed worth the tactical advantages gained in portability and maneuverability in close confines. The Services continue to seek small, but significant, improvements in all of their small arms, including the M4.

Changes to the hardware or ammunition can improve firearm performance, and research into the dynamics of the M4 is pointing the way to improvements. Additional benefit can be obtained by operator discipline in maintenance (lubrication) and controlling heat. Overheating is an especially crucial issue in M4 Carbine reliability and in barrel failure in all models.

Regardless of the rate of fire a soldier or police officer wishes to shoot, the designs and materials available require control of the firing rate except in the most critical circumstances. The potential of damage from overheating thus combines with the general need for ammunition conservation and accurate fire to force users, regardless of instinct, to maintain discipline over their firing rates. In the final analysis, tactics must bend to a number of influences, among which is physics.

Most importantly, carbine users must remember that there is no free ride: the advantages of short barrel length and an adjustable-length buttstock come at the expense of reduced reliability, increased sensitivity to differences in ammunition, reduced muzzle velocity, increased muzzle flash and blast, and less effective terminal ballistics.

In order to balance the needs for reliability, portability and tactical superiority, our customers are advised to:

1. Select carbines with barrels at least 16" long;
2. Select carbines with mid-length gas port locations (8" rather than the 6" of the M4);
3. To test and select ammunition that functions reliably in their short-barreled arms instead of purchasing based on price alone;
4. Conduct regular, thorough maintenance on their carbines;
5. Maintain fire discipline, using the minimum rate of fire needed to successfully resolve the tactical situation.

While there are differences in reliability between rifles and carbines, those differences don't account for the majority of malfunctions. The most common causes of malfunctions are poor maintenance and damaged (or low quality) magazines. Interestingly, both insufficient and excessive maintenance can cause malfunctions. Insufficient maintenance causes malfunctions rapidly as contamination slows the motion of the firearm's components. Excessive and/or improper maintenance may cause even more serious trouble by damaging critical components of the firearm. Common causes include the use of improper cleaning materials, tools, and processes intended to meet the "white glove" standards of insufficiently trained supervisors.

© 2012 ArmaLite, Inc. All rights reserved.   Used by Permission.

THE *NEW* AR-15 COMPLETE OWNER'S GUIDE

*Genuine Colt Buffers from Brownells; Upper, Rifle; Lower, Carbine.
Walt Kuleck Collection.*

*Genuine Colt buffer springs from Brownells: above,"fixed stock"; below, "sliding stock."
From USGI TMs, RIFLE: 11 3/4 Inches minimum to 13 1/2 inches maximum;
CARBINE: 10 1/16 inches minimum to 11 1/4 inches maximum.
Replace your spring when it collapses to the minimum.*

*Ever wonder what those Carbine buffer markings mean?
Left, original "standard" buffer, weight 3 oz.
Center, "H" buffer, weight 3.8 oz.
Right, "H2" buffer, weight 4.6 oz.
Not shown, "H3" buffer, weight 5.4 oz.
"Unmarked" contains three steel weights, "H" contains two steel weights and one tungsten
weight, "H2" contains one steel weight and two tungsten weights, and "H3" contains three
tungsten weights. Ist alles klar?*

THE RIFLE, COMPLETE

With all that in mind, why indeed are Carbines so popular? They *are* short and handy. When equipped with the customary adjustable collapsible stock, the Carbine can fit everyone from a young boy or girl to a burly bodybuilder. While the flat top receiver and railed handguard float tube are not necessarily exclusively for Carbines, the flat top and railed handguard allow the shooter to customize their sighting options much more effectively than the original carry handle upper. Perhaps most significantly, we've become used to seeing Carbines in news reports from "the field," and a large proportion of today's veterans "cut their teeth" on the M4 whilst in the service.

So, what are the practical consequences to the user of shortening the AR? Just this: the Carbine can be just a bit more finicky in function than the classic Stoner rifle design. Keep in mind that the Stoner system is a System. Everything is coordinated: the cartridge, the barrel length, gas port position, gas port size, buffer spring length, buffer, the lot. When the AR is shortened, all of these dimensions are changed. The wonder is that the AR design is sufficiently robust in engineering terms that it can tolerate this abusive manipulation.

Fortunately, AR manufacturers have generally got their Carbines right. One does not hear of widespread malfunctions with Carbines from reputable manufacturers. However, did we mention that the Stoner system was a System? In the real world, shooters do not restrict their Carbine use to 55 grain US-made ammunition. Steel case, heavy bullets, light bullets, European manufacture, any and all can upset the balance of the System. That imbalance can be revealed by the ejection pattern the shooter observes. If the shooter is committed to the ammunition that results in an abnormal ejection pattern, there are some steps she or he can take, as suggested by the following table:

Ejection Pattern	Cause	Solutions
12:00 to 3:00 (over the muzzle to directly to the right)	Overpowered/ Underdamped	Heavier Buffer Heavier Buffer Spring Heavier Carrier (M16) Adjustable Gas Block
3:00 to 4:30	Perfect Balance	Enjoy Perfection
4:30 to 6:00	Underpowered/ Overdamped	Fix Gas Leaks Lighter Buffer Lighter Bolt Carrier Lighten Buffer Spring

Another untoward manifestation of System imbalance is the failure to extract. The higher gas system pressures and shorter "dwell time," the time between the bullet's passage over the gas port and the beginning of the bolt's travel rearward, is a consequence of the shortened system. In simple terms, the bolt may be asked to pull the empty case out of the chamber before the case has had time to fully relax its grip on the chamber wall. If the residual pressure in the chamber is high enough, the case will stick. Because the AR bolt does not have primary extraction, the extractor and extractor spring have a more difficult job than in previous US gas operated service rifles. Consequently, extraction has been a weak link in the System. Colt and the US Army over the years have progressively increased the

THE *NEW* AR-15 COMPLETE OWNER'S GUIDE

The Benchmark Carbine: Colt LE6920. Why is this the "benchmark"? First, this is the civilian counterpart of the M4 Carbine, which Colt developed and for which Colt created the Technical Data Package (TDP) that defines the M4. The "real" military M4 has a 14.5", not 16" barrel, and has either full auto or burst mode in addition to SEMI-SAFE; thus, the 6920 is not true "Mil-Spec." However, Colt does make the 6920 using the same materials, processes and testing that they used to manufacture the M4. Walt Kuleck Collection.

strength of the extractor spring, dare I say it again, System. The extractor spring is comprised of a coil spring with an elastomer insert. Colt has apparently settled on a gold spring with a black color-coded insert. If the shooter experiences failures to extract, and the ejection pattern indicates that the gas system is properly "powered," installing a new Colt spring and insert (or a comparable spring system from another vendor) should solve the problem.

PITFALL:
If a strong extractor spring is good, isn't a stronger spring even better? There is such a thing as "too much" extractor tension.

TIP:
You can infer excessive extractor tension when you notice that the base of the cartridge case is found to have smeared the bolt face, and you have no signs of excess chamber pressure or overpowered gas system.

The Benchmark Carbine: Colt LE6920

Why is the Colt LE6920 the benchmark? First, it's the civilian-legal (in most states!) version of Colt's original M4. Colt developed the M4 and created the Technical Data Package (TDP) that defines the M4. Of course, the LE6920 is semiauto only, not select-fire nor three-round-burst capable. US law requires that a rifle have a minimum 16" barrel whilst the M4 has a 14.5" barrel. Never mind, when the cognoscenti refer to "Mil-Spec," it's the LE 6920 to which they refer.

NOTE:
We will not get into the minutia of Mil-Spec (Military Specification) and Mil-Std (Military Standard) definitions. You will find ample opportunity to Google discussions and, dare we say, no limit of controversies on the "Mil-" subjects therein. Knock yourself out.

TIP:
The high-round-count zealots will demand Colt bolt carrier groups with their military test protocol, genuine Colt extractor springs and inserts, and "H" and "H2" buffers in their Carbines. Colt is not the only vendor of these items, but if you seek purity of essence, you want Colt.

The accompanying photo essay details the specifics of LE6920 components and their markings. The LE6920 is shipped with a Magpul "MOE" (Magpul Original Equipment) PMAG 30 magazine (where legal) and Magpul MOE folding back up sight. Somewhat puzzlingly, this example was shipped with a push-button QD sling swivel. The puzzlement is that there is no place to plug in a QD swivel on the LE6920! No matter, now that photography has been completed, the standard Colt furniture will be replaced with Magpul MOE furniture, turning the LE6920 into an LE6920 MP-B ("B" for black).

Back in the bad old days of the Clinton Crime Bill, the legally-mandated loss of the bayonet lug was greatly lamented. However, when you attempt to affix a bayonet to the lug of a Carbine, you'll find that the barrel ring falls behind the flash suppressor, which is intended to support the ring. You'll need a 14.5" barrel if you ever want or need to "Fix Bayonets!"

Colt LE6920 Gallery

Colt LE6920 lower receiver legends. Note: "M4 Carbine." 'Nuff said. Walt Kuleck Collection.

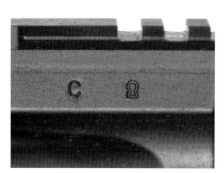

Left, LE6920 upper receiver marking. Right, "Circle 4" on hammer. What's that mean?

Left, "H"-marked buffer. Right, properly staked buffer tube (receiver extension) nut.

THE RIFLE, COMPLETE

Left, LE6920 barrel marking: "C" Chrome Lined, "MP" Magnetic Particle inspected, 5.56 NATO chambered, 1 in 7 twist. Right, "F"-marked front sight tower.

Left, "M16" bolt carrier. Right, properly-staked gas key screws. Note the greatly displaced metal.

Left, "C"-marked bolt carrier. Center, "MPC"-marked shot-peened, proof-tested, magnetic-particle-inspected bolt. Right, gold extractor spring with black insert.

THE *NEW* AR-15 COMPLETE OWNER'S GUIDE

Our exemplar of one approach to solving the Carbine's "problems": the ArmaLite SPR Mod 1 in Remington 6.8 SPC II. The solution? This Carbine has a "mid-length" gas system. The mid-length gas system literally splits the difference between rifle and customary Carbine gas systems, reducing the port pressure compared to the Carbine, if not to the level of the rifle.

THE RIFLE, COMPLETE

ArmaLite's Solution to the Carbine "Problem": The Mid-Length Gas System

Another approach to improving Carbine reliability was pioneered by ArmaLite in the '90's: the so-called mid-length gas system. As detailed in ArmaLite Tech Note 104 earlier, the mid-length gas system is one way of allowing a moderated gas port pressure compared to the carbine-length system. If the carbine-length gas system is so problematic, why did Colt design that length into the M4 Carbine? The reason is that with a 14.5" barrel, the M4 could be made to function well with the gas port position they chose while accepting the M7 and M9 bayonet.

> **PITFALL:**
> When you attempt to attach a bayonet to a Colt LE6920, for example, the distance between the bayonet lug on the front sight base and the flash suppressor is greater than the difference between the bayonet's lug latch and barrel ring. You need the shorter 14.5" barrel to bring the flash suppressor back to the point that the bayonet's barrel ring can rest on the body of the suppressor.

> **TIP:**
> If you are bound and determined to fix a bayonet to your non-NFA 16.5" Carbine, get a mid-length gas system.

When ArmaLite first introduced the mid-length gas system there was some concern that the mid length would remain a proprietary niche offering by a single vendor, ArmaLite. For example, barrels and handguards would be limited to whatever that vendor chose to offer. If for some reason that vendor chose to discontinue the product line, an owner would be left bereft. But, fortunately, the idea was too good to die, and good enough for others to adopt Thus, the ArmaLite mid-length has survived and thrived.

The ArmaLite SPR has another major deviation from the classic Stoner system: the "monolithic" upper receiver. This design integrates the upper rail of a classic handguard float tube with a flat top upper receiver. ArmaLite's implementation of the concept features interchangeable "rails"—smooth, half Picatinny (reversible to put the Picatinny front or rear), or full Picatinny.

The benefit of a monolithic upper receiver is that the top rail is one piece from charging handle to gas block. This design not only strengthens the join between the handguard and the upper receiver, it ensures that an optic mount that bridges the flat top upper and handguard rail sections enjoys perfect alignment of those sections, because there is but the one long section.

This particular ArmaLite SPR is chambered in 6.8 SPC, yet another variation from the Stoner system. We'll go into the somewhat long and tortuous history of the 6.8 in the Ammunition chapter, but suffice it to say that a mid-length gas system is probably a good idea with that chambering.

The ArmaLite mid length: a solution to the Carbine gas port pressure "problem."

Above and right: ArmaLite SPR Mod 1 Carbine in 6.8 SPC II. This rifle is equipped with A.R.M.S. 71L front and rear folding backup sights. Note the "Department of Defence (DoD) Acceptance" stamp applied to every complete ArmaLite rifle. No, the rifle isn't really DoD inspected, but it's a nice touch. Rifle Courtesy ArmaLite, Inc.

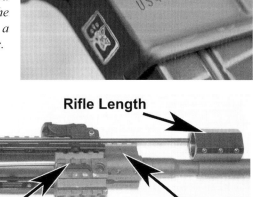

Here's the ArmaLite solution to the gas port pressure "problem" inherent to Carbine-length gas systems, the ArmaLite-pioneered mid length gas system; it splits the difference.

THE RIFLE, COMPLETE

The ArmaLite SPR Mod 1 is also characterized by its "monolithic" upper receiver. The top rail of the receiver runs right up to the gas block.

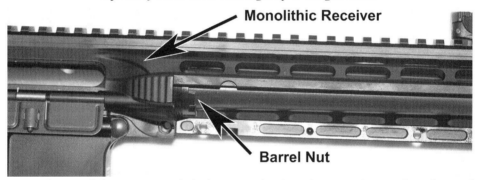

Here's the monolithic receiver with the bottom and right rails removed. Note the redesigned barrel nut made necessary by the monolithic design.

This closeup of the barrel nut shows that it's engaged by a special wrench much like the buffer tube nut.

THE *NEW* AR-15 COMPLETE OWNER'S GUIDE

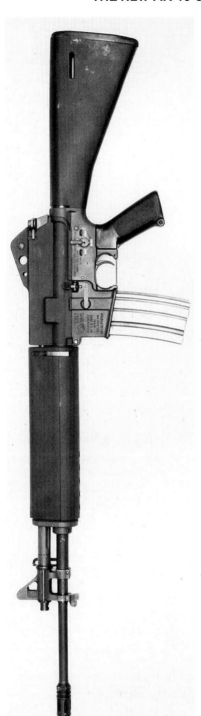

One of the first external piston ARs: the Colt "M16A2" of 1969.

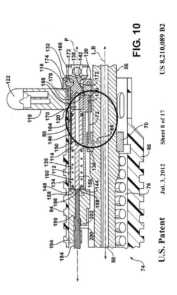

One of the latest: Brown's "BEAR," patented in 2012. Note the circled short gas tube that isolates the barrel from the gas cylinder; essentially free-floating the barrel nearly as well as does the internal piston system's long gas tube.

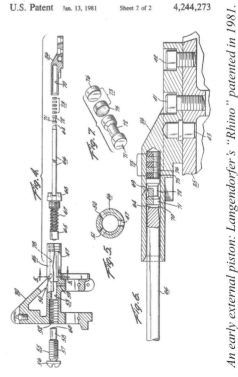

An early external piston: Langendorfer's "Rhino" patented in 1981.

THE EXTERNAL PISTON AR: A SOLUTION LOOKING FOR A PROBLEM?

Introduction

We have discussed the Stoner System in some detail in the History chapter, and reviewed some of the pros and cons of each. We may have left the impression that external piston systems are without significant merit, but that is not the case. If external piston systems are of value and deserving of consideration, what criteria can we use to make an informed decision about gas systems?

External piston systems are touted to provide several benefits. First among them is cleanliness. The internal piston system exhausts its gas into the upper and lower receivers, causing them to soot up. The gas brings not only combustion residue but also heat. Piston systems typically vent somewhere in the handguard area, keeping the receivers clean and cool. Sounds good, yes?

However, if fouling in the receiver were not accompanied by function issues, going from the simplicity of the direct impingement gas tube to a mechanically operated bolt carrier would be difficult to justify. The function issues in question are not those you might expect, i.e., the effects of fouling on the rifle's action. Rather, it is the shift to short barrels (as short as eleven, ten, even nine inches), along with the more widespread use of sound suppressors (commonly called "silencers") that have been the real drivers for gas piston ARs. The external gas piston system shines in short-barrel, e.g., under 16", applications such as the 11.5" barrel that appeals to SWAT entry teams. A well-designed piston system can accommodate not just the initial design pressure from the port, but also the changes in pressure due to gas port wear. Note that for us civilians these short barrels require NFA (National Firearms Act of 1934) registration as Short Barreled Rifles (SBRs) for ownership. Consequently, for the majority of AR shooters, the short-barrel functionality of the gas piston systems is not particularly relevant.

For much the same reason as tolerance of gas port pressure variations, external piston designs can function more reliably than the Stoner system when sound suppressors are installed. While suppressors are also NFA items, they are becoming more and more popular among non-military non-law enforcement shooters. Suppressors can help preserve the shooter's hearing, while reducing the annoyance of the sound of the shot to bystanders.

Finally, full-auto operation (NFA rears its ugly head again for most of us) brings its own set of stressors, not least of which is the rapid buildup of fouling and buildup of heat in the upper receiver and bolt carrier group, when ammo is expended at the rate of 750 rounds a minute over an extended period of time. Automatic fire generates not only fouling but also heat and more-rapid gas port erosion, both of which will increase the pressure seen by the gas piston at the port. Once again, the external piston system becomes worth a look.

So, why don't we all switch to external piston designs? Well...there is no such thing as a free lunch. External pistons exact a price, in weight, complexity, and...cost. External piston systems also potentially impose an accuracy penalty. Internal piston systems provide what is essentially a free-floated barrel when a handguard float tube is used. External piston

Our exemplar of another approach to solving the Carbine's "problems": the Ruger SR-556 external gas piston rifle. This is the SR-556 in 6.8 SPC. It's the rifle on Page 250, complete with "can" or sound suppressor. Fun in the sun! Walt Kuleck Collection.

Here's another SR-556. This is the SR-556VT, Varmint/Target, in 5.56mm. Walt Kuleck Collection.

systems burden the barrel with a gas block and some kind or another of pushrod system. Finally, external piston systems are challenged to match the accuracy of the internal piston system. One major manufacturer claims 1.0 MOA accuracy for their internal piston model, but only 1.5 MOA for its external piston counterpart.

> **NOTE:**
> The Adcor "Bear" gas system has an intermediate gas tube that connects the gas port in the barrel with the gas cylinder mounted to the handguard float tube.

OK, So All External Piston Systems are the Same, Right?

Note that when we talk of "external piston systems" for AR-type rifles, we are gathering a number of disparate principles under the tent. You can have long-stroke such as found in the Garand and AK, short stroke as in the SKS, cutoff and expansion as in the M14, and even a "gas trap"-like system.

Over the past thirty years, inventors and engineers have been seeking ways to supplant the AR internal piston Stoner system with one sort of external piston system or another. Some have devised means to convert existing AR uppers to an external piston system. However, there is a problem with the conversion approach. The dogleg in the impingement system's gas tube is the clue: the bolt carrier's gas key is not in line with the front sight base's gas "outlet"; the gas key is higher above the bore line. But, the problem is not just the gas key *per se*; the hole in the upper receiver through which an operating rod must pass, and the clearance for the gas key as the bolt carrier reciprocates in the upper receiver roof, are also fixed and higher above the bore line than the front sight base's opening.

Thus, more-or-less-direct conversions must incorporate an awkward "dog-leg" in their mechanism to accommodate the difference in elevation above the bore line. A "dog-leg" is not only aesthetically inelegant, it introduces bending moments in the actuating mechanism that must be accommodated by thick, heavy part sections and/or one or more intermediate bearing supports. Replacing the front sight base with a base or gas block with an outlet in line with the gas key and upper receiver gives a direct "shot" for the actuating mechanism, at the cost of incompatibility with "standard" AR handguard and float tube dimensions (e.g., see the "Rhino" patent on Page 156). Consequently, most current AR gas piston systems concede the need for a complete upper receiver system for straight-line action and handguards that clear the system.

Ruger's SR-556: Our External Piston Exemplar

An exemplar of the external piston AR is the Ruger SR-556. The SR-556FB is a completely modern AR-type rifle, with quality Troy front and rear sights and proprietary Troy rail handguard. The sophisticated gas system of the SR-556 is worthy of detailed description and discussion. The gas block has a gas regulator with four positions, including position "0" for complete gas cutoff. The default for most ammunition and circumstances is "2," with "1" and "3" available for reducing or increasing gas power, respectively. "One" is suggested for use with a suppressor, and "3" for use under adverse conditions. While the gas regulator adjustability is both useful and uncommon in gas piston ARs, it's the distinctive two-stage short-stroke gas piston that is a true innovation.

THE *NEW* AR-15 COMPLETE OWNER'S GUIDE

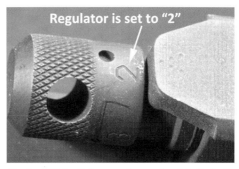

Setting "2" of the regulator, the "default."

SR-556 gas block. The gas port location splits the difference between the that of the conventional rifle and conventional carbine.

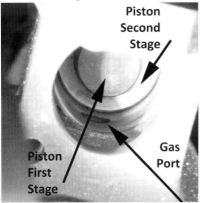

Pushing out the captive pin and aligning these flats allows removal of the regulator

Gas flows from the gas port to the piston first stage via a hole in the regulator body.

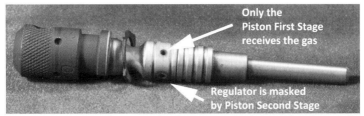

The piston is given initial impetus by the gas impinging on the piston's first stage.

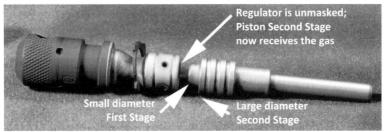

When the piston has moved 0.120" rearward, the gas also acts on the piston's second stage.

THE RIFLE, COMPLETE

The SR-556's gas piston has two "stages," a first stage piston with 0.055 square inches of area, and a second stage with 0.155 square inches of area (which includes, of course, the area of the first stage). As gas begins to move the piston via the selected hole in the regulator, the bolt carrier gets a relatively gentle start to its movement via the intermediate "transfer rod." In contrast, the abrupt pulse delivered by the internal piston system contributes to the extraction difficulties experienced by AR shooters if all is not perfect with the rifle and ammunition. The SR-556 piston's first stage, followed by the second stage that kicks in after the piston has moved 0.120 in. rearward and has unmasked the regulator, gives the bolt carrier and thus the bolt a progressive "push" that is relatively gentle on the extractor while giving the bolt carrier enough power to reliably cycle the bolt carrier group. A welcome benefit is a reduction in perceived recoil due to the "smoothing" of the gas system impulse. The SR-556 may look like other external piston ARs, but the two-stage system makes the SR-556 a big leap forward in AR external piston system design.

Because the gas is exhausted through the bottom of the gas block rather than conducted into the bolt carrier, the gas key is now superfluous. In its place is an integral abutment for the transfer rod (as Ruger calls the operating rod) to act on the bolt carrier. Because this is a dedicated upper and not a conversion, the abutment can be integral rather than a bolt-on replacement for the gas key. However, when the transfer rod is pushing on the abutment, because of the displacement of the abutment above the centerline of the bolt carrier, an upsetting (tilting) moment is generated that must be accommodated if the bolt carrier is not to bind in its bore in the upper receiver. Ruger's solution is to carefully hold the tolerances of the upper and lower receivers combined with a full-diameter rear bearing surface that is more than twice as long as the standard AR bolt carrier's surface. When combined with the lubricity of the hard-chrome finish of the bolt carrier, smooth function without binding is assured.

But...do we really need an external piston system in our AR?

The gas driver is just one part of an integrated system. As with most in life, it's a matter of compromise. The internal piston system shines in longer-barrel (16" and up) applications where accuracy, particularly at longer ranges, is the goal; you can free-float the barrel with the flimsy and flexible gas tube as the only restraint. The simplicity, light weight and low cost for the widely-available standardized parts of the internal piston system arguably make it the choice for most non-full-auto applications. There's literally nothing in the gas system to wear, seize, break, corrode or be lost in the mud beneath one's boots while cleaning it. But, the internal piston systems are more sensitive to ammo variations and do dump much of the exhaust gas into the upper and lower receivers.

If, on the other hand, the clean running of the external piston system, combined with its tolerance of ammunition and gas pressure variations are important benefits, the external piston system is the way to go. If you have a suppressor, you have yet another reason for an external piston setup. However, you do give up simplicity and must tolerate some added weight and cost. The SR-556 does keep the loose part count down to a minimum with only two relatively large parts that are removable. (Your author still has memories of scratching in the grass in search of the teeny tiny Lee-Navy extractor that falls out upon bolt removal [what was Winchester thinking? On shipboard, into the scuppers?].)

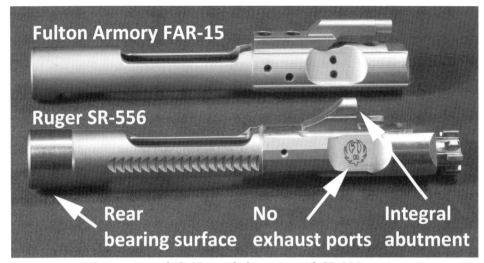

Comparison of AR-15-type bolt carrier with SR-556 carrier.

Because the SR-556 bolt carrier does not admit the operating gas, the carrier key is supplanted by an integral abutment against which the transfer rod presses. No gas coming in means that the carrier omits the exhaust ports of the AR-15-type carrier.

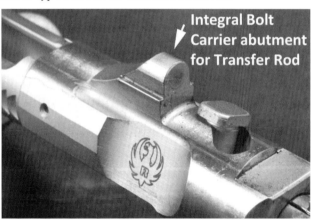

At the other end of the bolt carrier, the SR-556 carrier has a long bearing surface to counteract the upsetting moment (carrier tilt) caused by the action of the transfer rod at a distance above the bolt carrier axis.

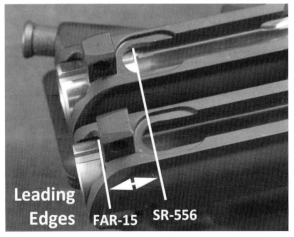

THE RIFLE, COMPLETE

While this may not be a consideration for some, it should be noted that there is no standard for external gas piston systems. Every system is different; some vendors have changed designs two or three times! The owner is locked into a particular vendor for support, and that's assuming that the vendor will continue to support early iterations. If not, you have a thousand dollar tomato stake. Thankfully, most current external piston uppers are compatible with standard AR-15 lowers.

So, if you don't fire 1,000 rounds in a session, particularly if it's not full-auto, and you have a civilian-legal barrel length, you might be better off investing instead in ammo and becoming more proficient rather than spending the money on an external piston AR. I'll submit that this will be the case for 99% of civilian shooters.

That having been said, this SR-556 is a wonderful piece of kit and a keeper for the author. It's not only technically elegant, it is aesthetically pleasing and a fine performer. In the end, it's up to you, the owner and shooter, whether a gas piston AR meets your needs, whether real or perceived.

Ruger SR-556C Carbine. The flash suppressor is machined into the end of the barrel, shortening it by the length of the flash suppressor. Walt Kuleck Collection.

Ruger SR-556CLA, "Carbine Light Adaptable." The CLA is an SR-556C variation with a (relatively, compared to the SR-556FB) lightweight float tube with user-configurable rails. Walt Kuleck Collection.

THE *NEW* AR-15 COMPLETE OWNER'S GUIDE

This AR is fitted with the uncommon USAF .22LR conversion kit with its white .22LR magazine. The upper receiver is a rare Colt Model 750 LMG upper. This upper differs from the common A2 upper in that it has a case deflector but no forward assist. Because a .22 conversion unit has no provision for the forward assist, this 750 was a natural choice as a host for the kit. Walt Kuleck Collection.

A 9mm Carbine based on a Professional Ordnance polymer upper and lower receiver set. Greg King Collection.

CHAPTER 6

CHAMBERINGS and CARTRIDGES

The AR: Flexible Launch Platform

The AR-type rifle nearly from the beginning has been adapted to cartridges other than the original .223/5.56-MM that had been designed for the original AR-15. The first caliber adaptation was to what would seem to be a natural, the rimfire .22 Long Rifle (.22LR). The US Army and Air Force each adopted a rimfire conversion, while Colt designed yet another. While .22LR conversions have the appeal of providing training on the AR system using inexpensive ammunition, the fact of the matter is that the AR-15's .223/5.56-MM barrel is not well adapted to the .22LR bullet. The .224" bore of the ".223" is larger than the .222" diameter of the .22LR bullet, while the slowest twist found in .223/5.56-MM barrels is 1 in 12", far faster than the 1 in 16" which is the standard for the .22LR. The lead bullets of the .22LR will often not even properly engage the rifling of the more common 1 in 8" and 1 in 7" twist barrels found in contemporary ARs. Thus, when a conversion unit is used, the bullet tends to skid down the barrel rather than spiraling down in conventional controlled fashion. Thus, .22LR conversion units have been generally supplanted by dedicated .22LR uppers, using a barrel chambered and rifled for .22LR bullets and a conversion bolt that doesn't require the bullet to free fly through the very long throat of the .223/5.56-MM chamber adaptor. In any case, a special magazine is required that fits the AR-15 magazine well on the outside and the much smaller (than the .223/5.56-MM) .22LR cartridge on the inside. The Army conversion kit used an insert for 20-round M16 magazines, while the Air Force unit had a special magazine that looked like an M16 magazine but hid a .22LR magazine mechanism inside.

The .22LR chambering, whether via adaptor or dedicated upper, functions by simple blowback. That is, there is no locking of the bolt; the bolt's rearward travel is controlled by the inertia of the mass of the bolt and the recoil spring. It was not a great leap to design dedicated uppers for other cartridges that could be adapted to blowback operation, specifically pistol cartridges such as the 9mm Parabellum (Luger) and .45 ACP. These adaptations were pioneered by Colt and Olympic Arms. The Colt conversion used a magazine well adaptor pinned into the lower receiver to accept pistol-cartridge-size magazines, for example.

While these rimfire and pistol cartridge chamberings were perceived to have value and provided the ergonomics and control protocols of the AR, their superficial external similarity to the AR design belied their complete deviation from the Stoner System internally. Consequently, while these are interesting variations, they cannot be considered true ARs.

However, this is not the end of the story. The AR has been adapted to a wide range of cartridges, from .204 Ruger to .500 Sledgehammer. We can characterize these variations three ways:

"Type 1" AR Chamberings: from left, .204 Ruger, .223/5.56-MM and .300 Whisper. Cartridge specimens courtesy Dick's Gun Room, Walt Kuleck Collection and Arlan's Guns & Ammo.

"Type 2" AR Chamberings: from left, .223 (for comparison), 6.8 SPC, 7.62x39, .450 Bushmaster and .500 Beowulf. Specimens courtesy Walt Kuleck Collection, Hornady, CorBon Ammunition and Arlan's Guns and Ammo.

"Type 3" AR Chamberings: from left, .223 (for comparison), .22-250, 7mm-08 and 7.62-MM (.308 Winchester). Specimens Courtesy Walt Kuleck Collection.

CHAMBERINGS and CARTRIDGES

1. Cartridges that employ the case head dimension of the .223/5.56-MM cartridges; consequently they use the same bolt face diameter, and require only a barrel change for use. "Factory" cartridge chamberings include:

- .17 Remington
- .204 Ruger
- .221 Fireball
- .222 Remington and .222 Remington Magnum
- .223 Remington (5.56x45mm)
- 6x45mm
- .300 Whisper/.300 AAC/Blackout

2. Cartridges that can physically function through the AR-15 lower receiver magazine well, but require a bolt as well as a barrel change; factory cartridges include:

- 5.45x39mm
- 6.5mm Grendel
- 6.8x43mm SPC (Special Purpose Cartridge)
- 7.62x39mm Russian Short
- .30 RAR (Remington AR)
- .450 Bushmaster
- .458 SOCOM
- .50 Beowulf

3. Cartridges that will not physically into fit the original AR-15 design, but will fit the original AR-10 design. Designers and manufacturers, starting with ArmaLite, looked to the AR-10 for inspiration. These cartridges include those based on the .308/7.62MM case, from .243 Winchester to .358 Winchester. We might call these AR-10-based rifles "big block ARs" to distinguish them from the original "small block" AR-15. Chevrolet aficionados will recognize the analogy.

In truth there's a fourth category: Super-size ARs designed for very large and long cartridges, including the .30-'06 and .338 Winchester Magnum. These are far from mainstream, not readily available, and if you need one, you most likely will know where to find it.

Military 5.56-MM Cartridges

The history of the military 5.56-MM cartridge begins in the 1950's, when Gene Stoner, huddled with Frank Snow of Sierra Bullet Co. to create the original bullet for the .223, a 55-gr Full Metal Jacket (FMJ) analogue of the bullet in the Cartridge, Cal..30, M1, originally designed for the M1903 Springfield rifle and M1917 and M1919 machine guns. The cartridge case was based on the .222 Remington cartridge; the .222 case was eventually lengthened by Remington to increase powder capacity and was originally called the ".222 Remington Special." The name was soon changed to ".223 Remington" to avoid confusion with Remington's new ".222 Remington Magnum, a similarly lengthened .222 Remington cartridge.

It would take a book to describe the evolution of the .223 Remington, its evolution into the .5.56-MM, and its subsequent development and production worldwide. Fortunately,

THE *NEW* AR-15 COMPLETE OWNER'S GUIDE

5.56-MM US Military Cartridges: from left, 55-gr M193, 62-gr M855 "green tip," 77-gr Mk 262 Mod 0 and 62-gr. Mk 318 Mod 0 "USMC 'SOST'." Walt Kuleck Collection.

.223 Remington Commercial Cartridges: from left, .22LR (yes, we know, it's not a .223, but it's there for comparison), .40-gr "Varmint" bullet (the .22LR bullet is 40-gr, so now you see why the .22LR started the lineup), 52-gr, 62-gr, 68-gr and 77-gr. Cartridge specimens courtesy CorBon, Dick's Gun Room and Walt Kuleck Collection.

CHAMBERINGS and CARTRIDGES

for those interested in the gritty details of the AR-15/M16's cartridge, there is such a book: ***The History and Development of the M16 Rifle and Its Cartridge***, by David R. Hughes. Alas, Hughes' book was printed in an edition of only 500 copies in 1990, and is now very hard to find and costly when a copy is located. For the serious historian, though, Hughes' book is indispensable.

The US military has standardized five variations of the 5.56-MM "ball" cartridge. The first was the 55-gr M193. The second, as briefly detailed in the History chapter, is the 62-gr M855 with steel penetrator and identifying green tip. The third is the 77-gr Mk 262 developed for long range work by Special Operations troops. The fourth is the 62-gr Mk 318, developed to penetrate intermediate barriers such as car bomb windshields while retaining antipersonnel effectiveness. The fifth is a variation of the M855, the M855A1. This last variation is touted by its developers to be the best yet, but its detractors are equally vocal. It would seem that "green" concerns were an impetus to the 'A1's design, as it is "lead-free."

Other cartridges have been offered as superior replacements to the 5.56-MM, such as the 6.8 SPC and 6.5 Grendel. To date, the US Military has chosen to progressively enhance the 5.56-MM's effectiveness via bullet design rather than a costly rifle upgrade.

PITFALL:
While the commercial .223 Remington and 5.56-MM share initial development, they are not completely interchangeable. The 5.56-MM cartridge requires a more generous chamber neck area and throat, or leade, compared to the .223 Remington. You can shoot .223 Remington cartridges in 5.56-MM chambers, but the 5.56-MM should not be used in .223 Remington chambers; excess chamber pressure will almost surely result, with the prospect of rifle damage and personal injury. You have been warned!

.223 Remington: Most Versatile Cartridge of All Time?

From the early beginnings of the .222 ArmaLite/.222 Remington Special/.223 Remington in 1957 to today, the .223 Remington has been adapted to many sporting, hunting, law enforcement and just fun purposes. There are 35-gr explosively expanding Varmint bullets, to 80-gr VLD (Very Low Drag) bullets for long range target work. Bullets for expansion, penetration, and expansion after penetration—the so-called "barrier blind" rounds—are now on offer.

Before the .223 Remington, the .30-'06, itself a long-running US Military cartridge, was surely a candidate for "most versatile." .30-'06 cartridges with bullets from 110-gr for varmints to 220-gr throwbacks to the .30-40 Krag and the .30-'03 progenitor of the '06 can be bought off the shelf. This 2-to-1 ration of bullet weights has now been exceeded by the .223 Remington with a 2.5+-to-1 ratio. There's not much a .223 can't do inside of, say, 600 yards or to harvest game up to 200 pounds.

THANKS:
To CorBon, Dick's Gun Room and Arlan's Guns and Ammo for cartridge specimens at a time when AR ammo was hard to come by.

THE *NEW* AR-15 COMPLETE OWNER'S GUIDE

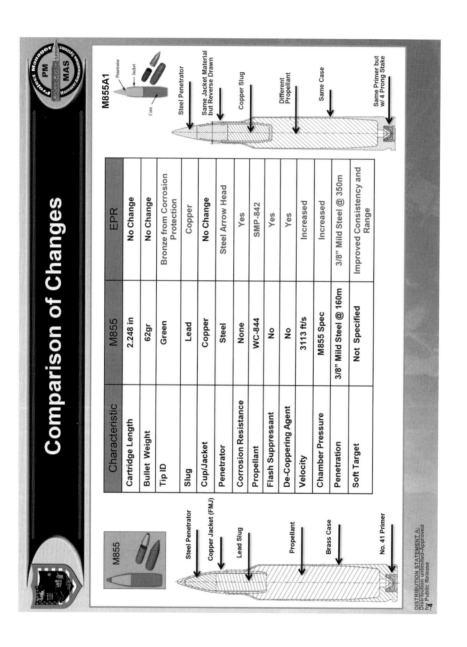

CHAMBERINGS and CARTRIDGES

Enhanced Cartridge Development

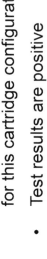

5.56mm Ball, Carbine, Barrier - MK 318 MOD 0

- New projectile developed from technology utilized in current law enforcement projectile
  - Front of bullet is designed to help defeat barrier
  - Back of bullet is solid copper and acts as a rear penetrator
- Short barrel propellant was specifically designed for this cartridge configuration
- Test results are positive
- Cartridge is compatible with various 5.56mm firearms
- Projectile can be manufactured on conventional bullet assembly machinery and it can be assembled on high speed loading equipment

DISTRIBUTION STATEMENT A. Approved for public release; distribution is unlimited

THE *NEW* AR-15 COMPLETE OWNER'S GUIDE

When one contemplates the novelty of the .308 AR, one should keep in mind that the AR started as a .308, or rather, 7.62-MM NATO rifle. It's the 5.56-MM that is the novelty! Or, one could so argue.

CHAMBERINGS and CARTRIDGES

Deja Vu All Over Again: The .308 AR

The Federal "Assault Weapons Ban" (AWB) hampered development of the AR platform for calibers not very closely related to the .223/5.56-MM. The law had proscribed new manufacture of "large-capacity feeding devices" for semiautomatic rifles. "Large capacity" was defined by the legislation as greater than ten rounds. While there was a sea of "pre-ban' (manufactured prior to September 1994) twenty- and thirty-round magazines for the AR-15-type rifle in 5.56-MM or .223 Remington caliber, magazines for other calibers could not be produced with capacities greater than ten rounds. Since consumers demanded what they deemed "normal-capacity" (twenty rounds and up) magazines for their ARs, manufacturers had little incentive to tool up for calibers that were not closely based on the .223 Remington case (most .223-case-based cartridges would feed from of existing "normal capacity pre-ban" magazines).

With the expiration of the AWB in 2004, the AR landscape changed dramatically. AR-type-rifle manufacturers were finally able to offer newly-made normal-capacity magazines for cartridges whose case bodies are larger than the .223, opening the door to a plethora of new calibers for the AR platform. This opened the way to design AR-type rifles that leave the AR-15 platform behind, in favor of a scaled-up AR-type rifle that can accommodate calibers in the .308 Winchester/7.62-MM family, as well as cartridges of similar length, such as the new Short and Ultra-Short Magnums. Before the sunset of the AWB, the popularity of these rifles was greatly hindered by the lack of proper magazines at a reasonable price. This "magazine gap" led to the adaptation of more-readily available magazines, such as those originally for the M14 and FN-FAL rifles, to these larger AR platforms. Neither solution proved to be completely satisfactory. Now that the availability of .308 ARs is expanding (one might almost say "exploding"), we now have what we might call ".308 ARs," the "big blocks" of the AR family.

Genesis of the "Big Block" ARs

The genesis of the AR family began with what we now term "battle rifle" cartridges rather than the now-familiar lower-power cartridges developed for select-fire assault rifles. Gene Stoner's early rifles, such as the Stoner M5 and M6, were chambered in .30-'06 almost of necessity, since .30-'06 was the standard US military cartridge of the time. The first AR-10s were in fact chambered in .30-'06 using BAR magazines, since the T65 cartridge had yet to be formally adopted.

The early AR-10s looked little like today's AR-15 except for the straight buttstock and high sight line. But, by the time the AR-10 was submitted for US Army testing and placed into production, its operating system (multi-lug bolt locking into the barrel extension, balanced gas expansion internal piston system) makes the AR-10 recognizably the forerunner to today's AR-15.

The original AR-10 had very limited success due to the market and political climate of the time. Since the US Army did not adopt the AR-10, foreign countries were reluctant to consider it, particularly as the AR-15 could be had, in many cases, with US subsidization.

THE *NEW* AR-15 COMPLETE OWNER'S GUIDE

The Stoner 63 was the 5.56-MM development from the 7.62-MM Stoner M69W and 62. Why the name "M69W"? The Stoner weapon system used the same receiver as the heart of as many as eight different weapons, from carbines to fixed machine guns. Some of these configurations required that the receiver be inverted; "M69W" reads the same upside down as rightside up!

CHAMBERINGS and CARTRIDGES

On the civilian side, the American public was not ready for an exotic aluminum and plastic firearm. Despite its adoption by the US military, even the semiautomatic AR-15 got a slow start in the civilian market. It wasn't until the evolved M16 finally succeeded in Vietnam, and Vietnam vets began returning, that the AR-15 began to get traction. The final impetus was the development of the National Match float tube system; it and the success of the AR-15 in Service Rifle competition fostered the AR-15's progression to ubiquity and widespread acceptance. The incorporation of the AR into the fabric of American shooting made the .308 AR not only acceptable, but almost inevitable.

Knight and Stoner Lead the Way

After his time at ArmaLite and some consulting for Colt, Gene Stoner continued his arms designing career at Cadillac-Gage, where he began to develop a series of "modular weapon systems." These families of small arms included rifles, light machine guns and general-purpose machine guns, all of which used the same core components and which, like a martial Lego® set, could be configured to fill a variety of roles. The advantage of this approach was to simplify logistics, as different small arms would have a high degree of component commonality with each other.

Stoner's first "family," the M69W/Stoner 62 system, was in 7.62-MM. Unfortunately, Stoner's history with the AR-15 was repeated. First, the military was not interested in a battle-rifle-cartridge system, and second, even when redesigned for 5.56-MM as the Stoner 63 and strongly endorsed by the Navy SEALS, the US Army rejected the Stoner design. Stoner went on to cofound ARES, a small arms design boutique in Ohio. While there, Stoner created further advanced light machine guns and rifles, but none went into production.

When Cadillac-Gage exited the arms business, Reed Knight, of Knight's Manufacturing Company (KMC), purchased the Stoner 63 tooling from Cadillac-Gage. KMC produced 100 Stoner 63 receivers before the Gun Owner's Protection Act legislation of 1986 froze the National Firearms Act registry, so that no further civilian machine guns could be manufactured.

It's likely that Stoner and Knight became acquainted at some point during the Stoner's Cadillac-Gage or ARES years, particularly with KMC's acquisition of the Stoner 63 design. In the event, Stoner joined with Knight in 1990. According to Gary Paul Johnston, Stoner must have been a ".30 caliber kind of guy," since Stoner first designed the AR-10 and Stoner 62 in 7.62-MM, but left Jim Sullivan and others to reformat both systems for 5.56-MM. Stoner's projects with KMC included the SR-25, a 7.62-MM AR-15-type rifle, the first such rifle to enter production since the AR-10 forty years previously.

The SR-25 was designed to use as many M16 components as possible (a reported 60% commonality), since KMC considered commonality with components already in the US military logistics system to be a valuable selling point for US military adoption. The SR-25 has in fact been adopted by the Navy and USMC as the Mk 11, and by the Army as the M110. In its military guise, the SR-25 has seen action in Afghanistan and Iraq, especially by "Tier 1" Special Operations units.

The SR-25 was also designed to use a variation of the original AR-10 magazine. The AWB on "normal capacity" magazines is one factor that made civilian ownership of the SR-25

USMC Mk 11. Knight's Armament Company (KAC) Photograph.

US Army XM110 (SASS). KAC Photograph.

US Navy SEALs train with Mk 11s. KAC Photograph.

CHAMBERINGS and CARTRIDGES

problematic before the AWB sunset in 2004, because very few "normal capacity" magazines were in the civilian sector prior to the ban. Under the provisions of the AWB legislation, new magazines could be supplied only to military and law enforcement customers. Since the sunset of the ban, new "normal capacity" magazines are now plentiful and affordable.

KMC established an affiliated company, Knight's Armament Company (KAC), to manufacture and market both 7.62-MM SR-25 and 5.56-MM SR-15 (and select-fire SR-16) rifles in a wide variety of configurations. The SR-25 is manufactured with a forged lower receiver and extruded upper receiver in flattop configuration. It is currently available in a wide variety of rifle and carbine configurations for the civilian market.

ArmaLite Recreates the AR-10

When Mark Westrom of Eagle Arms seized the opportunity to acquire the rights to the ArmaLite name and the proprietary information that remained, he changed the name of his company to "ArmaLite," while retaining "Eagle Arms" as a brand name. Eagle Arms had already been producing a 5.56-MM AR-15-type rifle, the M15, but now, even though Colt retains rights to the trademark "AR-15," ArmaLite could proudly mark its rifles "ArmaLite."

Along with the rights to the ArmaLite name, Eagle Arms also acquired rights to the AR-10 trademark, which Colt had let lapse with the collapse of the original AR-10's marketing effort nearly forty years before. Thus, with the names "ArmaLite and "AR-10" in hand, a rifle must surely follow. And, it did.

Rather than simply dust off the original AR-10 blueprints, which would have produced a rifle with lines unfamiliar to those accustomed to seeing AR-15s, Westrom appears to have begun with an eye to producing a familiar "AR-15" silhouette, but with improved internals to handle the power of the .308. For example, the AR-10 has a clever variation on the theme of the standard Stoner bolt, one that compensates for the "missing lug" at the extractor, consequently allowing a more equal distribution of forces among the remaining lugs. Instead of carrying over the standard AR-15 gas tube as does the SR-25, the AR-10's gas tube was designed for the .308's pressure curve, and gives more gas key engagement.

With the goal of producing a more robust rifle than the SR-25, ArmaLite put less emphasis on M16 commonality than did KMC/KAC. ArmaLite did position itself to serve the SR-25 user base with SR-25 component commonality at a higher "assembly" level, e.g., bolt carrier and upper receiver assemblies. Product improvements to the latest generation of ArmaLite rifles have continued with an eye to increasing their parts and accessories commonality with the 5.56-MM ArmaLite M15s.

Since the development of the new AR-10 was being pursued somewhat unluckily at the beginning of the AWB era, magazines became crucial to the viability of the project. In the civilian market an AR-10 with ten-round magazines would have limited appeal. The two most available "normal capacity" 7.62-MM magazines were the FN-FAL, particularly in "metric" form, and the US M14. ArmaLite's engineers chose the M14 magazine and created a two-piece lower receiver "mule" with an easily modified magazine well to help determine the "perfect" magazine position and angle. As the M14 magazine is originally a "rock and lock" design compared to the straight in-and-out AR-15 design, M14 magazines

THE *NEW* AR-15 COMPLETE OWNER'S GUIDE

Retro, before retro was cool. ArmaLite not only "recreated" the AR-10 (keep in mind that, strictly speaking, only an ArmaLite can be an "AR-10"), but offered a variant, the "AR-10B" (not to be confused with the later "B"-model AR-10s) that sported an under-carry-handle charging handle and brown furniture as a tribute to the first AR-10s. ArmaLite originally moved the charging handle to the rear of the receiver because the original under-the carry-handle charging handle got literally "too hot to handle" after firing a magazine or two worth of rounds through the rifle. Catalog page from Walt Kuleck Collection.

CHAMBERINGS and CARTRIDGES

ArmaLite AR-10 SASS (upper)

ArmaLite AR-10T Carbine (right)
Yes, that's an AR-10T in Iraq! (inset, above)
Photographs Courtesy of ArmaLite.

THE *NEW* AR-15 COMPLETE OWNER'S GUIDE

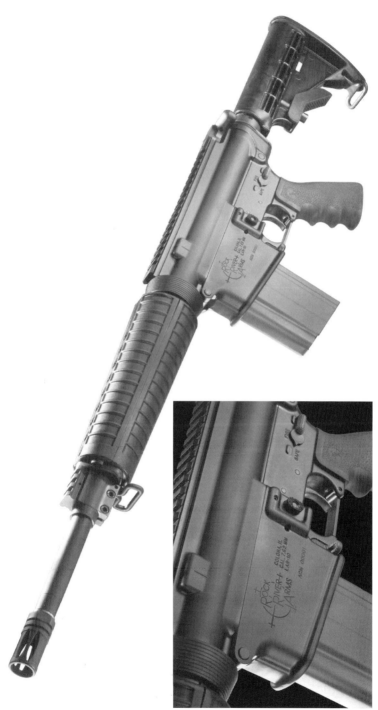

Rock River LAR-8 Mid-Length A4 (above), Rock River Receiver Closeup (left). Photographs Courtesy of Rock River Arms.

CHAMBERINGS and CARTRIDGES

required modifications to engage the AR-15-type magazine catch. A further modification was required to allow a redesigned magazine follower to engage the AR-15-type bolt stop. This magazine modification procedure sufficed to bring the AR-10 to market, but remained an inconvenience for AR-10 buyers. With the sunset of the AWB, ArmaLite is now able to manufacture new magazines designed specifically for the AR-10. No longer is it necessary to modify M14 magazines except in those states that still follow the provisions of the 1994 Federal ban. More recently, ArmaLite has offered a variation of the AR-10 that accepts the now nearly universally accepted updated SR-25 magazine first offered by DPMS.

Just as with the original AR-10, US military orders seem to have eluded ArmaLite, though ArmaLite has filled contracts for law enforcement agencies, including the ATF. AR-10s continue to be under evaluation by the US military; some of those, as well as some privately-purchased AR-10s have appeared "in the sandbox." Outside the US, the Canadian Special Forces did adopt a version of the AR-10T as their sniper weapon, and ArmaLite enjoys substantial foreign military sales to other countries.

The AR-10 proudly carries the heritage of the AR-10 into the 21st century, doing justice to the ArmaLite name.

Bushmaster Has a FAL Moment; Rock River Steps In

During the dark days of the AWB, magazine availability was a concern for designers of new autoloading military-style rifles, since the consumer expected not only a detachable "high capacity feeding device," but also one that was of normal capacity. As noted earlier, the only 7.62-MM NATO magazines manufactured and commonly available prior to the ban on normal capacity magazines were those for the FN-FAL and M14. The designers of what is now the Rock River LAR-8 decided to adapt the AR concept to use FAL magazines.

Both the FAL and the M14 magazines are of the "rock to lock" design. That is, the magazine is inserted slightly angled towards the front of the rifle; the top front of the magazine is "hooked" to the top front of the magazine well. In the case of the M14, the "hook" is the op-rod-spring-loaded nose of the operating rod spring guide. One inserts the magazine angled forward and hooks the nose of the spring guide into a hole in the top front of the magazine. With the front of the magazine engaged, the magazine is then rocked rearward, where a protrusion on the rear of the magazine is captured by the magazine catch at the top rear of the magazine well.

The FAL magazine works much the same way, with the exception that the hook is on the top front of the magazine, and the "hole" is a recess in the top front of the magazine well. There may be little to choose between the two magazines' locking arrangements, but the very low cost of the huge pool of FAL magazines makes the FAL magazine an attractive alternative to the much less common and thus more costly M14 magazine.

In contrast to the "rock and lock" approach, the AR was designed for "drop free," or "straight in and out" magazines, secured by a magazine catch that engages a slot in the side of the magazine, much like that of a Model 1911 pistol. Thus, the magazine well of the AR-10 and AR-15 was designed for this type of magazine. Since the AR lower receiver is aluminum, the steel hook of the FAL magazine would be engaging a recess in the aluminum

DPMS Panther LRT-SASS Rifle (top).
DPMS Panther TAC20 (bottom).
Photographs Courtesy of DPMS, Inc.

CHAMBERINGS and CARTRIDGES

magazine well. It's likely that the steel magazine hook would rapidly "wear out" any recess provided for it in aluminum.

The Bushmaster designers avoided the wear problem of the FAL magazine hook on the receiver by relying solely on the magazine catch at the rear of the magazine to secure the FAL magazine in the AR receiver. Since the magazine is secured only in a downward direction, unlike the AR magazine, which is secured both upward and downward, the magazine does move about when firing. Bushmaster's lower receiver had to be lengthened compared to the AR-10 or SR-25 in order to accommodate the FAL-style magazine catch, but the catch, as well as the FAL-style bolt stop, was made ambidextrous. The result is a rifle that indeed uses very inexpensive magazines, but for which certain compromises—magazine stability and receiver length—were required to accomplish this feature.

Bushmaster eventually exited the .308 AR market; Rock River Arms picked up the design, refining and enhancing the original and offering it as the "LAR-8." Rock River has made both steel and polymer magazines available for the LAR-8. For someone who is a FAL fan, or who just wants something a little different, the LAR-8 is an intriguing option.

DPMS Goes Back to Basics

While the DPMS .308 AR may have been later to the market than others, its development started in 1994, with one of the first prototypes being used to bag an Alaskan mountain goat in 2002. DPMS designed a straightforward "back to basics" rifle using the same magazine design as the original AR-10 and the SR-25. DPMS had extensive experience manufacturing AR-15 magazines, so the development of magazine tooling for a .308 AR-type rifle was a "natural." DPMS decided to make their magazine compatible with the original AR-10 and the SR-25. With the sunset of the AWB, DPMS "standard capacity" magazines became a boon to the magazine-starved SR-25 owner.

DPMS' "Panther LR-308" series includes the expected variations of barrel weights and lengths and float tubes, but does not include any models with the conventional AR-15-type "A2" upper. DPMS does offer a detachable A2-style carry handle for their flat top upper. One of DPMS's upper receivers has an ejection port cover and a case deflector with integral forward assist. This forward assist differs from the AR-15/M16, in that it acts on the rear of the bolt rather than engaging serrations in the bolt carrier. Combine the forward assist upper and the detachable carry handle, and you have a credible 'M16A2" appearance, at least where the upper receiver is concerned, without the need to tool up for an A2-type receiver.

LR-308 upper receivers are extruded from aluminum and then machined. Current (as of this writing) LR-308 rifles have a higher, thicker upper receiver than did early rifles. The lower receiver is machined from forged aluminum. The lower accepts AR-15 fire control and other lower receiver components, with the exception of the necessarily longer pivot and takedown pins and magazine catch screw. The greater diameter of the .308 cartridge requires a wider receiver, which in turn demands longer pins and screw.

DPMS rifles and upper receiver assemblies are available not only in .308 Winchester, but also .243 Winchester, .260 Remington, .338 Federal, and 6.5 Creedmore. Thus, the DPMS owner has a variety of not only upper receiver configurations to contemplate, but also the

THE *NEW* AR-15 COMPLETE OWNER'S GUIDE

Fulton Armory 18" Rifle (above), 16" Carbine (below) Walt Kuleck Collection.

CHAMBERINGS and CARTRIDGES

choice of (as of this writing) five calibers. DPMS' direct and straightforward approach to the .308 AR-15-type rifles allows DPMS to offer a quality rifle at a very attractive price.

Fulton Armory Wades In

Fulton Armory had been a manufacturer of 5.56-MM/.223 Remington AR-15-type rifles (the FAR-15) for a number of years. Fulton Armory addresses the market of the shooter who wants a custom rifle with typical Fulton Armory innovations, at a very competitive price.

In 2005, Fulton Armory began the development of a .308 AR. The original design goals included the use of unmodified FN-FAL magazines. Nearly two years of engineering and prototypes led to the conclusion that the steel "hook" of the FAL magazine was essentially incompatible with the aluminum AR-15-type receiver, and incorporating a FAL-type rear magazine catch would require an unacceptable lengthening of the receiver. Fortuitously, the end of the AWB meant that DPMS could bring forward a "standard capacity" magazine suitable for .308 ARs, and the decision was made to design the new Fulton Armory rifle to use the DPMS magazine.

In addition to adopting the DPMS magazine, Fulton Armory realized that the lack of standards in the .308 AR world was hindering the development of the .308 AR marketplace. Consequently, Fulton Armory teamed with DPMS to not only standardize on the DPMS magazine, but also to make Fulton Armory upper and lower receivers 100% compatible with their DPMS counterparts. This means that Fulton Armory rifle owners can exploit the range of DPMS upper receiver assemblies, and vice versa.

The introduction of the new Fulton Armory FAR.308 Titan took place in January, 2007. In keeping with Fulton Armory's tradition, the Titans are uniquely configured to meet the needs of the discriminating .308 AR shooter. Titan options include the state-of-the-art Geissele trigger and Magpul Titan PRS buttstock.

The Titan lower receiver is forged aluminum, and, like the DPMS receiver, accepts AR-15 internals except for the pivot and takedown pins, and magazine catch screw. The bolt stop is of a new, robust design to suit the DPMS-compatible magazine and the forces of the .308 caliber cartridge. The new Titan continues the Fulton Armory priorities of quality and content at an affordable price.

The Fulton Armory/DPMS "Standard" has caught on in the industry to a great extent, with Remington and Bushmaster (not surprisingly, because the latter two and DPMS became part of the same corporate family) getting on board. Other vendors have adopted the receiver interface standard, while more have designed their .308 offerings to accept the DPMS magazine.

Ruger Combines Paradigms

Possibly one of the best applications for the external gas piston system is for the big-block AR. There is a lot more energy required to cycle the action of a big block, and a lot more energy to absorb from the .308-class cartridges and up. Ruger's take on the combination, adapting their "soft-touch" piston to the .308, is particularly advantageous in harnessing

THE *NEW* AR-15 COMPLETE OWNER'S GUIDE

Ruger SR-762; barrel marked ".308/7.62." Walt Kuleck Collection.

CHAMBERINGS and CARTRIDGES

that energy for the useful work of running the gun without beating it or the shooter in the process. This may become one of the author's favorites.

Closing Thoughts

Since the "rebirth" of the AR-10-type rifle in the early '90's, the AR has become "America's Darling," used for all manner of purposes well beyond its original combat applications. Now, everything from prairie dogs to elk and paper bull's-eyes to steel silhouettes are within the purview of the AR shooter, with cartridges from .22LR to .50 caliber. Of course, the original "tactical" uses of the AR remain.

The magic of the AR has proven to be its adaptability and versatility. In its early years, the "Swiss Army Knife" or "Men's Barbie Doll" aspects of the AR's modularity was at the fore. Today, it's not just "change to a different upper for a different purpose," or "add a gadget," it's taking the AR concept and expanding its range of application to more effective cartridges in both of the original chassis sizes, and supplanting Stoner's original system with legacy gas system concepts, for better or worse.

Frankly, the author, as was the case with so many others in the '70's and '80's, dismissed the AR as an unworthy successor to the M1 and M14, ill-suited to purposes beyond equipping small-statured soldiers for jungle combat. Boy, was he wrong. The AR can be unnaturally accurate, is incredibly versatile, and just a blast to shoot.

The only real threat to the AR as a standard for America's shooters is political. It's up to the American shooter, nay, the American citizen, to do whatever possible to thwart the misguided efforts of the narrowminded to proscribe the ownership of "America's Gun." Be sure to do your part to defend our liberty and our freedom to choose!

Yep, it's a Ruger, and yep, it's in .308/7.62 NATO!

THE *NEW* AR-15 COMPLETE OWNER'S GUIDE

*Picatinny Rail Bottle Opener/Sling Mount.
Photograph Courtesy Ace Limited.*

*Picatinny Rail Chain saw by Panaceax.
Photograph Courtesy panaceax.com.*

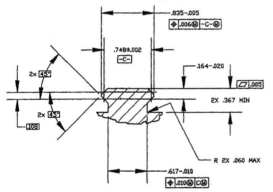

*Mil-Std 1913 Accessory Mounting Rail Profile.
Compare to the STANAG 4694 drawing found in the following pages.*

FIGURE 1. ACCESSORY MOUNTING RAIL PROFILE

Mil-Std 1913 Recoil Groove Profile.

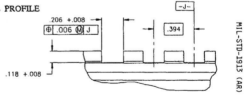

Note
1. Groove dimensions apply to all grooves. The number of grooves are dependant on application.
2. Center to center dimension applies between adjacent grooves.

FIGURE 2. Recoil groove

ACCESSORIES and ACCOUTREMENTS

CHAPTER 7

ACCESSORIES and ACCOUTREMENTS

Introduction

The subject of accessories, upgrades, enhancements and accoutrements for the AR-type rifle is sufficiently broad that an entire book could be devoted to them. It would be a boring book, though, and rapidly outdated as manufacturers are constantly introducing new products and allowing "legacy" products to fade away. The proliferation of "add-ons" for the AR was greatly facilitated by the development by Dick Swan of what became the "Picatinny Rail." When rails were added to handguards, particularly handguard float tubes, the floodgates were opened. Now you can get everything from a bottle opener to a cordless mini electric chain saw! A cursory perusal of the Internet will turn up any number of pictures depicting "clown car" ARs festooned with every manner of gadget.

The magic of Dick Swan's innovation was to create a simple, robust interface specification that would accept equally simple and robust mounting attachments. In the years since Dick's Swan/Weaver rail was standardized at Picatinny Arsenal via Mil-Std 1913/NATO Standards Agreement 1913, hence, "Picatinny Rail," the Rail has become not just a military standard but a worldwide universal mounting system for optics and accessories on all types of rifles, shotguns and handguns.

The first implementations of Swan/Weaver/Picatinny Rails (hereafter we'll just call them "Rails") on handguards offered full-length Rails on all four sides. This was done presumably for two reasons. First, the simplest way to make a handguard float tube of this type was by extrusion. Aluminum was forced through a die to create a railed tube that might be several feet long. This tube was then cut to length and machined for cross slots and barrel nut and so on.

The second, and more relevant reason for the shooter, was that the great expanse of rail permitted maximum flexibility in number and position of accessories to be attached to the rail, whether on the top, bottom, or either or both sides.

This early implementation did have some drawbacks, however, for example the simple round tube had to be of a certain diameter, if uniform all 'round, to clear the gas tube. When the rail heights were added to this diameter, you now had a bulky, heavy tube that was difficult for some shooters to grasp just because of its size, and uncomfortable for most with all those sharp rail and cross slot edges. This latter led to the development of rail covers of various types, which you'll see in many of the photographs in this volume.

As the popularity of the AR increased following the expiration of the Crime Bill in 1994, the increased market began to make a practical business proposition of innovating the application of Rails to AR handguards. Diameters were reduced, with an elevated section on top to clear gas tubes. Modular rail arrangements were devised, allowing the user to attach only the lengths and numbers of Rails needed or desired. These measures have increased comfort and reduced weight and bulk.

THE *NEW* AR-15 COMPLETE OWNER'S GUIDE

MIL-STD-1913 / STANAG 4694

The differences between MIL-STD-1913 and STANAG 4694 are:

- Metric drawing.
- Added some new necessary measurements and tolerances.
- Adjustment of some measurements.
- Reduction of straightness tolerances with approx 50%.

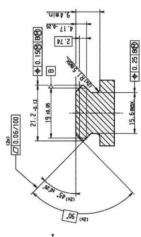

As of May, 2009 MIL-STD 1913 was replaced by STANAG 4694. One change in the spec was converting to metric dimensions.

ACCESSORIES and ACCOUTREMENTS

NATO Army Armaments Group

Recommendations

- On a typical Mil-Std-1913 rail the grabber is clamping the rail on the v-angles.
- Our tests have shown that this does not provide good repeatability.
- We recommend instead that the top surface is used as a reference and alignment of the grabbers.
- Our tests have shown that this provides excellent repeatability.

Typical US MIL–STD-1913 Rail/Grabber Interface

NATO Rail/Grabber Interface

The second, more significant change, was to change the clamping surfaces from the tops and bottoms of the "vees" to the bottoms of the vees and the top surface of the rail—without sacrificing backward compatibility.

VLTOR KeyMod Handguards. Photograph Courtesy VLTOR.

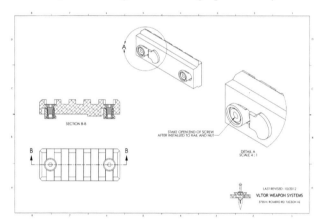

Page 4 from KeyMod Spec. Drawing Courtesy VLTOR.

*CMMG Handguard with KeyMod-mounted bipod
Photograph Courtesy CMMG.*

ACCESSORIES and ACCOUTREMENTS

But, for some the modular Rail handguard was not enough. Many accessories needn't be attached to the rifle by Rail, particularly those for whom removal was routine: bipods, for example. In recent years at least one serious competitor to the Rail system has been introduced: the KeyMod system.

The KeyMod system was devised at VLTOR Weapon Systems by Eric Kincel. During its development John Noveske of Noveske Rifleworks approached Eric to the end of creating an alternative to the Rail. Todd Krawcyk of Noveske enhanced the accessory lock/antirotation nut and Noveske adopted the system.

The KeyMod system has been put into public domain. The system has been adopted by dozens of manufacturers and accessory suppliers. We can expect a growing range of offerings incorporating the KeyMod system into the future. You can find the latest specifications and drawings for the KeyMod system via VLTOR.

Because the original Rail system is the US Military—and indeed, international NATO—standard, expect the Mil-Std 1913—and now the STANAG 4694—Rail to continue to be an important and common interface for AR accessories. There are millions of ARs with Rails in citizens' hands, after all.

NOTE:
An irony of sorts is that one of the first accessories to be offered in the KeyMod system is likely to be...a section of Rail!

Magazines

For the first thirty years or so of the AR-15 and M16, AR shooters had the choice of twenty- or thirty-round military pattern magazines. While there were early polymer magazines, particularly the Israeli Orlite and Canadian Thermold, the polymer magazines never really caught on. Most shooters felt they were deficient in fit, function or durability...or all three. The burning question at the time was, "Which US military surplus/contract overrun magazines are any good?" That's because between 1994 and 2004 no new "standard capacity" (greater capacity than ten rounds, that is) magazines could be made for citizen acquisition. Thus, AR owners were forced to search for magazines made prior to 1994, which in practical terms meant finding surplus military magazines. Sadly, some of these military magazines didn't work very well at all.

Fortunately, in September 2004 the Crime Bill's "Assault Weapon" ban expired, including the ban on the manufacture of standard capacity magazines for citizen purchase. Consequently, we are awash in quality magazines, both metal and plastic. The highest quality polymer magazines are more durable, e.g., harder to crush and less affected by the environment. That is, they won't rust or otherwise corrode, and when made of proper polymers, retain their strength and robustness in both arctic cold and desert heat.

The standard capacity magazine for the 5.56-MM AR platform now holds thirty rounds. Twenty round magazines are still offered; for certain purposes, e.g., Service Rifle match competition, the shorter mags are either preferable or mandated. We have also seen the development and offering of magazines of up to 100 round capacity. These large capacities

THE *NEW* AR-15 COMPLETE OWNER'S GUIDE

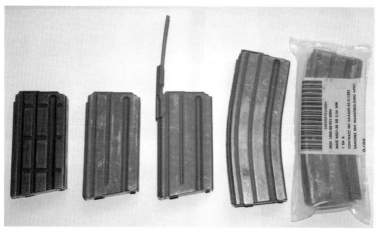

Left to Right: Armalite (Colt) Waffle .223, Colt 5.56, Adventure Line with stripper clip and guide, Kay, and Sanchez. Walt Kuleck Collection.

L to R: Radway Green (UK), Imperial Defense Services (UK), Heckler & Koch, FN (USA). Walt Kuleck Collection.

L to R: Beretta (IT), "8448674," DPMS, Brownells 30 rnd, Brownells 20 rnd (note the curve, these are made with "universal" 30/20 rnd tooling), AR Stoner. Walt Kuleck Collection.

ACCESSORIES and ACCOUTREMENTS

L to R: MWG Comp-Mag 10, Fulton Armory 10-rnd plastic waffle, Bushmaster 10-round "Assault Weapons Ban" mags. Walt Kuleck Collection.

L to R: Military Blank, "20-" and "10-rnd" Single-Loading "Bob-SLEDs." Walt Kuleck Collection.

L to R: Ramline Mini-14/AR Combo, Orlite, Thermold, TAPCO, Lancer L5, Troy Battlemag. Walt Kuleck Collection.

L to R: Magpul PMAGS: Gen 1, Gen 2 (Window), Gen 3, Gen 3 (Window). Walt Kuleck Collection.

THE *NEW* AR-15 COMPLETE OWNER'S GUIDE

C Products Beta C-Mag; 100 rounds. Surefire offers box mags with 60 and 100-round capacities. Heavy and somewhat cumbersome unless you have a heavy-barrel full auto.

Even accessories have accessories. Pictured here: "Green" 30-round mag followers, magazine dust covers, Mag-LuLa magazine unloader/loader, single-loading snap-in platform, MagCinch magazine coupler, and replacement springs and floor plates.
Walt Kuleck Collection.

ACCESSORIES and ACCOUTREMENTS

There is no NATO rifle!

- During the tests the US M16A1 was a control weapon.
- You can often see reference to:
  – NATO/STANAG magazine.
  – NATO/STANAG flash hider.
  – NATO/STANAG bayonet.
- There is currently no such thing!

You read it here; there is no "NATO Magazine." While a draft standard, STANAG 4179, was written for a "NATO Magazine," it was never ratified and died without adoption.

ArmaLite's Recommended Magazine Evaluation Protocol

INSPECTION:

1. Use a new magazine of known high quality as a standard to compare to used magazines.
2. Inspect the used magazine for cracks or dents, especially in the feed lips. Some dents or bends can be carefully straightened.
3. Check the spring for "dipback." Dipback is a tendency for the rounded ends of the spring to bend down instead of up as they curve between the straight side sections. Look at the spring so that a straight section on the left side of the magazine is pointed straight into your eye, and would look like a period if it didn't have a curve in the way. That curve should look level or slope slightly upward to the right. If it curves slightly downward, the spring displays dipback and may produce unreliable operation. Check all of the curves. Dipback is common, especially on early magazines, and is undesirable.
4. Check the top coil for proper position. The top coil is bent toward the inside to enter a hole in the follower. The turned-in end of the top section of coil should be level with or less than .070 below the straight section on the opposite side of the spring.
5. Green followers are preferred to black followers.

TESTING THE MAGAZINE:

Testing spring pressure. Place two cartridges in the magazine. Press the top round down about 1/8-inch. When released, the top round should return to full contact with the feed lips. If it fails this test and has a black follower, replace the follower with a green one and retest. Failure doesn't mean that the magazine won't work, but does mean that it should be tested for reliability.

Reliability test. This is the key test of the magazine. Test fire the magazine using 40 rounds in 10 cycles of 4 rounds each (this test should be conducted during normal practice so you don't waste the ammunition.):

1. Load 4 cartridges into the magazine.
2. Release the rifle's bolt carrier group so that it is in the forward, locked position. Insert the magazine into the rifle and charge the rifle by pulling the charging handle fully to the rear and releasing it.
3. Fire the four cartridges.
4. Repeat 9 more times.
5. Reject the magazine for tactical use if the rifle malfunctions in any of the 10 firing cycles. Reserve the magazine for practice until it proves reliable in actual use.

MONITORING AFTER THE TEST:

Every practice or training session is a magazine test. Use good ammunition and a rifle known to be reliable, and always mark the magazines on the bottom each time the rifle fails to feed. If only one or two magazines show marks, the magazines are probably the problem. If all of the magazines accumulate marks at about the same rate, the rifle is probably unreliable. Magazines that accumulate marks that can't be blamed on the rifle cannot be depended on in an emergency.

© 2003 ArmaLite, Inc. All rights reserved.

ACCESSORIES and ACCOUTREMENTS

may be for most beyond the point of diminishing returns. Thirty or seventy rounds more than the standard capacity add weight and bulk, and are of most value when used with a squad automatic-oriented AR such as the USMC M27 Infantry Automatic Rifle (IAR).

So, you've made your choice and purchased some magazines. It would be prudent to determine if any are less than reliable. The magazine, after all, is a sophisticated and somewhat complex mechanism upon which the entire operation of the rifle depends. If the magazine does not function flawlessly, neither will the rifle. Without a magazine, even the finest AR becomes a rather cumbersome single-shot straight-pull rifle. To help guide your evaluation of your magazines, ArmaLite has published a magazine test protocol reproduced here. It would be a good idea to put your magazines to the test before betting your life on them.

Slings

AR-type rifles can be equipped with all manner of slings and carry straps. The author has ARs with Andy Langlois' (Andy's Leather) Ching and Rhodesian sings, great choices for hunting. The classic military M1907 sling, in either leather or modern Biothane, can be used not just by Service Rifle match shooters, but by any classically-trained rifleman/woman who knows how to "sling-up" for position-shooting stability. Strangely, these long-established highly useful choices are overlooked by today's shooters in favor of modern "tactical" slings. These modern slings come in three flavors: one point, two point and three point. Three point tactical slings have pretty much faded from the scene due to their complexity of installation and use, leaving two- and single-point slings.

> **TIP:**
> If your rifle is intended primarily for "home defense," you may wish to consider whether or not you really want to sling it. It's all too easy to get yourself all tangled up in the wee hours of the morning when you're not firing on all eight cylinders. Even if you get the strap on your body right-side-up, you still risk snagging on lamps, doorknobs, flower pots, all the trappings found in your house.

> **POINT of CLARIFICATION:**
> To the classically trained rifleman/riflewoman, the use of the term "sling" is potentially misleading. When we think "sling," we think of the M1907 military sling, which is very effective for steadying the rifle when sitting, kneeling or prone. Modern tactical "slings" are more accurately carrying straps, adjustable to position the rifle conveniently for presentation, or alternatively to allow the rifle to get out of the way when transitioning to a sidearm, for example.

American practice historically has been for slings to be mounted on the bottom of the stock front and rear. This approach doesn't work well for AR-type rifles with their prominent pistol grip and protruding box magazine. These protrusions dig into the back if the rifle is slung over the shoulder. The solution is to mount the sling swivels on the side of the rifle. Not only does the AR now lie flat across the back, if the shooter releases the rifle from firing position it no longer flips upside down.

A further refinement to the AR sling has been the advent of Quick Detach (QD) sling swivels. A cottage industry for designing and manufacturing QD sling swivel sockets, from

THE *NEW* AR-15 COMPLETE OWNER'S GUIDE

Single point sling clipped to a receiver back plate adaptor. Walt Kuleck Collection.

Two point sling. Note inset with QD sling swivel socket bolted to side rail. Walt Kuleck Collection.

ACCESSORIES and ACCOUTREMENTS

those that bolt to Rails to those that "plug into" Magpul butt stocks has emerged. Whatever form they take, QD swivels are a modern convenience that's worthy of consideration.

Single point slings are usually mounted to the rear of the lower receiver in some fashion. Illustrated is a single point sling with an HK-style snap hook connector and matching accessory back plate with loop. A single point sling such as this with an elastic "bungee" section can provide isometric resistance to presentation, providing at least the impression of enhanced stability.

PITFALL:
The major drawback to single point slings, and for some, a disqualifying characteristic, is that when you release the rifle the muzzle points downward—toward the shooter's lower leg, ankle or foot. Not safe, thus not a good idea.

CLICHE CLARIFICATION:
Modern usage of "to shoot oneself in the foot" is to indicate a foolish error. However, the phrase dates back to the trenches of WWI, where war-weary soldiers were tempted to self-inflict a minor wound so as to be allowed to leave the front lines. Shooting oneself in the foot became a cliche based on this sad reality.

CLICHE CORRECTION:
The more appropriate cliche would refer to quick-draw competitors of yore who discharged their Peacemakers before clearing the holster, perforating their sit-upons. That's why quick draw petered out with steel-lined holsters and wax bullets. But, we digress.

Two point slings are generally affixed to the side of the handguard and the side of the butt stock near the butt plate. The better two point slings have a quick adjustment capability, such as the Vickers Combat Applications Sling preferred by many in the special operations community, and the author. The Vickers sling has a clever quick adjustment for length that adds neither complexity nor bulk. You'll see the Vickers sling on many of the author's rifles illustrated in this book.

Lights and Lasers

Another class of popular enhancements for the AR platform is illumination: white light "flashlights" and laser designators. The latter are usually called laser "sights." These illuminators can be integrated into various components of the rifle, e.g., handguards or hand grips, or "scabbed on" with clamps.

Flashlights have become more and more powerful over the years. Where once 60 lumen lights were considered bright, now we see 600, 700, even 800+ lumen lights. With the development of LED emitters, battery life has been dramatically increased even with the spectacularly increased light output.

PITFALL:
Where weaponlights are concerned, it may be a case of bigger not necessarily being better. Outdoors, the brighter may be the better. Indoors, however, the proximity of light-colored surfaces, i.e., walls, may mean that when you switch on your 800

*Rail Light Mount from Magpul.
Walt Kuleck Collection.*

Front Handgrip Light Mount with Surefire flashlight. Surefire and others offer integrated grip/light/laser systems. Walt Kuleck Collection.

ACCESSORIES and ACCOUTREMENTS

Streamlight light/laser combination with rail mount. Walt Kuleck Collection.

Surefire integrated handguard/weaponlight, updated with LED lamp head; Note the tape switch. Clamped to the barrel is a laser. Walt Kuleck Collection.

THE *NEW* AR-15 COMPLETE OWNER'S GUIDE

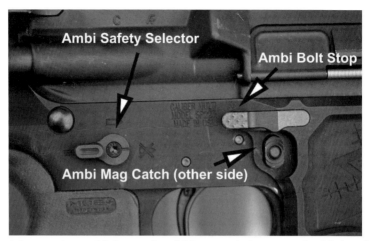

Seekins Precision receiver with integral ambidextrous bolt stop and added ambi safety selector and magazine catch. Walt Kuleck Collection.

Extended charging handle latch, used to allow charging even with a large scope sight eyepiece "in the way." Walt Kuleck Collection.

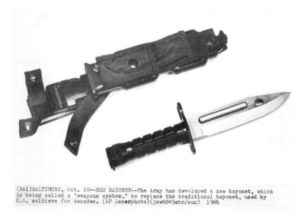

The bane of hoplophobes: M9 Bayonet.

ACCESSORIES and ACCOUTREMENTS

lumen light in your home, you, the "operator," are as instantly blinded as your interloper.

TIP:
Try your weaponlight setup in your house before making a final configuration decision for your home defense rifle/Carbine. Avoid unpleasant surprises.

TIP:
"Integrated" illuminators typically have controls and control paradigms oriented towards use by a weapon operator. Adapting an everyday carry flashlight to your weapon may be enticing, but its controls may be awkward when the light is on the weapon.

TIP:
Whatever the arrangement you choose, make certain you practice with your illumination equipment until its operation is second nature. The last thing you want to say to an intruder is, "Excuse me for a moment while I get this light on to blind you."

PITFALL:
Illumination equipment requires batteries. Batteries wear out. Most illuminators use CR123-size cells that are not generally found at Lowes or Walmart. Stock up and be ready to change them frequently. Your author buys them by the dozen, and is always surprised when a light goes dim; it seems so soon!

Other Neat Stuff

There is so much you adapt to your AR-type rifle that its impossible to even scratch the surface. From front to back, there are muzzle devices, front sights, handguards and handguard float tubes, the aforementioned lights and lasers, rails, sling mounts, bipods, hand stops, front hand grips, front hand grips with integral bipod, add-on magwells, ambidextrous controls, enlarged trigger guards, lower receiver rear plates with various sorts of sling attachments, butt stocks—and a plethora of accessories for butt stocks!

But, keep in mind...that bottle opener and chain saw. Who can live without them?

The penultimate accessory (next to the chain saw)? 37mm flare launcher. Greg King Collection.

THE *NEW* AR-15 COMPLETE OWNER'S GUIDE

Rifle Parts and...

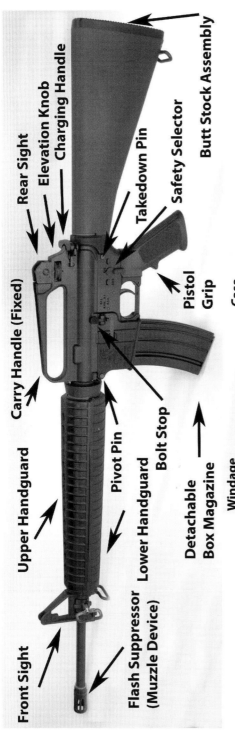

Where They Are

CHAPTER 8

OPERATING

Principles of Operation

The AR-15 is a gas operated, air cooled, semiautomatic box-magazine-fed centerfire rifle. With the bolt forward, the cycle of operation begins by inserting a loaded magazine into the magazine well. The charging handle is then drawn fully back, pulling the bolt carrier and bolt with it. As the carrier moves rearward, it pops open the ejection port cover, if the cover was closed. When the charging handle is fully back, abruptly release the handle. Do not "ride" the handle forward; release it decisively.

When the charging handle is released, the bolt carrier carries the bolt forward, stripping the top round from the magazine. As the bolt carrier continues forward, the bolt face pushes the cartridge forward into the chamber. When the cartridge case "bottoms out" in the barrel's chamber, the bolt stops but the bolt carrier continues forward for about a further 1/2 inch. During this movement the cam pin, which connects the bolt with the bolt carrier, rotates the bolt into locking position, where the locking lugs in the bolt enter their corresponding recesses in the barrel extension. As the bolt carrier reaches the end of its travel, it forces the bolt forward such that the extractor hook in the bolt face pops over the cartridge base and engages the cartridge case's extractor groove.

When the charging handle is pulled rearward, it also causes the bolt carrier to cam the hammer back into the cocked position, where it is engaged by the trigger. The selector can now be placed in the "SAFE" position. The selector cannot be turned to "SAFE" unless the hammer is cocked.

At this point the rifle is ready to fire. If you do not wish to fire the rifle immediately, the selector should be placed on "SAFE." When the selector is on "SAFE," its shaft is intended to block the trigger from movement. When you are ready to fire the rifle, be certain it is pointed in the direction in which you want to shoot. If the selector is turned to "SAFE," turn it to "FIRE." Then you may aim and squeeze the trigger.

When the trigger is squeezed, it releases the hammer, which is rotated forward sharply under the influence of the hammer spring. The hammer strikes the rear of the firing pin, which is freely floating. The firing pin flies forward and detonates the primer. When the cartridge discharges, the bullet is propelled down the barrel under the influence of the rapidly expanding hot gas produced by the burning propellent.

As the bullet passes by the gas port in the top of the barrel (covered by the front sight base or the gas block), hot gas is allowed to pass through the port, into the front sight post or gas block, and thence into the gas tube. The gas flows down the gas tube towards the upper receiver, where it flows into the carrier key on the top of the bolt carrier. The carrier key's inside diameter is slightly larger than the gas tube's outside

Quiz: How many different ARs are shown in this chapter? Can you identify them? Answers at the end of the chapter.

THE *NEW* AR-15 COMPLETE OWNER'S GUIDE

Warning!
Beware of Dangerous Procedures!

Before storing, disassembling, cleaning or handling your AR, **be certain that the magazine is removed and the chamber is empty!** In that order! Use both a visual and a tactile inspection (poke a finger into the chamber as well as peering into it).

Your AR-15 may discharge negligently if it is dropped muzzle down with a loaded chamber. This is true regardless of the position of the hammer or safety.

Never cock your AR without setting the selector lever to "SAFE" until the moment you are about to shoot.

When the bolt carrier is latched open and a loaded magazine is installed, **the rifle is in an unsafe condition.** Jarring it may cause the bolt carrier to close and load the chamber.

Be certain that the cam pin is installed in the bolt group upon reassembly; if it is not, the rifle will fire and **will explode**!

Do not exchange or switch bolt assemblies from one AR-15 to another without checking for proper headspace. **Failure to do so may result in injury or death.**

If your rifle stops firing with a live round in the chamber of a hot barrel (misfire), **remove the round fast.** However, if you cannot remove it within ten seconds, remove the magazine and wait fifteen minutes with the rifle pointed in a safe direction (downrange). If the round "cooks off" you can avoid injury. However, **keep your face away from the ejection port** when clearing a hot chamber.

Use only ammunition that is manufactured to US or NATO specifications.

If your bolt fails to unlock and you try to free it by banging the butt stock on the ground, **keep yourself clear of the muzzle.**

If there is water in the barrel, do not fire the rifle. **It could explode.**

If a noticeable difference in sound or recoil is experienced, stop firing! Either can be an indication of an incomplete powder burn and/or a bullet stuck in the bore.

OPERATING

diameter; thus the key envelopes the gas tube and overlaps it by about 1/2". The gas flows down the key into the carrier, which is forced rearward (while the bolt is pressed forward against the cartridge case head) by the pressure of the gas within. As the carrier moves rearward the cam pin rotates the bolt, unlocking it from the recesses of the barrel extension. The now-cooling gas is vented primarily out the holes in the carrier provided for the gas' exhaust.

The carrier continues to move rearward, bringing the now-unlocked bolt with it, and drawing the empty cartridge case with the bolt. As the case leaves the chamber, the case is rotated out the ejection port by the plunger ejector located in the bolt face. The rearward movement of the carrier also rotates the hammer rearward, which is caught by the disconnector hook. Releasing the trigger at this point transfers the hammer from the disconnector to the trigger. The hammer is now cocked.

The rearward motion of the bolt carrier assembly is retarded by the buffer spring. The buffer cushions the final travel of the bolt carrier assembly. The buffer spring then begins to return the carrier assembly to battery. If there is a cartridge in the box magazine, the bolt will strip it and chamber it. The rifle is now ready to fire. If you do not immediately intend to fire that round, move the selector from "FIRE" to "SAFE."

If the box magazine is empty, the magazine's follower will trip the bolt catch, which will capture the bolt carrier assembly, holding the latter back and open. When the empty magazine is replaced by one containing cartridges, pressing the bolt catch will allow the bolt carrier assembly to complete its forward travel, chambering the topmost cartridge. This may be done with the selector turned to either "SAFE" or "FIRE." If the selector is set to FIRE and you do not intend to immediately fire a round, set the selector to "SAFE."

DANGER!
If you drop the rifle muzzle down with a chambered cartridge, the inertia of the floating firing pin may negligently discharge the chambered cartridge, regardless of the position of the selector. Be aware!

When you have finished shooting, remove the magazine, lock the bolt carrier back with the bolt catch, clear the chamber both visually and tactilely and set the selector lever to "SAFE." Push the charging handle forward until it locks.

Normal Operation

The accompanying diagrams show the steps to be followed during normal operation, beginning with the "Preventive Maintenance and Checks" or "Preflight." Note that the selector may be turned to "safe" only when the hammer is cocked. The diagrams on show alternate chambering procedures, depending on whether the bolt is locked open or is closed when the magazine is seated.

If Your Rifle Stops Firing

A failure to fire has two main causes; first, the rifle has failed to feed a cartridge into the chamber. Second, there is a cartridge in the chamber but it fails to discharge. The rifle will fail to feed if the bolt does not pick up the top round in the magazine, or

THE *NEW* AR-15 COMPLETE OWNER'S GUIDE

Preventive Maintenance Checks and Services

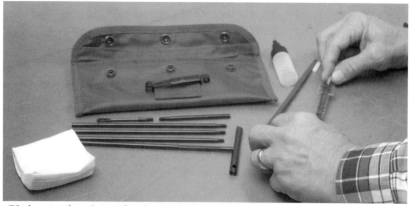

The GI cleaning kit. Jointed rods aren't the best, so pull it, don't push it when you use it..

2. Remove the magazine, cycle the bolt several times, check that the chamber is clear.

1. Run a patch through the barrel to remove excessive oil. Drop the rod into the breech, then pull the patch through from the muzzle.

3. Point the muzzle in a safe direction, move the selector to "safe," pull the trigger. The hammer should not fall.

4. Point the muzzle in a safe direction, move the selector to "fire," pull the trigger. The hammer should fall.

OPERATING

Operation: Loading and Chambering a Round

5. Point the muzzle in a safe direction. Push the magazine upwards until the magazine catch engages and holds the magazine.

6. Tap upward to make sure the magazine is seated tightly.

7. Pull down on the magazine to ensure that the magazine is firmly latched.

THE *NEW* AR-15 COMPLETE OWNER'S GUIDE

Operation: Loading and Chambering a Round (continued)

Note: Magazines may be inserted with bolt open or closed.

Chambering with Bolt Assembly Open:

8a. Depress bolt catch.

8b. Tap forward assist to ensure bolt is fully forward and closed.

Chambering with Bolt Assembly Closed:

9a. Pull charging handle fully rearward.

9b. Release the charging handle.

9c. Then, tap forward assist to ensure bolt is fully forward and closed.

Never "ride" the charging handle. Let it go forward on its own.

NOTE: If you are not firing the rifle immediately, set the selector to "safe" and close the ejection port cover.

OPERATING

the bolt may have failed to extract the previously fired cartridge case and now cannot chamber the next round. In either case, the challenge is to quickly clear the rifle so a live round can be chambered.

If there is a cartridge in the chamber that has not discharged, the cause may be a faulty cartridge or fault in the hammer or firing pin of the rifle. If the cartridge is faulty, the immediate action should be to replace the cartridge with another, which will hopefully fire. If it does not, then you should cease fire, clear the rifle and examine it carefully to find the fault.

If your rifle fails to fire when the trigger is pulled, the diagrams describe the actions you should take to get your rifle quickly back into action. These actions are SOP (Standard Operating Procedures) for Marine Corps shooters. Some authorities recommend alternate procedures.

For example, rather than "Slapping" the magazine base to see if the magazine is fully seated, "Pull" on the magazine to see if it is fully latched. If it is not, it will begin to come out of the magazine well. If it does, push it firmly upward until you feel it latch. Pull again to make sure it is indeed latched. If the magazine comes free again, the magazine catch may be worn, broken or out of adjustment. Cease firing and clear the rifle. Ensure that the catch rather than the individual magazine is at fault by trying several unloaded magazines in the rifle. If the magazine is not at fault, inspect the magazine latch and correct the problem.

When checking the chamber for the presence of a cartridge, be careful not to put your face in line with the ejection port. You may get hot brass in the face, or worse if the chambered round decides to "cook off" at the critical moment. Whenever you are releasing the charging handle to chamber a round, you should <u>decisively release</u> it, allowing the buffer spring and buffer to drive the bolt carrier and bolt forward. As the charging handle works only to pull the bolt carrier assembly rearward and cannot push it forward, any hesitance in releasing the charging handle from its full-rearward postion will only retard the carrier assembly's forward motion. You want the full force of the carrier assembly driven by the buffer spring working for you to strip the top cartridge from the magazine and fully chamber it.

The forward assist and its use has been a source of controversy from the earliest days of the M16, and carries over to the AR-15. Right up to the 1990's Colt was supplying AR-15 rifles without the forward assist. Gene Stoner resisted the idea of the forward assist, believing that allowing troops a means to force a cartridge into the chamber would lead to troops doing just that, possibly creating a depot-level jam. The Army was adamant, and a forward assist became standard with the M16A1. The Air Force remained opposed to it while the Marine Corps was indifferent.

The forward assist works on a ratchet principle. A toothed hook at the end of the forward assist mechanism engages serrations on the bolt carrier. This hook is hinged so that it will push the carrier, but not pull it. So despite the short stroke of the forward assist assembly, repeated actuations can move the bolt carrier practically through its full

Immediate Action

If your rifle stops firing, perform the following immediate actions:

1. SLAP *upward to make certain the magazine is properly seated.*

2. PULL *charging handle rearward all the way back.* OBSERVE *ejection of case or cartridge.* CHECK *chamber for obstruction.*
WARNING: Do not load with a hot chamber!

3. *If cartridge or case is ejected,* RELEASE *charging handle to feed a new round. Don't ride the charging handle forward.*

4. TAP *forward assist.*

5. *Now,* FIRE. *If the rifle won't fire, look for trouble and apply remedial action (next page).*

OPERATING

Remedial Action
WARNING:

If your rifle stops firing with a live round in the chamber of a hot barrel, remove the round FAST. However, if you cannot remove it within ten seconds, remove the magazine and WAIT fifteen minutes with the rifle pointed in a safe direction. This way you won't get hurt by a round possibly "cooking off." Regardless, keep your face away from the ejection port while clearing a hot chamber!

If your rifle fails to fire after performing steps 1 through 5, check again for a jammed cartridge case.

If a case is in the chamber, tap it out with the cleaning rod.

Bullet Stuck in Bore
WARNING:

If an audible "POP" *or reduced* RECOIL *is experienced during firing, immediately* CEASE FIRE! *Then, (1) remove the magazine, (2) lock the bolt to the rear, (3) place the selector on the* "SAFE" *position and (4) visually inspect and/or insert a cleaning rod into the bore to ensure that there is not a bullet stuck in the bore.*

THE *NEW* AR-15 COMPLETE OWNER'S GUIDE

Troubleshooting

Problem	Check For	What to Do
Won't Fire	Selector on SAFE.	Put Selector on FIRE.
	Improper assembly of firing pin.	Assemble Correctly: *Retaining pin goes in back of large shoulder of firing pin.*
	Too much oil in firing pin recess	Wipe out with pipe cleaner.
	Defective Ammo.	Remove and discard.
	Too much carbon on firing pin or in firing pin recess.	Clean.
Bolt Won't Unlock	Dirty or burred bolt.	Clean or replace.
Won't Extract	Broken extractor spring.	Replace.
	Dirty or corroded ammo.	Remove. Push out stuck case with cleaning rod.
	Carbon in chamber.	Clean chamber.
	Fouling or carbon in extractor recess or lip.	Clean.

OPERATING

stroke. The proper use of the forward assist would seem to be as depicted in picture 8b on page 212: tapping it to ensure that the bolt is fully forward. Using it to force a reluctant cartridge into the chamber is best left to the battlefield, where the soldier has nothing to lose and everything to gain by getting that round loaded.

If All Else Fails...

If you have a spent cartridge case in the chamber that just won't come out by cycling the bolt, allow the rifle to cool. Sometimes the contraction of the brass case after cooling will be enough to allow it to come free, sometimes even of its own weight. If the rifle is cooled down and the case still refuses to come out, then the judicious use of a cleaning rod may be necessary. Caution! If there is a live round rather than a spent case in the chamber, you have a situation fraught with peril. Take the rifle to a gunsmith who specializes in AR-15s and see what he can do with it. Don't attempt to tap a live round out from the muzzle with a cleaning rod!

As you are firing your AR-15, if you hear a different sound or feel reduced recoil, cease fire! You may have had a "squib" cartridge that has left a bullet in the bore. Clear the rifle and confirm with a cleaning rod that the barrel is clear. If there is a bullet stuck in the bore, once again you should take the rifle to a gunsmith and have him remove the bullet. It is all too easy to attempt to pound the bullet out with the cleaning rod, have the cleaning rod slip to one side of the bullet tip, and end up with both a bullet and a cleaning rod stuck in the bore!

Troubleshooting

Don't you love that word in the firearms context? As a rule, troubleshooting should never be necessary in a cleaned, lubricated and properly maintained rifle. The AR-15 in particular has been developed into a robust system that requires little "fiddling" or "adjusting" to operate properly for extended periods. There are few components that fail with any frequency. The extractor and gas rings are the only two that come to mind. Of course, anything can and will fail.

The first steps in troubleshooting are also the first steps you should use to evaluate an AR-15 or to preflight it prior to shooting. Once you are satisfied that these basic checks have been passed, you may proceed to troubleshoot your rifle.

Performing the troubleshooting procedures shown assume that you have mastered the basic disassembly procedures shown. If you have not, we would suggest that you turn to those illlustrations before beginning troubleshooting.

The gas rings function much like the piston rings in an automobile engine. Like piston rings, they must be staggered to minimize blowby. They also must be "broken in" just like the rings in your car. And finally, they do wear out. The gas rings are one of the primary causes of "short stroking," particularly when they are new and not yet broken in. Several Service armorers suggest putting a drop of oil in each carrier exhaust hole after installing new gas rings, to help them seat properly. Can't hurt!

Troubleshooting

Problem	Check For	What to Do
Won't feed	Dirty or corroded ammo.	Clean or discard safely.
	Dirty magazine.	Clean.
	Defective magazine.	Replace.
	Too many rounds in magazine.	Take out excess.
	Action of buffer assembly is restricted.	Take out buffer and spring and clean.
	Magazine not fully seated.	Adjust magazine catch. PRESS BUTTON on RIGHT SIDE TURN CATCH on LEFT SIDE Turn catch clockwise to tighten and counterclockwise to loosen.
Double feed	Defective magazine.	Replace.

OPERATING

Troubleshooting

Problem	Check For	What to Do
Won't chamber	Dirty or corroded ammo Damaged ammo. Carbon in chamber or on gas tube.	Clean or discard safely. Replace. Clean.
Won't lock	Dirt, corrosion or carbon buildup in barrel locking lugs.	Clean lugs.
Won't extract	Frozen extractor. Restricted buffer assembly. Restricted movement of bolt carrier group.	Remove and clean. Remove and clean. Remove, clean and lube. Before putting bolt back in, make sure that the gas tube fits into carrier key and that the carrier moves freely.

Troubleshooting

Problem	Check For	What to Do
Short recoil	Gaps in bolt gas rings not staggered.	Stagger ring gaps 120 degrees apart.
	Carbon in chamber or on gas tube.	Clean.
	Q-tip or pipe cleaner stuck inside carrier key.	Remove foreign material. Will probably require removing carrier key, removing the stuck material, reinstalling and restaking the carrier key.
Bolt fails to lock after last round	Dirty or corroded bolt latch.	Clean.
Selector lever binds	Faulty magazine.	Clean.
	Needs oil.	Lubricate.
	Dirt or sand under trigger.	Clean.

OPERATING

Troubleshooting

Problem	Check For	What to Do
Bolt Carrier "hung up"	Round jammed between bolt and charging handle and/or double feed.	1. Remove magazine. 2. Push in on the bottom of the bolt latch. 3. Bang rifle butt on the ground. Bolt should lock to rear. 3. While bolt is held to the rear, the round should fall out through the magazine well.

THE *NEW* AR-15 COMPLETE OWNER'S GUIDE

Clear Your Rifle

Point rifle in a SAFE DIRECTION. *Place selector on* SAFE. *If weapon is not cocked, lever cannot be turned to* SAFE.

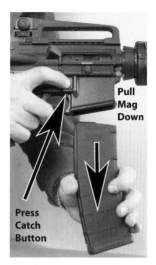

Remove magazine

To lock bolt open, pull charging handle rearward. Press bottom of bolt catch and allow bolt to move forward until it engages bolt catch. Return charging handle to forward. If you haven't already, place selector lever on SAFE.

Check receiver and chamber to ensure these areas contain no ammo.

With selector lever pointing to SAFE, *allow bolt to go forward by pressing upper portion of bolt catch.*

OPERATING

Another supposed source of low gas system power, exhibited in "short stroking," is a clogged gas tube. Let's set that straight right now: gas tubes don't clog. They don't. Unless, of course, you try to clean them with a pipe cleaner, in which case the pipe cleaner invariably gets stuck in the gas tube. Then you have to replace the gas tube anyway. Why not eliminate the middleman and just put in a new gas tube if you think it's clogged? It won't be, but if you feel better, so be it!

The carrier key, though, is a component that can have carbon buildup. Again, this is probably not as common as some think; but if it makes your feel better, go ahead and clean it. If you get your "worn bore brush" stuck in the carrier key, however, you'll likely be replacing the key. Note that the carrier key screws must be staked after tightening.

Disassembly

The focus of this book is on the new AR-15 shooter, or one who wants a single source for all the fundamentals. Therefore, we'll limit disassembly to the level to which most users should limit themselves. If you wish to take your AR down to the last pin and spring, **The AR-15 Complete Assembly Guide** will have the information you need.

Disassembly begins with properly clearing your rifle. We cannot emphasize this too much, nor repeat it too often. As with any autoloading firearm, the clearing sequence begins with removing the magazine before cycling the bolt. Once you have removed the magazine, you then open and lock back the bolt. With the bolt locked back, you must perform a visual and tactile examination of the chamber and lower receiver, including the magazine well, to ensure that no ammunition is present. The only thing possibly worse than a negligent discharge is an out-of-battery negligent discharge. With the former, you *might* hurt someone else; with the latter, you *will* hurt yourself! When you have assured yourself that the rifle is clear, allow the bolt carrier assembly to go fully home. If it's not fully forward, you will not be able to break the rifle open.

The military manuals suggest that at this point you should remove the handguards. For routine (vs. thorough) maintenance, this step is not strictly necessary. You should remove the handguards when you feel the need to clean and oil the barrel under the handguards, perhaps after exposure to rain or other environmental contaminants. The "buddy system" shown is convenient, but it is possible to remove the handguards single-handedly. The secret is to use both hands to pull down the delta ring (A2) or slip ring (A1), then pop one or the other handguard out at its rear using whatever digits you can free for the task. It's even possible to remove one hand from the ring to pop out the handguard once the ring is pushed down; it's a bit easier to keep it down against its spring than it is to push it down initially. However, the handguard tool shown makes an otherwise onerous task a piece of cake!

Whether or not you choose to remove the handguards at this stage, your next step is to break the rifle open and separate the upper and lower receiver assemblies. Regardless of the type or manufacturer of your AR, the takedown pin at the rear of the receivers will be of the captive push type. Pushing it from left to right (from the shooter's perspective) will disengage the takedown pin from the left side of the lower and from the upper. The

THE *NEW* AR-15 COMPLETE OWNER'S GUIDE

Disassembly
The "Buddy System"

Place the rifle on the butt stock and press down on the delta ring (slip ring) with both hands.

Have your buddy pull the handguards free.

NOTE: The new (A2) handguards are identical and can be interchanged top or bottom.

Install the handguards using the same system.

Who are we kidding? This is what it really looks like!

Get one of these handguard tools; they make it easy.

1. Push takedown pin as far as it will go. Pivot upper receiver from lower receiver.

2. Push receiver pivot pin.

3. Separate upper and lower receivers.

4. Pull back charging handle and bolt carrier.

OPERATING

pin will be held captive by the right side of the lower. Don't try to remove it further. At this point you can swing the receivers apart on the front, pivot pin. Note that if the bolt carrier assembly is not fully forward, the receivers will not open.

M16s and all clone AR-15s use a second captive push pin, much like the takedown pin, for the front, pivot pin. Its operation is identical to that of the takedown pin. Push the pin through from left to right as far as it will go, but don't try to remove it all the way.

Colt, in its infinite wisdom, in the early days of the AR-15 chose to use a screw arrangement rather than a captive push pin for its receiver pivot pin. You can readily identify this pin because it has a straight-slot screw head on each end. This type of pin is removed by using two screwdrivers, one to hold and one to screw. Make very certain that you use a perfectly-fitting screwdriver in each slot. The screw heads are not particularly hard, so it's easy to damage the screw slots.

Once you have your Colt factory takedown pin out, you may wish to replace it with an aftermarket push pin. The aftermarket pins have a spring-loaded ball detent that allows them to function nearly identically to the military-type captive pin, though it will not be captive. Note that Colt has used two diameters of "screw pin"; most early rifles have an oversize pin. Late production "post-ban" guns have a "screw pin" the same diameter as the military-type pin, so get the proper size push pin.

WISE PRECAUTION:
> When the receivers are separated, push the pivot and takedown pins back into place flush with the lower receiver. This way you don't risk dropping the receiver on a pin and breaking the pin out of the receiver wall. Doing so would junk the receiver.

The next step in disassembly is the removal of the bolt carrier assembly and the charging handle. The military manual instructs you to remove the bolt carrier assembly and charging handle once the receivers are separated. Of course, when the rifle is "broken open," you can remove the bolt carrier assembly and charging handle then; your choice. Once the bolt carrier assembly is out of the rifle, the charging handle can be removed. The charging handle has flanges on each side of its shaft. These flanges engage slots in the upper receiver. Once you remove and replace the charging handle a few times you'll instinctively "feel" where the interruptions are in the slots; these gaps permit you to raise the charging handle up, back and out of the receiver ("up" when the upper receiver is inverted, "down" when the upper receiver is right-side-up).

During the next step, removal of the firing pin, it's important to reemphasize that one should not spread or squeeze the legs of the firing pin split-pin-retainer. It looks like a Cotter pin so the temptation is to mess about with it. Anyone who's used a Cotter pin will reflexively want to bend the firing pin retainer. The firing pin retainer is not a Cotter pin. The tension that the retainer's split legs put on the sides of the bolt carrier hole into which it's s inserted is crucial to keeping the pin in place. The retainer made of steel, so if it works its way out to the left because its tension has been reduced it's very likely to scar the inside of the aluminum upper receiver. It might even contribute to a jam.

Disassembly

Remove bolt carrier and bolt.

PULL BACK AND UP

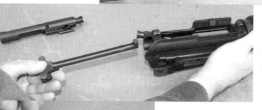

Remove charging handle.

Remove firing pin retaining pin.

DO NOT OPEN OR CLOSE SPLIT END OF PIN

PUSH IN *to put bolt assembly in locked position.*

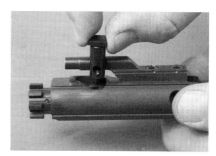

Drop the firing pin out of the rear of the bolt carrier.

GIVE CAM PIN a 1/4 TURN AND LIFT OUT.
Remove cam pin.

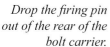

Remove bolt assembly from bolt carrier.

OPERATING

Once the firing pin is dropped out the rear of the bolt carrier, the cam pin is removed to free the bolt. Note that the bolt must be in the rearward, locked position with respect to the bolt carrier for the key to be removed. You will quickly see that the cam pin has to be in the rear of its track for it to clear the carrier key.

The cam pin can be a bit of a challenge to remove. For one thing, the cam pin is nestled tightly below the carrier key, so you don't have any clearance to spare as you pull the cam pin up and out. Further, the cam pin can be very difficult to turn and then to pull out if it's been a while since the bolt carrier assembly has been thoroughly cleaned. You may find it necessary to use a tool to grasp and turn the cam key the 1/4 turn required to remove it. If you do, make certain that you use nothing that will mar the cam pin, the carrier, or the carrier key. Pad the jaws of the pliers or whatever tool you use.

Once the cam pin is out, the bolt will come out the front of the bolt carrier, and routine disassembly of the bolt carrier group is complete. The first time you do this, you might want to closely examine the bolt carrier group's ingenious design. The cam track in the bolt carrier rotates the bolt to lock and unlock as the bolt carrier reciprocates during firing. The cam pin retains the bolt while the firing pin retains the cam pin. The firing pin retainer is the key to the puzzle.

The bolt need not be routinely disassembled unless a thorough cleaning or parts replacement is required. Both the ejector plunger and the extractor are retained with spring pins. The military manual addresses the removal of only the extractor. The extractor is an Achilles heel of the AR, and one should be familiar with its removal and replacement. The ejector plunger rarely goes bad; however, its removal is similar in principle to that of the extractor. The ejector's retaining pin is notably smaller, though.

Military manuals suggest the use of the firing pin to remove the extractor pin. While this works fine, there is the chance that you will damage the tip of the firing pin. If you do deform the firing pin tip, it is much more likely to pierce a primer and cause gas leakage. For that reason, we recommend that you acquire the proper size pin punch to use for ejector pin removal. Save the firing pin technique for an exigent field expediency situation. If your rifle is equipped with a titanium firing pin, don't use it as a tool under any circumstances. Titanium pins are more readily damaged than the standard steel pins.

The final step in disassembly is to remove the buffer and spring. The buffer retainer is a collared plunger that sticks up just far enough to keep the buffer from exiting the receiver extension under the tension of the buffer spring. Depressing the buffer retainer will allow the buffer and spring to come out.

Reassembly

"Reverse to reassemble." Bet you've heard these words before. In the case of the AR-15, though, there is a great deal of truth to them. As you proceed, keep in mind the following tips and tricks.

The extractor of the AR is a critical part and one worth some extra diligence. Before replacing it, be certain that both it and the bolt recess into which it fits are perfectly

Disassembly
THESE STEPS TO BE TAKEN ONLY WHEN DIRTY OR DAMAGED

NOTE:
Press rear of extractor to check spring tension.

Remove extractor and spring assembly.

Check spring, update/upgrade if needed or desired.

Remove extractor pin. Use firing pin if punch unavailable.
DO NOT DAMAGE TIP OF FIRING PIN

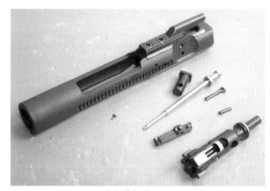

Disassembled bolt components.

Depress buffer retainer pin.   *Ease buffer and spring past pin.*

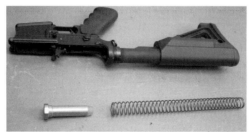

Lower receiver assembly field stripped.

OPERATING

clean. Examine the extractor itself to ensure that it's not cracked or chipped. You might want to use a magnifier to do this. You might also wish to supplement the spring and rubber insert with the "D-Fender" or the "Crane O-Ring." These small polymer inserts increase the extractor force several-fold and could prevent an untimely jam.

Before you insert the bolt into the bolt carrier, "stagger" the gas ring gaps so that they do not line up. They should be offset 120^0 from each other around the bolt. With the bolt installed, <u>do not forget to install the cam pin</u>! The cam pin is the means by which the bolt is locked to the barrel upon firing. If the bolt isn't locked, it will allow the full force of the discharging cartridge to be unleashed upon the upper and lower receivers of the rifle, surely wrecking them. In the process you will receive serious injury.

While you must never attempt to fire an AR-15 without the bolt cam pin, you must also *never* attempt to close the bolt via the bolt carrier without the firing pin and firing pin retainer! You might be tempted to do so when, for example, checking headspace with a stripped bolt. You could very likely get an unpleasant surprise: a jammed bolt carrier. The bolt will be closed and locked, with no way to get it out. Your author is not certain why the cam pin hangs up under this circumstance, but it can and will. You have been warned. Always insert the firing pin and firing pin retainer even if you're just checking headspace.

While we're on the subject of the firing pin and firing pin retainer, be sure that the firing pin is fully forward before inserting the retainer. It's easy to insert the retainer in front of the collar on the firing pin rather than behind it as is proper. The hammer will jam under the firing pin if you attempt to fire the rifle with an misinserted retainer. To check for proper insertion, check the position of the collar; the AR-15 bolt carrier is cut away underneath to the point that the collar is visible. M16 carriers are not cut away, so you can't see the collar; however, you can in either case just tip the bolt up. If the firing pin falls out, you get to pull the retainer and put it back in—correctly, this time!

When you join the upper and lower receivers, it's best to cock the hammer and put the selector to "Safe" before closing them together. Doing so will avoid possible damage to your hammer hooks. Also, be sure that the bolt carrier is fully forward. If the rear of the bolt carrier is protruding even a little bit the receivers will not close. If the fit between the upper and lower receivers is tight, or if you have inserted the little Accu-Wedge that's so popular, you may have to rest the buttstock and pistol grip on a firm surface while pushing down on the carry handle to get the takedown pin to pop all the way in.

Magazine Disassembly and Reassembly

The following pictures illustrate the simple procedures to disassemble your magazines and put them back together. You should treat your magazines to some periodic maintenance, primarily cleaning them thoroughly and coating them inside and out with a preservative such as Tetra Oil or CLP.

Answer: Three: a Bushmaster, a Fulton Armory FAR-15 and a Ruger SR-556.

Magazine Disassembly and Assembly
GI-Pattern Magazine

Push each cartridge... ...*forward and out...* ...*until the mag is empty.*

Remove the ammo from the area.

Now that the mag is empty,

push in on the baseplate retainer. *Slide the baseplate off; control the spring.*

Carefully release the spring. *Pull the spring out of the mag body.*

OPERATING

Remove the follower.

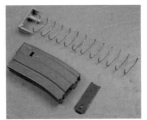
The disassembled magazine; now, reassembly.

Orient the follower as shown.

Insert the follower...

...get one side under the magazine body's tabs on that side...

...push the follower down past the tabs on the other side.

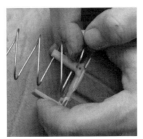
Engage the spring into the follower.

Push the follower in...

...until the spring is all the way down.

Slide the floor plate onto the body...

...until the floorplate "pops" into place.

The assembled magazine.

Magazine Disassembly and Assembly
Polymer Magazine (Magpul PMag)

The popular PMag.

Push in the locking plate tab...

...pulling the floorplate forward...

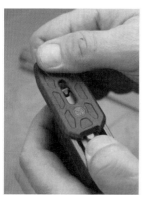

...with one thumb on the locking plate...

...to capture the spring.

Slowly let the spring out...

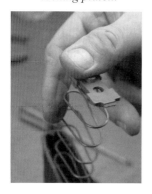

..until the tension...

...is released.

Pull the spring and follower out of the magazine body.

OPERATING

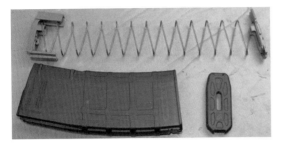

The magazine disassembled. Now, to assembly.

Engage the spring and follower.

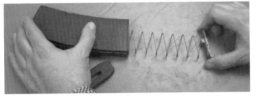

Slide the spring and follower into the mag body until....

..the locking plate enters the body.

Hold down the locking plate.

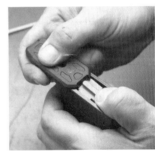

Start the floorplate...

...onto the mag body...

...until the locking tab snaps into place.

Done!

THE *NEW* AR-15 COMPLETE OWNER'S GUIDE

The solution to a clean rifle without cleaning it to death. The big rig is Hornady's Hot Tub; as this staged photo shows, it will accept a 16" upper. If you need to clean a longer upper, you can do the back half and the front half sequentially by hanging the upper at an angle. Perched on the Hot Tube is Hornady's small cleaner, perfect for bolt carrier groups and small budgets. Walt Kuleck Collection.

MAINTENANCE

CHAPTER 9

MAINTENANCE

Cool Tools

In our decades of working with and studying the AR, we've run across a number of tools that make living with ARs a lot easier and more fun. Let's explore some of the standouts.

Cleaning

Let's get something clear right from the start:

AN ENDURING TRUTH:
More rifles are worn out by cleaning than by shooting.

Every generation or so an officer or noncom from our armed forces sits down and writes in a military professional journal: "More rifles are worn out by cleaning..." Obsessive cleaning, unless done with the greatest care and the delicacy of a brain surgeon—or a High Master High Power Shooter—may well be counterproductive in the long run.

TIP:
Please do not write to the publisher if you disagree. Many shooters gain hours of zen-like contemplation, not to mention self-satisfaction and self-confidence in their equipment from OCC...Obsessive-Compulsive Cleaning. We respect dissenting opinions on the matter. But, one should keep in mind that the AR is based on a well-developed military rifle that has gained a hard-won reputation for durability. It's not a benchrest rail gun.

So...what do we really mean by, "Don't"? What we mean is, don't clean what's not dirty. What's "dirty"? "Dirty" is when foreign matter threatens the function of the rifle. For example, in the Mideast it would be prudent to brush and flush the sand out of the guts as often as is practical in a given tactical situation.

Nonetheless, there is something in an AR that gets about as dirty as dirty can be, particularly an internal piston rifle: the bolt carrier group. When you shoot the AR, there's a lot of carbon buildup on the bolt and in the carrier. When there's enough carbon fouling, the rifle slows down; then you know it's time to get the crud out. There are a lot of carbon scraping aids available, many of which are quite effective. But, there is a shop tool now available that makes a pleasure out of an otherwise onerous task: the ultrasonic cleaner.

If all you want to do is clean the bolt carrier group this quick and easy way, a small ultrasonic cleaner is offered by Hornady and others, primarily for cartridge case cleaning by reloaders, but well adapted to small parts cleaning. One high-round-count AR shooter of the author's acquaintance shoots with a sound suppressor on the muzzle; he swears by his little Hornady ultrasonic cleaner. A few minutes and he's got a bolt carrier group that's squeaky clean.

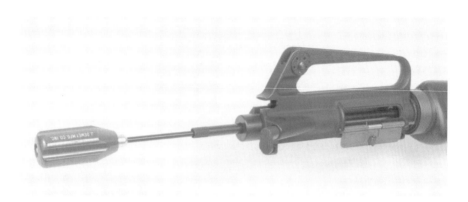

Here's the recommended "conventional" cleaning setup: a good coated rod and a bore guide for the breech. Walt Kuleck Collection.

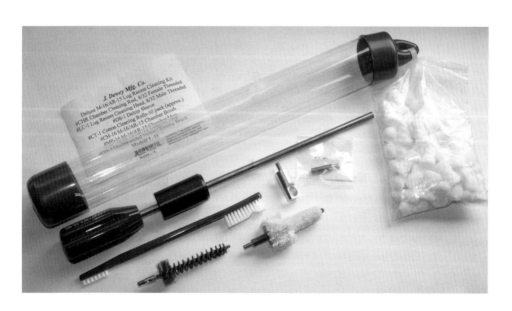

The Dewey kit for chamber cleaning. Actually, the chamber isn't that hard to clean. It's the bolt locking lug recesses in the barrel extension that harbor the products of incomplete combustion.

MAINTENANCE

But, what about the rest of the upper? Hornady has an answer for that too: the Hornady Hot Tub. The Hot Tub strikes a balance between capability and cost. By making the Hot Tub just big enough for a 16 in. upper, the investment required makes the Hot Tub accessible to many shooters. If an individual just can't justify the investment in this tool, there's no reason he or she couldn't organize a group of friends to share a Hot Tub. Life just got a lot easier.

We should also point out that properly used, ultrasonic cleaning won't wear out your rifle. Just sayin'.

Well, OK, you don't have an ultrasonic cleaner. What you should have is a good one-piece coated cleaning rod, such as the Dewey, and a bore guide to allow cleaning from the breech to the muzzle. One problem area in the AR is a consequence of the multi-lug bolt: the locking recesses in the barrel extension. Fortunately, there are tools to help in this area. Sticking with Dewey, the Dewey Chamber Lug Recess Cleaning Kit has everything you need to get the crud out of the chamber extension. As for the bolt carrier group, there are is a wide range of tools available to help ease the chore of scraping the carbon off the bolt and out of the bolt carrier.

But, let's keep one thing in mind: more rifles are worn out by cleaning... Most of the time it's sufficient to flush the inside of the upper and lower receivers with a spray gun cleaner, wipe down the outside of the upper and lower receivers and bolt carrier group, and run a patch through the bore after a shooting session.

Periodically, of course, a thorough detail cleaning after field stripping and detail stripping the bolt carrier group is in order. How often is "periodically"? It will probably take several thousand rounds for the rifle to get to the point where it begins to get sluggish; that's your cue. Now, you may consider this rifle abuse; if so, please feel free to clean as often as your conscience nags you. We simply suggest that "perfection is the enemy of 'good enough'"; if the rifle is clean enough, save the white-glove treatment for your drill instructor.

Out in the Field

Not all cleaning and upkeep can take place in your clean, well-lighted workshop. You really should have something in your pocket that will keep you in the fight. While we strongly recommend only the use of a good quality coated one-piece cleaning rod such as the Dewey, a one-piece rod will not fit in a pocket; but, a good pull through kit, such as one by Otis can come in handy when clearing the bore is necessary. One thing that will destroy a barrel pronto is a bore obstruction; a field cleaning kit *will* fit in the pocket. Don't leave home without one.

HISTORICAL NOTE:

Doreen Garrett was pursuing a "very smart deer," as she put it, through a swamp when a hidden root tripped her up. With her grandfather's Winchester 94 full of mud, she discovered she and her dad had no good way to get that mud out of the bore. While warming up in camp that night, she determined to solve that problem for herself and for all hunters. At age sixteen, Doreen created what became the "Whole Kit and Kaboodle," a portable cleaning system that has blossomed into a

Sometimes you just have to get in that bore and clean out the crud and mud. The Otis field cleaning kit fills the bill, even including a dedicated carbon scraper, the "B.O.N.E. Tool," and lubricant. Walt Kuleck Collection.

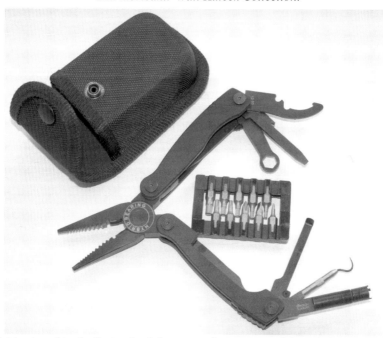

The Multitasker, this the Series 3. It has everything you need for "light" in-field support, including an A2 front sight tool! Don't leave home without one. Walt Kuleck Collection.

MAINTENANCE

very successful enterprise: Otis Technologies. Otis? Otis is Doreen's dad. Now you know the rest of the story.

PITFALL:
When using a pull-through, be sure that you don't allow the cord or cable to contact the bore; keep the cord or cable centered in the muzzle as you pull it through from the breech to the muzzle. Otherwise, you'll wear the muzzle the way Tommies did to their SMLEs during WWI.

We should also mention the BoreSnake, cleaning swab and brush all in one. Toss it in the washing machine when it gets dirty. Just don't use too aggressive a copper cleaner; you may dissolve the brushes imbedded in the 'Snake.

Of course, a cleaning kit can't handle all the jobs that may arise; for that we need something mechanical. A good multitool such as the MultiTasker is invaluable. The Multitasker is seriously weapon-centric. If something goes amiss with your AR, chances are you can fix it with this tool. You can even scrape that carbon out of the bolt carrier group and adjust your A2 front sight. We haven't found anything better; now that we have one, we won't leave home without it.

In the Shop

Back at home base, there are a few items that you might find handy. It's not unusual to find takedown and pivot pins that are hard to push through. If you use a punch or other expedient tool, you risk slipping off the end of the pin and marring the receiver finish. There is a cute little pin pusher you can get that will get those tight pins moving without damaging the rifle.

Once the rifle is apart, you will need a way to keep the upper and lower receivers under control while you work on them. There is a variety of jigs and tools to allow a vise to serve you as a "third hand." These can facilitate accessory and upgrade installation, and even bore cleaning with your one-piece rod. Be certain you clean from the breech to the muzzle, and use a chamber bore guide.

While a combination tool such as the Multitasker might have a useful field expedient buffer tube nut spanner, you should have a bench "combo tool" suitable for your rifles and Carbines. When we say "suitable," we mean with the correct barrel nut wrench and buffer tube spanner. One of the author's very early Carbines has a buffer tube nut that takes an early spanner with round, not square, tooth. Better not lose that wrench!

When you drop the hammer in your AR, the hammer blow is cushioned by the bolt. When you drop the hammer with the upper receiver opened or removed, the full blow of the hammer falls on the rear of the mag well, where the wall is thin. A few too many such blows and your lower is toast. The solution is a mag well hammer block from Brownells. Just as we suggest pushing the pins back in to avoid damaging the upper, one of these cool tools is not a bad idea for protecting your lower from egregious ruination.

While we're on the subject of bench tools, because detail cleaning includes extractor and ejector removal, a bolt vise is a good idea. With it, you can easily remove and replace the ejector pin while keeping the ejector itself under control.

THE *NEW* AR-15 COMPLETE OWNER'S GUIDE

The Boresnake, cleaning for field or bench. Walt Kuleck Collection.

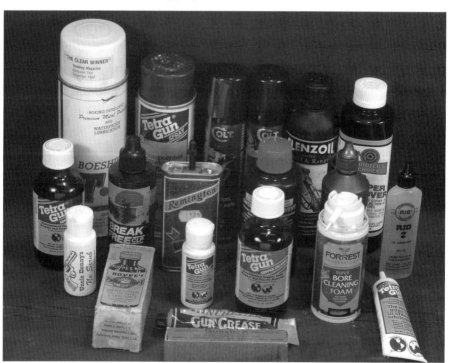

This is a part of the collection of cleaners, lubricants and preservatives the author has accumulated over...let's just say a number of decades. Which is best? Dunno. I don't think any are really bad. Heck, in a pinch, get some drops of oil off the dipstick from your truck, car or motorcycle. You might recognize this shot from **The M1911 Complete Owner's Guide**. *Walt Kuleck Collection.*

MAINTENANCE

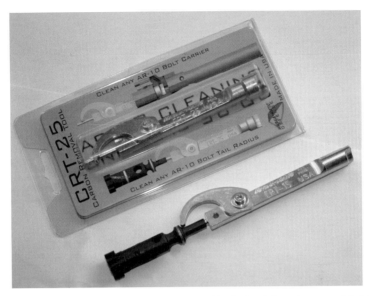

These carbon scrapers from Magnamatic are suitable for both bench use and field carriage.. Below is the 5.56 model, above, the 7.62/.308. It's a bit more elegant a carbon scraper than the MultiTasker, but if you have the latter, you're still well-served. Walt Kuleck Collection.

Here's another carbon scraper, this from Talon complete with carrying case. The component at the bottom has a number of useful functions in addition to carbon scraping. Walt Kuleck Collection.

THE *NEW* AR-15 COMPLETE OWNER'S GUIDE

Remember that sequence of pictures in the Operating chapter, where we used a tool to make non-float tube handguard removal simple? Here's a closeup. Walt Kuleck Collection.

Ever have a tight takedown or pivot pin? Here's the solution. Walt Kuleck Collection.

MAINTENANCE

If you're going to work on your upper or lower, holding it in a vise with the Wheeler upper receiver tool (above) or the Peace River Arms lower receiver tool (lower) will make a convenient "third hand." Walt Kuleck Collection.

This is a sample of the "combo tools" accumulated by the author over the years. Take note of the arrow; it points to the round lug on this early DPMS tool that fits the early collapsible stock buffer nut on one of the author's rifles. Just like his tool for the three-prong M16 flash suppressor, no, you can't have it. Walt Kuleck Collection.

THE *NEW* AR-15 COMPLETE OWNER'S GUIDE

OK, so we've exhorted you to make sure your gas key screws are "properly staked"; well, here's the "proper staker." This bench tool from Brownells is similar to Michigun's original MOACKS, the "Mother Of All Carrier Key Stakers." Michiguns replaced the original MOACKS with their MOACKS II, smaller and more versatile. Michiguns also has a Pocket MOACKS, for those who want to be able to restake their screws in the field. All are highly recommended. Get 'em from Brownells or M-Gun.com. Walt Kuleck Collection.

Yeah, we know, some guys just hammer a nail part way into the bench and lean on the bolt. We like this bolt vise for removing the ejector pin. It's elegant, and avoids damaging the bolt or oneself. Walt Kuleck Collection.

MAINTENANCE

This odd-looking item is a mag well hammer block from Brownells. If you play with your trigger with the upper open or removed, you'll need something to cushion the hammer's blow on the mag well. Sooner or later, probably sooner, without a block such as this, you'll break out the back of the mag well. Bad juju. Walt Kuleck Collection.

Here's how the hammer block fits into the mag well, going in from the top. The hammer now has something to hit besides the thin, fragile mag well rear wall. The cognoscenti will be able to identify the trigger assembly. Walt Kuleck Collection.
P.S.: It's a Jewell.

THE *NEW* AR-15 COMPLETE OWNER'S GUIDE

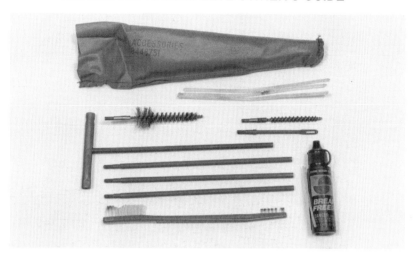

Just to remind you, here's the GI field cleaning kit, this time with butt stock pouch. It's an interesting accessory to accompany your AR collection, but please don't actually use it to clean your rifle. Walt Kuleck Collection.

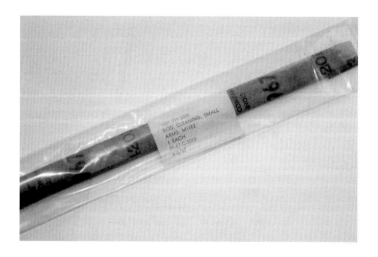

An M11E2 GI sectional cleaning rod. It's still in the original clear plastic package, wrapped in VPI (Vapor Phase [rust] Inhibitor) paper. It's still sealed, because it's a collectible artifact, not for use. Walt Kuleck Collection.

MAINTENANCE

"Make sure the carrier key screws are properly staked." You've probably heard that more than once. So, how do you do that? A loose key will take you out of the game. Years ago, you were forced to resort to freehand work with a punch and a hammer. Today, we have some pretty slick tools to make staking those screws quick and easy. Pioneered by Ned Christiansen of Michiguns, one of these tools is a "must-have" for the serious AR shooter.

Lubrication

Lubricating the AR-15 is as controversial a subject as cleaning. Heck, ask three experienced AR shooters how to best lubricate their rifles, and you'll get four opinions. Here's ours, for what it's worth.

The AR likes to run "wet." By that, we mean liberally oiled. Not only will this lubricate the rifle, but also keep fouling soft. Black powder shooters will recognize the principle. So, we want the rifle well-lubricated; but where?

Put a dab of oil on the bolt body, smear it around the shaft and around the lugs. Make sure that the piston rings—oh, we mean "gas rings"—are well lubricated. Get some lubricant on the cam pin; that steel part runs in the aluminum upper receiver.

Run a line of lube along each side of the top and each side of the bottom of the bolt carrier, where the bolt carrier runs in the upper and lower receivers. When it's convenient, give the buffer spring a healthy coat of grease; that will attenuate the "sproinggg" that some ARs emit as the bolt buffer compresses and relaxes the spring.

The fire control group doesn't *need* lubrication; it will migrate down from the bolt carrier group. If you really must, use a high-pressure grease on the contact points of the hammer, trigger and disconnector.

TIP:
We cannot overemphasize this truism: "ARs will run dirty, but the will *not* run dry. Lube 'em!

So, there you have it. Keep it simple; the AR is not a delicate flower. Just give it loving attention, but not so you love it to death.

Some of you may be curious as to what the author used to clean and lube his ARs. Here it is; Tetra Gun. We were introduced to Tetra Gun by Clint McKee of Fulton Armory quite a long time ago; what's good enough for a custom service rifle builder is good enough for us. Walt Kuleck Collection.

THE *NEW* AR-15 COMPLETE OWNER'S GUIDE

Yep, there it is: a suppressed full auto shorty. Note the cases in the air. Thanks to Rick Linke for the firearm and the photo. Rick Linke/Arlan's Guns & Ammo Collection.

CHAPTER 10

FORBIDDEN FRUIT

Why Can't You Have a Suppressed Full Auto Shorty?

Well, actually, you can, and may. You just have to have very deep pockets, at least for the select-fire or full-auto part. Thank Al Capone, Dutch Shultz, Pretty Boy Floyd, John Dillinger and the like.

> **NOTE:**
> Despite his nickname, purportedly bestowed by his wife so he would appear menacing, "Machine Gun" Kelly never had a machine gun.

The notoriety of the 20's and 30's gangsters led the US Congress to pass, and President Franklin D. Roosevelt to sign, the National Firearms Act of 1934 (NFA 34 or NFA). This legislation regulated by taxation the ownership of certain classes of weapon, including machine guns, silenced weapons, short barreled (under 16") rifles and short barreled (under 18") shotguns. There's a lot more to the NFA, such as regulating forward vertical hand grips on pistols, but they're only tangentially related to the AR world so we shall leave it to the reader to explore the NFA's exotica if there is interest so to do.

While the price of tax stamps—the NFA was originally under the authority of the Internal Revenue Service; it was a "tax," you see—hasn't increased since '34, there are other factors that have made machine guns specifically increase exponentially in price. First, in 1968 the Gun Control Act of '68 (GCA '68) halted the import of machine guns. Thus, only domestically manufactured machine guns could be sold to the general public. Enterprising gunsmiths imported machine gun parts sets, building everything from Maxims to Stens with domestically manufactured receivers, in addition to simply building entire machine guns such as Thompson M1928s, Ingram M10s, Stemple M76s and the like. Alas, when the Gun Owner's Protection Act of 1986 (GOPA) was passed, during the dead of night the so-called Hughes Amendment was added by a suspect voice vote. The Amendment ended the sale of newly-manufactured machine guns to the general public. With a fixed supply and an ever-increasing demand, prices for machine guns will continue to rise steadily for the foreseeable future; in many ways, a better investment than even gold. They're still mining gold, after all.

> **NOTE:**
> Although the supply of machine guns has been frozen, there is no current limit on the supply of silencers, nor on short-barreled rifles. Thus, prices for "SBR-ing" an AR or equipping one with a silencer remain quite reasonable, though a transfer tax is imposed on each individually. The exception is a machine gun, which is not regulated as to barrel length. SBR and silence a semiauto AR, though, and you pay two taxes: one for the SBR and one for the silencer.

Here he is again. The author was pleased to find his Elite Iron 7.62x51 suppressor worked well on his 6.8 SPC SR-556. Magpul stock, Leatherwood scope, Andy's Leather "Rhodesian" sling. *Walt Kuleck Collection.*

FORBIDDEN FRUIT

Machine guns have been entered into a national registry under NFA '34 since 1934. Transfers of machine guns and other articles regulated under NFA '34 must be approved by the Bureau of Alcohol, Tobacco, Firearms and Explosives (BATFE) of the Department of Justice and a transfer tax paid. Your local "NFA Dealer" will be pleased to walk you through the process, which is not particularly forbidding but which can take an age to progress through the BATFE bureaucracy. SBR-ing an AR requires a similar approval process, as does acquiring a silencer.

Silencers/Sound Suppressors

Contrary to popular film and fiction, it isn't really possible to silence an AR completely. While the report from the muzzle can be attenuated by 20 to 30 dB or so (it is left to the reader to delve into the details), unless the bullet is traveling at less than about 1200 feet per second (fps, actually 1126 fps at "standard temperature and pressure": 68 degrees Fahrenheit at sea level) the bullet's sonic boom, perceived as a sharp "crack," is undiminished.

> **NOTE:**
> A suppressor aficionado and manufacturer from Central Ohio, JD Jones of SSK Industries, decided to solve the sonic bullet problem by devising a series of cartridges that propel heavy bullets at under 1200 fps. His ".300 Whisper," a .30 caliber cartridge on a shortened .221 Fireball (itself a shortened .222 Remington) case, has proven to be a winner in the AR.

Because each silencer you acquire requires an application, transfer tax and lengthy approval wait, it makes sense to use a given silencer on a number of rifles. The author has both autoloading and bolt action rifles threaded for his .308 silencer, for example. One silencer for each caliber is really all you need, unless you plan to shoot two rifles at once.

> **TIP:**
> In previous chapters we have noted that external piston ARs are much more pleasant to shoot suppressed than are internal piston versions. The added back pressure created by the silencer increases the exhaust gases emitted from the gas system; it's much more comfortable for the shooter if the gases are exhausted at the gas block rather than the bolt carrier. If you do choose an external piston rifle, one that has an adjustable gas system is better adapted to that increased back pressure. For example, the author's Ruger SR-556, which is normally set to "2," functions quite well on setting "1" when suppressed.

Short Barreled Rifles/SBRs

The "Short Barreled Rifle" is an arbitrary legal artifact. Legislation has defined the minimum legal barrel length for a rifle as 16". Most rifle manufacturers make their barrels somewhat longer than 16", e.g., 16.1" or 16.5", just to be on the safe side.

> **NOTE:**
> There is also a minimum rifle overall length, but for the purposes of this discussion the barrel length is the gating parameter.

THE *NEW* AR-15 COMPLETE OWNER'S GUIDE

Not all shorties are SBRs; this is a "pistol." Be sure you start with a lower designated as a pistol, not a rifle, unless you want to get dinged for an unregistered SBR! When you fill out the form for the lower, if you're doing the build, be sure the 4473 says, "Pistol." Greg King Collection.

Here's an M16. Why the collapsible buttstock on a rifle? So it will fit the locking bracket in a Charger Police Pursuit. Property of a Law Enforcement Agency.

FORBIDDEN FRUIT

PITFALL:
> The discussion in this chapter is limited to Federal law and regulations. Your state may have its own restrictions; for example, machine guns are not permitted in the State of California, silencers are prohibited in Minnesota, SBRs are illegal in New York, and Illinois denies citizens ownership of all three. You may also be subject to municipal restrictions. Check your laws; of course, a "Class III" dealer will not deal in forbidden weapons wherever you are.

The Federal restriction on barrel length is particularly relevant for AR owners, because the military M4's barrel length is 14.5". Therefore, to faithfully build a semiauto analogue of the M4, one must go through the process to register an AR lower receiver as an SBR. Thereafter, an upper receiver assembly with any barrel length desired may be installed and used on that registered receiver.

PITFALL:
> We must make it clear that it is the lower receiver that is registered and defines the SBR, not the upper receiver assembly. Once a lower is registered, more than one upper receiver assembly may be acquired for installation on that registered lower. You cannot install an upper receiver assembly with a barrel length less than 16" on any unregistered AR receiver you might own, only on a registered lower receiver.

PITFALL:
> If you have in your possession a barrel or an upper receiver assembly with a barrel of less than 16" length, and do not possess an SBR-registered lower receiver, you will be considered to have an unregistered SBR regardless of whether or not you ever install the short barrel on anything. Don't buy that short barrel until you have your registered receiver with the proper paperwork in hand!

Really short barrels, less than 14.5", can be a real functional challenge. Configuring and operating a really short SBR can be a chore, and is something of a specialty in the AR world. Expect to see rapid gas port wear and consequent overgassing of the system. This is another area where an external piston system may make more sense than an internal piston system.

SBRs lose muzzle velocity and energy, but gain in the fun factor category. They do have some specialized uses in restricted quarters, but for general use, a conventional 16" Carbine may make the most sense.

Select Fire and Full Auto
—Or, How to Turn Dollars into Decibels

Full auto is the *ne plus ultra* of NFA firearms. We have earlier discussed the cause of the steadily increasing value of full auto weapons: a fixed supply and growing demand. Consequently, full auto ownership requires a substantial investment. A genuine full auto Colt AR-15 or civilian M16 requires a *very* substantial investment. Keep in mind that USGI M16s have never been released for civilian ownership. You will see "M16" marked NFA ARs, but they will also bear the mark of the Class III manufacturing gunsmith who welded a cut lower back together again and registered the final product.

THE *NEW* AR-15 COMPLETE OWNER'S GUIDE

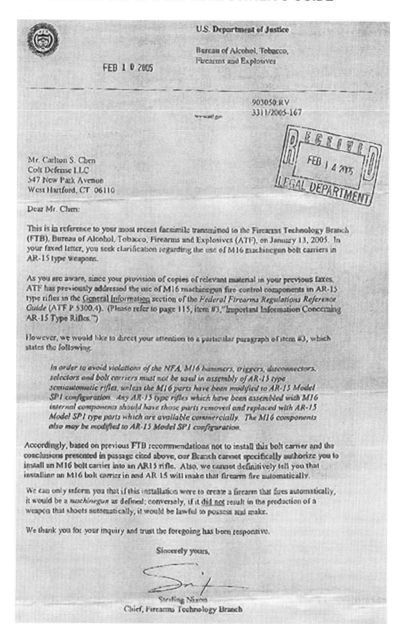

BATFE letter to Colt re: M16 "machine-gun" bolt carriers. Why was Colt insisting on installing an M16 bolt carrier in their semiautos? Because the 16" Carbines run better with the heavier M16 bolt carrier, that's why. Now you know.

FORBIDDEN FRUIT

a cut lower back together again and registered the final product.

One can reduce the required investment somewhat by acquiring a converted AR, that is, a semiauto that was converted to select fire by a licensed machine gun manufacturer and registered prior to the close of the NFA registry in 1986. Possibly the least expensive route is purchasing a registered Drop In Auto Sear (DIAS). Just don't drill that auto sear pin hole in an unregistered receiver. It's a serious felony with serious time.

However, as they say, "It's not the cost, it's the upkeep!" If you're paying a buck a round, every 30-round magazine dump will be $30 for less than ten seconds of noise. Machine guns are a great way to quickly transform dollars into decibels.

When Colt introduced the AR-15 SP1 "Comanche" (a name that appeared only on the first printing of the manual), the firm went to great lengths to alter the hammer, trigger, selector, and bolt carrier to satisfy the Technical Branch of the BATFE. While the BATFE had not yet refined the policy, "Once a machine gun, always a machine gun," the BATFE Technical Branch wanted to make certain that the conversion of an SP1 into an M16 would not be straightforward. Colt went so far as to increase the diameter of the pivot (front) pin so that M16 upper receivers would not simply interchange onto the SP1 lower. Then, they omitted the auto-sear clearance cut in the SP1 upper to hinder the conversion of SP1 lowers to machine guns, at least where SP1 uppers were to be used. In those early days of 1964, Colt did not sell either uppers nor lowers separately, a concept that is almost incredible today.

A consequence of Colt's efforts to restrict the SP1 to semiauto fire only was the BATFE's eventual doctrine that possession of M16-specific (that is, full auto) components was in itself *prima facie* evidence of the possession of a machine gun.

BATFE WARNING:
> "In order to avoid violations of the NFA, M16 hammers, triggers, disconnectors, selectors and bolt carriers must not be used in assembly of AR-15 type semiautomatic rifles, unless the M16 parts have been modified to AR-15 Model SP1 configuration. Any AR-15 type rifles which (sic) have been assembled with M16 internal components should have those parts removed and replaced with AR-15 Model SP1 type parts which are available commercially. The M16 components also may be modified to AR-15 Model SP1 configuration."

Now, you may ask, how does Colt get away with the use of M16 bolt carriers in their LE6920 and other AR-15 variants? In a letter to Colt, the Chief of the Firearms Technology Branch essentially says, "We can't tell you it's permitted to have an M16 bolt carrier, but if the intent isn't there and the result isn't a machine gun, then we won't stop you."

So, there you have it; a capsule summary of the Forbidden Fruit of the AR world. Now, I wonder how long it would take to save up for a ....

SINCERE THANKS
To Rick Linke of Arlan's Guns and Ammo for rifle exemplars, internal AR machine gun parts and unmatched "Class III" dealer service.

THE *NEW* AR-15 COMPLETE OWNER'S GUIDE

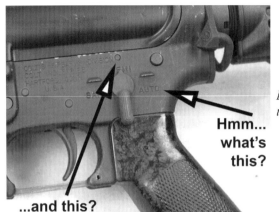

Hmm... what's this?

...and this?

Let's see...it says, "AUTO"...and there's an extra pin...

Ahh...there's the answer. It's an M16! Trivia question: what's wrong with this legend? It says, "M-16" when it should say "M16." No wonder some of the Army manuals have it wrong, also. Sigh. This is the M16 illustrated earlier.

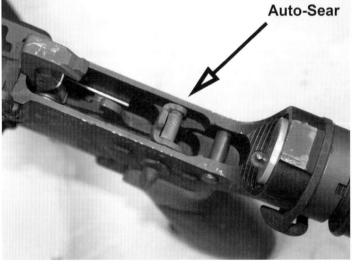

Auto-Sear

That's where the pin goes, to retain the auto-sear. If your receiver has a hole for this pin, it's a machine gun regardless of the components inside. It's a machine gun whether or not the auto sear is there. It better be registered!

FORBIDDEN FRUIT

Left, Colt semiauto SP1 hammer; right, Colt M16 auto hammer. Danger, danger.

Above, M16 bolt carrier; below, SP1 bolt carrier. Note the longer cutout on the SP1 bolt carrier.

M16 hammer and trigger. Note the rear lug that interfaces with the auto-sear.

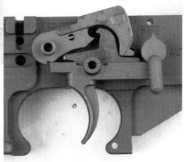

Here's another view., including the selector. Unless you have a registered machine gun, avoid these machine gun parts.

Here's a three-round burst fire control group. Note the three-lobe cam alongside the hammer, and the parallel disconnectors.

A closeup of the machine gun selector. Note how much more complex it is than a semiauto safety selector.

THE *NEW* AR-15 COMPLETE OWNER'S GUIDE

Really Old School Optics!

Here is a Colt SP1 from the first full year of production, equipped with an original Colt 4x carry-handle-mounted scope. The carry handle forces the scope user to suffer a very high sight line that turns one's cheek weld into a "chin weld." The desire to scope the AR led experimenters to whack off the carry handle and devise sundry means of adopting conventional scope mounts to the flattened top of the upper receiver. A decade or so of development resulted in the flat top railed upper receiver that dominates the AR world today.

Walt Kuleck Collection.

CHAPTER 11

INTERESTING STUFF NOT ELSEWHERE CLASSIFIED
Old School Optics

In those pre-flat top days, long eye relief optics were adapted to the A1 and A2 upper receivers via "scout"-type mounts. Here's a C-More reflex sight with integral carry-handle-based mount. A.R.M.S. offered a similar mount with a rail where the C-More is here. Walt Kuleck Collection.

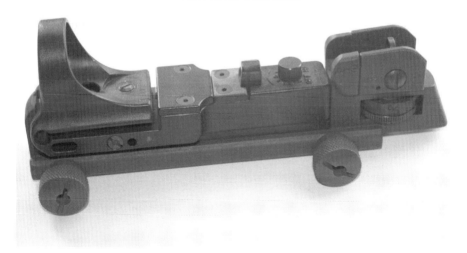

Another C-More offering from back in the day: the C-More "Tactical," a C-More sight with integral A2 iron sight for mounting on a flat top upper receiver. This example was offered by Colt in a Colt-branded box. Walt Kuleck Collection.

THE *NEW* AR-15 COMPLETE OWNER'S GUIDE

Old School Night Vision

More history. Today we're accustomed to seeing night vision quite routinely, from green-tinted Operation Iraqi Freedom combat footage to black and white Ghost Hunters episodes. But, back in the late '60's and early '70's night vision was akin to sorcery. This is the second generation of Vietnam War-era night vision, the AN/PVS-4. As old as it is, the 'PVS-4 is still a useful tool. This Israeli-surplus unit is rail mounted via an A.R.M.S QD mount.

Walt Kuleck Collection.

INTERESTING STUFF NOT ELSEWHERE CLASSIFIED
Charging Handle Variations

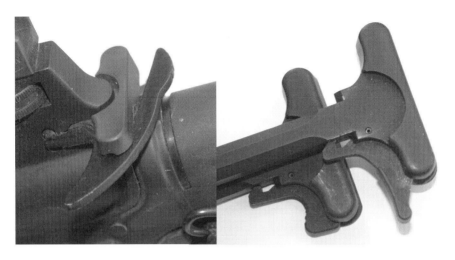

Various charging handles and charging handle catches are available to make the latch easier to "hit" either in a stress situation or when the latch is obscured by a scope ocular, for ambidexterity, or...to keep the latch out of the way. On the left, an extended ambidextrous latch, one of the author's favorites. On the right, a comparison between a standard latch (left and lower) and an extended latch (right and upper).
Walt Kuleck Collection.

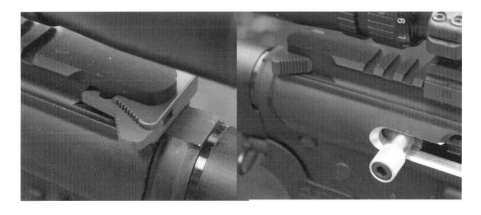

So, what was that about keeping the latch out of the way? On the left is a reproduction early "delta" latch. It's almost inaccessible under that big scope ocular. Why would we do such a thing? On the right, we see the answer: this is a side-cocking upper receiver. A vestigial latch is appropriate for this application. Walt Kuleck Collection.

Potpourri

Here's a really cool accessory for your AR: a 37mm flare launcher. If you don't look too close, it kinda looks like an M203. Unlike the M203, this example clamps to a lower Picatinny rail. Greg King Collection.

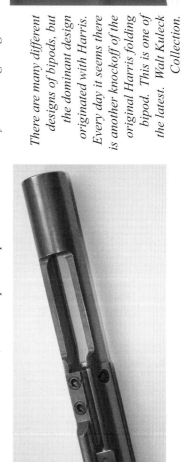

There are many different designs of bipods, but the dominant design originated with Harris. Every day it seems there is another knockoff of the original Harris folding bipod. This is one of the latest. Walt Kuleck Collection.

The ultimate of lubricity and fouling repulsion: the Fail Zero Boron Nitride bolt carrier group. Walt Kuleck Collection.

INTERESTING STUFF NOT ELSEWHERE CLASSIFIED
Magazine Loading Made Easy

Loading an AR magazine, even a thirty-rounder, is not a particularly difficult job. However, do it all day long without a loading aid, and the task gets old really fast—not to mention your thumbs get really black. The solution is the MagLULA.
Walt Kuleck Collection.

Some 5.56 ammo comes on stripper clips. Why go through the multiple steps of stripping the clips, then loading the mags with loose rounds? The solution here is the StripLULA.
Walt Kuleck Collection.

THE *NEW* AR-15 COMPLETE OWNER'S GUIDE
Chinese Copies

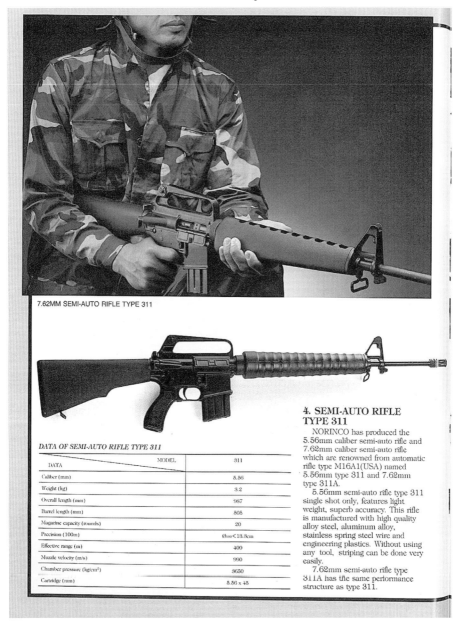

7.62MM SEMI-AUTO RIFLE TYPE 311

DATA OF SEMI-AUTO RIFLE TYPE 311

DATA	MODEL	311
Caliber (mm)		5.56
Weight (kg)		3.2
Overall length (mm)		987
Barrel length (mm)		505
Magazine capacity (rounds)		20
Precision (100m)		$\varnothing_{100}$ < 13.3cm
Effective range (m)		400
Muzzle velocity (m/s)		990
Chamber pressure (kg/cm^2)		3650
Cartridge (mm)		5.56 x 45

4. SEMI-AUTO RIFLE TYPE 311

NORINCO has produced the 5.56mm caliber semi-auto rifle and 7.62mm caliber semi-auto rifle which are renowned from automatic rifle type M16A1(USA) named 5.56mm type 311 and 7.62mm type 311A.

5.56mm semi-auto rifle type 311 single shot only, features light weight, superb accuracy. This rifle is manufactured with high quality alloy steel, aluminum alloy, stainless spring steel wire and engineering plastics. Without using any tool, striping can be done very easily.

7.62mm semi-auto rifle type 311A has the same performance structure as type 311.

While at the Ministry of Defence Pattern Room in Nottingham, England, the author had the opportunity to actually handle one of these Norinco Chinese copies. Note the "improvements" in furniture seen in the lower picture, including the ribbed handguards, curved pistol grip and butt stock with weak hand grip notch. Also note that it's offered in "7.62," presumably 7.62x39mm.

INTERESTING STUFF NOT ELSEWHERE CLASSIFIED
Disappearing Act

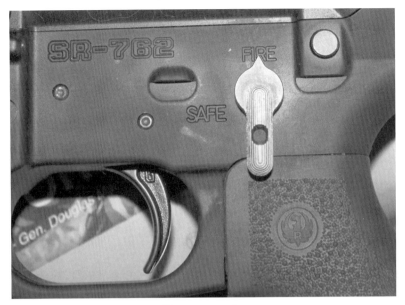

Now you see it...

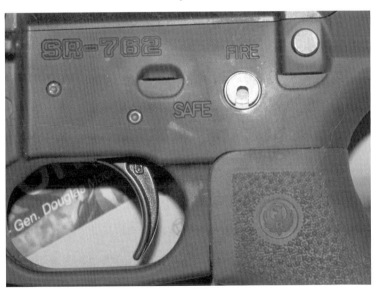

Now you don't. The AMBI selector from AMBI Products. Use a bullet tip or similar tool to depress the catch in the selector lever to slide the lever off. Set the selector to SAFE, *remove the lever from the shaft, and unauthorized users are locked out. The shaft is designed to accept the lever on the right end of the shaft for lefties, or get two levers and install a lever on each side for true ambidexterity. Recommended. Walt Kuleck Collection.*

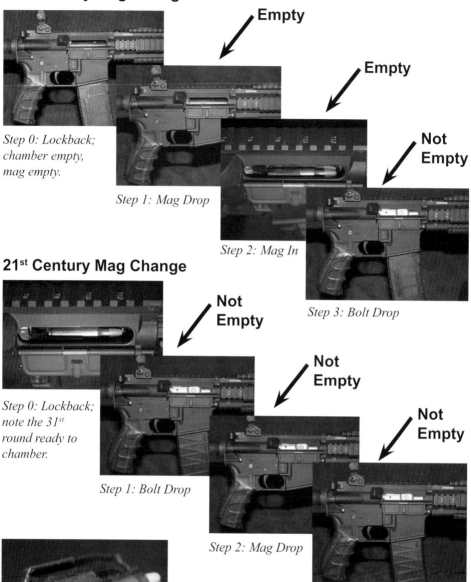

INTERESTING STUFF NOT ELSEWHERE CLASSIFIED
Paradigm Shift!
NEVER HAVE AN EMPTY GUN!

Rarely is a product introduced that turns shooting literally on its head; the Maklarbak "Time to Change Mag" (TTC-MAG) is just such a product. For many seroys shooters, the possibility of an empty gun is sufficiently distressing that in a "tactical" situation they will eject a partially expended mag, replacing it with a full mag whenever possible. This procedure is known as the "Tactical Reload." While the gun is never empty, the wastage of cartridges and magazines can be significant, with partially used but still useful mags littering the ground.

Maklarbak, a Danish company that channels their Viking heritage, turned the "empty gun" problem inside out. For a hundred years or more, the conventional protocol for a semi-automatic firearm with detachable box magazine has been to shoot to slide or bolt lockback, drop the empty mag, insert a fresh mag and lastly release the bolt or slide, chambering a fresh round. The firearm is thus returned to action.

The fly in this particular kettle of worms is that the chamber is empty between the first and last step of the process. Should a threat appear, the shooter may find himself or herself literally in a world of hurt with an empty gun. The TTC-MAG swats that fly.

Here's how it works; the TTC-MAG has a very clever follower, the "T-Follower," that trips the AR-15-type rifle's bolt stop on **the next to last round**. The bolt lock-back tells the shooter that he or she has "had his thirty" (with apologies to James Bond in ***Dr. No***; Bond to Denton: "That's a Smith and Wesson, and you've had your six."), but with an available 31st round ready to chamber. The shooter drops the bolt, chambering the 31st round, then drops the now-empty mag, inserts a fresh mag and carries on, *with his or her gun never empty.* This is the beauty of the Maklarbak concept. The T-Follower's spring-loaded bolt stop trip also aids ejection, while reloading with a closed bolt supports the magazine's lips.

Thus, *Every* Mag Change is Like a "Tactical Mag Change," with Never an Empty Gun!

A great idea, no? Hold on there, Pilgrim. What has been ingrained in every semiauto shooter since time, or at least the 20th century, began? The bolt locks back on an empty mag. With the chamber empty, the shooter drops the empty mag, grabs and inserts a full mag, drops the bolt, and is prepared to recommence fire. Note, of course, that between the bolt lock back and the bolt drop—an empty gun. But, this sequence is that to which we have become accustomed. So, to benefit from the TTC-MAG we have to unlearn one sequence (that begins with an empty gun) and learn another (wherein the 31st round ensures a loaded gun throughout). It's the same number of steps, just in a different order. Furthermore, you don't have two different reload "feels," the bolt back 20th Century reload, and the bolt forward tactical reload. With the TTC-MAG, every reload feels the same.

If you're up to the challenge, get yourself a gross of T-Followers—Maklarbak offers followers, or complete mags if you prefer—and start (re) training. You might well benefit from the comfort that comes from never having an empty gun.

THE *NEW* AR-15 COMPLETE OWNER'S GUIDE
No More Just Hangin' Around

The Sling Band-It gathers up all that loose webbing with hook 'n loop straps that release with the natural motion of deploying the sling.

OUCH!!

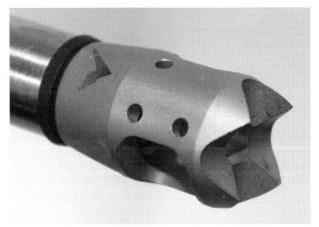

Rainier Arms offers this cute short muzzle brake with razor-sharp tines.

From Russia with Love

Colt ammo, from Russia, with love!

INTERESTING STUFF NOT ELSEWHERE CLASSIFIED
A Promising Second Act

Randy Luth, founder of DPMS, is back! Here's his lightweight rifle buttstock, adjustable for comb height and length of pull. An even lighter version eschews the adjustable comb and butt plate, revealing the skeleton stock underneath.

Double Your Pleasure, Double Your Fun!

Magpul's magazine coupler, as sturdy as the PMags it marries. What's it good for? Ohio residents, for example, suffer from a 30-round limit for semiauto centerfire rifles and can't take advantage of 60-round Surefire mags, alas. Here's a practical alternative that gives you 60 rounds on the rifle or Carbine.

THE *NEW* AR-15 COMPLETE OWNER'S GUIDE
Get a Grip

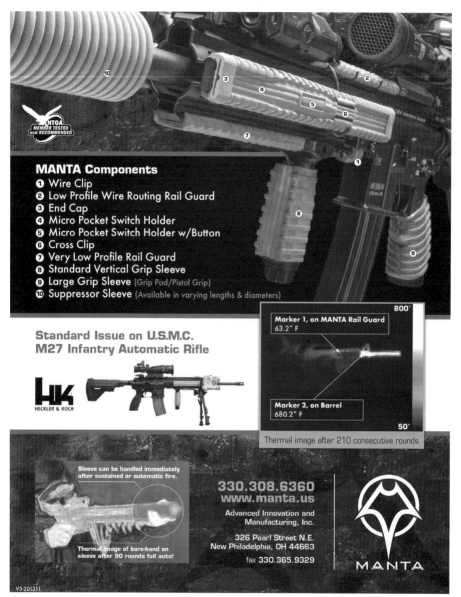

If you have rails, you need rail covers. Why? Try shooting a "naked" four-rail-hand guard-equipped AR for a hundred rounds or so; if your hand isn't bleeding, it'll hurt. By far, to date, the best rail cover that the author has found is from Manta Rail. The USMC thinks so, too, specifying the Manta Rail covers for the M27 IAR. Once you snap a Manta cover on your rail and hold it, you'll strip off all your other rail covers on all your other rifles and replace them with Mantas. That's what your author has done. The Manta Rail cover is that good.

INTERESTING STUFF NOT ELSEWHERE CLASSIFIED
Cool to the Touch

The Manta cover has not only the best "feel" of any other rail cover the author has tried, the Mantas also are very effective insulators. Check out the infrared picture inset into the Manta flyer shown at left. Note how the rail cover has attenuated the temperature of the barrel by an entire order of magnitude! The Manta material is so effective, Manta is also offering suppressor covers to protect the shooter and his or her equipment from the hot "can."

This has to be seen to be believed. Here the shooter can actually hold the rifle by the can—after running three 30-round magazines full auto in rapid succession, a full 90 rounds in just a few tens of seconds. Don't try this at home without a Manta suppressor cover!

THE *NEW* AR-15 COMPLETE OWNER'S GUIDE
The "Last AR"—
The Last AR assembled during the writing of this book, that is!

Here's a showcase of AR components and accessories. From the left, a Ranier Arms shorty muzzle brake, Yankee Hill low profile gas block, PRI carbon fiber handguard, Midwest Industries QD sling swivel mount, ArmaLite upper receiver; ATI Omni composite lower receiver (polymer body with aluminum rear section encompassing the receiver extension). Magpul mag coupler with PMags, Norgon Ambi Mag Catch, Rock River Arms Star selector/safety, Magpul pistol grip and Luth-AR MBA adjustable butt stock.

INTERESTING STUFF NOT ELSEWHERE CLASSIFIED
The "Last AR"—
The Last AR assembled during the writing of this book, that is!

More goodies can be seen on the right side, including Target Sports Rail to Sling Stud adaptor; Winchester-branded Harris Bipod clone, Battle Arms Development pivot and takedown pins, Fail Zero bolt carrier group (visible in ejection port), Target Sports QD Scope Mount under a Brunton scope, and Bravo Company Ambidextrous Gunfighter Charging Handle. The barrel is from White Oak, 1 in 7 twist with .223 chamber as confirmed by Michiguns' .223/5.56? Gage.

THE *NEW* AR-15 COMPLETE OWNER'S GUIDE

The 21st Century AR: an enhanced Colt LE6920. Upgrades include Magpul handguards, Magpul forward grip, thirty-round Magpul PMAG, Magpul pistol grip, Magpul CTR butt stock, and EOTech 552 holographic sight. Walt Kuleck Collection.

THE FUTURE OF THE AR
CHAPTER 12

THE FUTURE OF THE AR

The Last of the Line?

The AR-15 is very likely the last US Service Rifle that will be available to American civilians, albeit in semiautomatic form only. However, as "warfighter of the future" concepts continue to be developed, we will see multi-spectrum sensors linked to helmet vision blocks (and to higher command as well) used to sight what under it all may still be an M4A1!

We've Never had it Better

Brownells, the preeminent supplier of tools, parts and supplies to the shooting trade, reports that the three most popular platforms for maintenance and upgrading are the M1911 pistol, the Ruger 10/22® rifle, and the AR-15! In that respect, the future couldn't look brighter. Every day, it seems, a new part, accessory, or concept is introduced to enhance the AR-15 system or increase the shooter's enjoyment with it. Between the time this book was put to bed and its release from the publisher less than three months later, there will be at least a dozen new products aimed at the AR owner and shooter. Some of them will even be worthwhile!

What We Can Look Forward To

Compare the original SP1 to the upgraded LE6920; the AR-15 has come a long way in just over 50 years. The next 50 years could be just as exciting as the last, if we can only manage to keep our ARs.

The Future is Up to You

If some day the AR-15-type rifle is banned, shooters will have no one to blame but themselves. If we want to preserve our rights, we (sad to say) will have to work for them. The four million (projected) members of the NRA should be forty million; the rolls of the Jews for the Protection of Firearms Ownership, the Gun Owner's Action League and the Second Amendment Foundation and all the rest should be no shorter. We have the numbers; we could have the political power, if we had the will.

Inform yourself and vote. Inform your neighbors, friends and relatives. Help them see which way the wind is blowing, that the loss of one right is the loss of them all. Let it be known you are a shooter, and gun owner, and yes, AR-15 enthusiast. Take away the power to demonize by showing that we are not the demons.

If we fail to uphold the gift of the Constitution bestowed upon us by the greatest statesmen of all time, we will deserve our fate: to have only pictures of our guns, as the Japanese do.

The future of the AR-15 world, and indeed of the world as we know it, is up to you. Get involved.